D1831781

Colonial Lucknow
Burra Sahib and *Chota Hazry*

Colonial Lucknow

Burra Sahib and *Chota Hazry*

PC Sarkar

KALPAZ

Published by

Kalpaz Publications
C-30, Satyawati Nagar,
Delhi – 110052
Ph.: 011-47034999, 9811692060
www.kalpazpublications.com
E-mail: kalpaz@hotmail.com

Distribution Network
www.gyanbooks.com
India, USA, Canada, UK, Australia, France

© Author

All rights reserved. No part of this work may be reproduced, stored, adapted, or transmitted in any form or by any means, electronic, mechanical, photocopying, micro-filming recording or otherwise, or translated in any language, without the prior written permission of the copyright owner and the publisher. The book is sold subject to the condition that it shall not, by way of trade or otherwise, be lent, resold, hired out, or otherwise circulated without the prior publisher's written consent in any form of binding or cover other than that in which it is published.

Copyright of the vintage images, if any, as reproduced in this book, rests with the original owners; any infringement is purely unintentional.

ISBN: 978-93-5722-591-5 (HB)
First Published, 2024

Printed at: Gyan Press, Delhi.

The views and opinions expressed in this book are author(s) own and the facts reported by them have been veri ied to the extent possible, and the publishers are not in any way liable for the same.

Colonial Lucknow:
Burra Sahib* and *Chota Hazry
Author: PC SARKAR

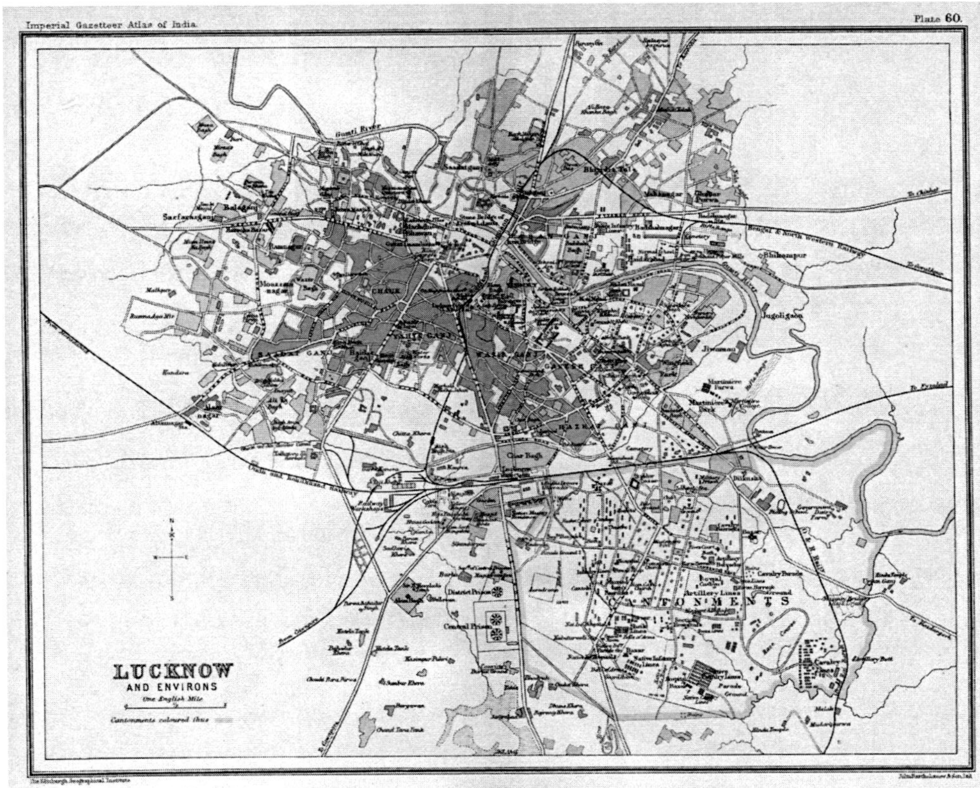

Lucknow and Its Environs, 1924, Imperial Gazetter Map of India, Edinburgh Geographical Institute

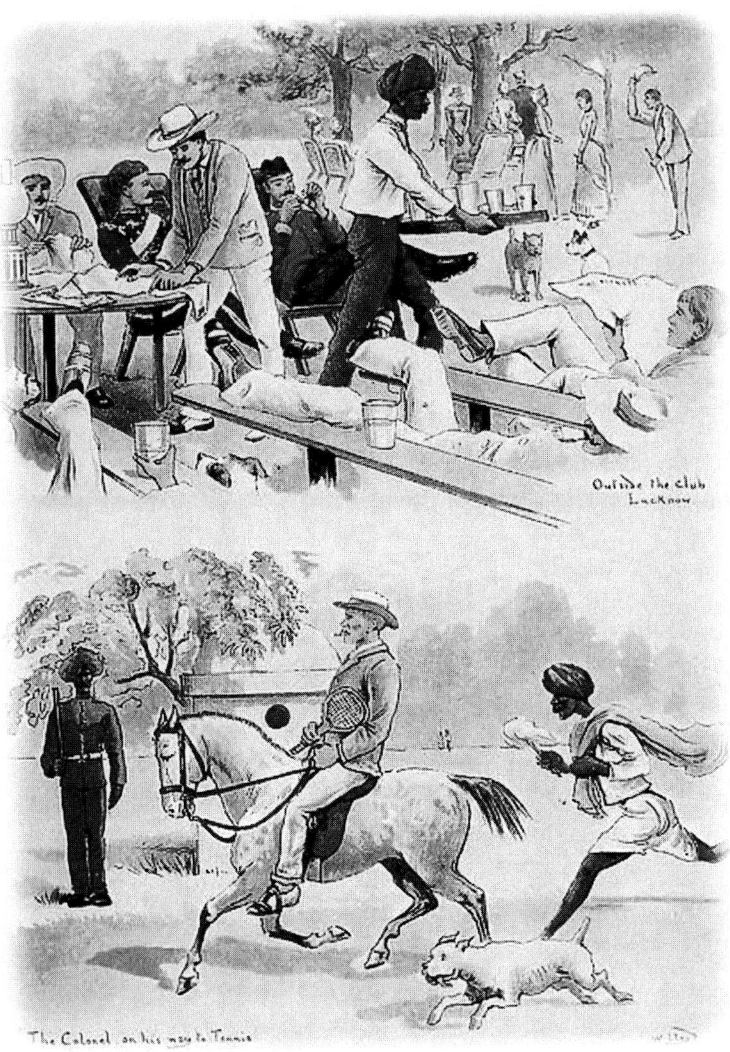

Colonialism was made possible, and then sustained and strengthened, as much by cultural technologies of rule as it was by the more obvious and brutal modes of conquest that first established power on foreign shores...

- Shashi Tharoor,
An Era of Darkness: The British Empire in India (2016)

Contents

List of Figures

CHAPTER - V

CHAPTER - VIII

Introduction

The "Nawabi" phase of Awadh (and Lucknow) commenced from 1722, with the advent of Sa'adat Khan Burhan-ul-Mulk and culminated with Wajid Ali Shah being deposed in 1856. We shall not go into the technicalities of who was a *Subadar,* who was a *Nawab,* who was a *Nawab Wazir* and who was a *Badshah* - terms which generally confound the casual reader. Come what may, this Safavid family from Nishapur or Neyshabur (Iran) successfully administered the territories of Awadh for more than 130 years; it left such an impression on the political, cultural and even architectural landscape of Awadh that it is talked and written about till today. The British East India Company first made inroads into Awadh after Shuja-ud-Daula's defeat in the Battle of Buxar in 1764 and assumed indirect control of the territory, although it was still, for all practical purposes, a state of the Mughal empire at Delhi. This devious form of "colonialism" or indirect rule lasted for 92 years, before being formalised into Company rule from 1856, which could not last for more than a year after which the First War of Independence broke out in 1857. After being on a limbo for about 18 months, the British regained control of Awadh, and commenced their rule in right earnest, not by the East India Company but directly by the Crown. This "Imperial" rule would last for about 89 years, after which, India gained independence. Thus, direct British rule or the *British Raj* lasted for about 90 years in Awadh (and Lucknow).

It is important to recognize that the British had predominantly achieved victory in their confrontations with various kingdoms and principalities throughout the Indian subcontinent, including Awadh. For the British, Lucknow, with its considerable riches, symbolised merely the "fruits of conquest." They viewed themselves as "victorious" heroes of war, part of a civilised society, while perceiving the indigenous people, the rightful owners of the land, as the "enemy," essentially portraying them as uncultured, and uncivilised. The manner in which the victorious British treated the local populace was reprehensible; however, from their perspective, they believed they were justified in their actions. Historically, the victorious are never generous with the vanquished. So to expect equanimity and generosity from the conquerors would have been a futile exercise. And, yet, one cannot deny the contributions of the *neo* rulers, however harsh they might seem to be. The colonial legacy of Lucknow (and elsewhere) is too prominent and too long-lasting to be simply wished away. Conversely, it is also true that the British Raj was focussed on extending benefits and comforts to its own community and looked down upon the locals as serfs who provided a support system. The bloody rebellion had created an atmosphere of resentment, fear and mistrust between the victorious and the vanquished; hence it was imperative that "safe" pockets, away from the grime of the native quarters, should be created for the European community to reside in, enjoy their liesure activities and even purchase groceries. This resulted in the creation of the "Civil Lines", the various planned markets and the new Cantonment in Lucknow. The swift deployment of troops was essential in the event of any future indigenous uprising; therefore, the construction of wide roads and bridges was vital, along with the railways to facilitate the transport of both personnel and military equipment. Additionally, an efficient postal and telegraph system for communication was of utmost importance. Adopting the native system of education was, of course, out of question - therefore, schools had to be built, which would serve the dual purpose of providing western education and promoting religious conversion. It was felt that the natives were basically heathens, the *Hindoos* with their peculiar orthodox practices and the Muslims being fanatics - hence a profusion of churches of all denominations was of paramount importance, in order to ensure that the European and Eurasian populations could participate safely in religious congregations of their choice and engage in prayer as devout Christians.

Without any bias, it must be regretfully accepted that Nawabi Lucknow, like any oriental city of those times, had lacked wide open boulevards for free movement, public spaces (Nawabi gardens were confined for use by nobility), sound sanitation and hygiene practices, availability of modern medicines, supply of clean drinking water and viable communication systems for its citizens. The British sought to correct all of these, with their own Victorian values coupled with contemporary ideas emerging due to rapid industrialisation in Europe. An undercurrent of hypocrisy also pervaded, especially regarding moral values. For example, enjoying the performance of skimpily clad *Hotcha Girls* during a stage show in colonial *Huzrutgunj* was permissible but a dance performance by a native *nautch* (dancing) *girl* was considered unacceptable, as the latter were fundamentally viewed as prostitutes. It goes on without saying that no nautch girl worth her salt would ever be skimpily dressed during her public performance or even in her daily routine. However, those were tumultuous times, characterised by unfounded beliefs stemming from a restricted understanding of indigenous life, during which reason and fairness were often overlooked.

A vast array of literature and numerous publications exist describing and analysing the Nawabi era of Lucknow, providing detailed insights into the art and culture of that illustrious period (including the author's own published works on the subject). Additionally, there is also a plethora of works addressing various facets of the *British Raj* in India authored by esteemed scholars. However, there is a notable scarcity of literature focused on "Colonial Lucknow," with only Oldenburg's work (1984) covering merely two decades of colonial governance in the city (1856 - 1877). This lack of comprehensive documentation of the colonial period is perplexing, given the substantial contributions made by the British towards the enhancement of Lucknow, including landscaping, the establishment of public amenities, the creation of institutions, and the construction of remarkable architectural works between 1858 and 1947, many of which are still extant today. The influx of European settlers, which began in small numbers and then rapidly increased, encountered distinct challenges in this historically rich yet now deteriorating medieval city. Many "settled" Europeans found themselves displaced during the upheaval of 1857-58, and the subsequent arrival of European officials and their families at Lucknow faced their own unique experiences and challenges. Despite the existence of records detailing these narratives, they have yet to be documented for broader understanding or dissemination.

This book is not intended to be a comprehensive treatise or historical account of those tumultuous times; instead, it represents a modest endeavour to chronicle certain overlooked challenges, experiences, and successes of Colonial Lucknow from 1856 to 1947, aiming to present this information to readers in an interesting yet succinct manner.

Chapter - I

Evolution of a City

Pre-Nawabi, Nawabi and Colonial Lucknow

Purists often argue that whenever the city of Lucknow is mentioned, the discussion invariably veers around its Nawabi phase, and the long lasting impression that Nawabi rule (1722 - 1856) left on the city's landscape, culture and more importantly, on its citizens and their lifestyles, which persists till today. That other than the Nawabi phase, the city must have had a pre-Nawabi phase, which should also be taken into account - and if historical records are not available, then bardic traditions intertwined with mythology (and religious texts) should also be accepted as source material. So be it.

The name Ayodhya or *Ájúdhiá* was apparently derived from the Sanskrit word, *Ajud* meaning unvanquished as also *Aj*, a name for Brahma, the Creator. But *Ájúdhiá* was also called *Oudh*, which in Sanskrit means a promise - in allusion it is said, to the promise made by Lord Ram, when he went in exile, to return at the end of 14 years. (Carnegy, 1870). The ancient city of *Ájúdhiá* was ruled by Lord Ram, the 57th descendent of Raja Manu. This dynasty of the *Suryavanshi kshatriyas* (a warrier race tracing their lineage from the Sun), founded by Ikshvakú or *Ikṣvāku,* ruled through three *yugas*: *Satya, Treta* and *Dwapara*, till the present *Kalyug*. It is believed that after the fall of the *Suryavanshi* rulers of Ayodhya, the countryside relapsed into wilderness, during which, the devotees and anchorites of Lord Ram dispersed and survived, spending their lives in prayer and meditation. To such persons are ascribed the foundation of many settlements of the region. For example, Madiaon was originally inhabited by Mandal Rikh or Mandavya *rishi* and Juggaur could be attributed to Jagdeo or Jogi Jagdev, a *yogi*, both of whom had received grants of land from King Janmejaya, the son of Parikshit and the grandson of Pandava Yudhisthir. Nighohan was established by Nagusha, originally of Ayodhya. It is also claimed that the rulers in far-off Jaipur, Jodhpur, Udaipur and other princely states also descended from the same dispersed people of Ayodhya.

There is mention that the kingdom of *Kosala* existed in the region, which was later encompassed in the Magadh Empire. Kosala is described as a kingdom extant during the times of King Janak of Mithila. It extended in the north to the foot hills of Nepal, and to the east, it was bounded by the river *Sadanira* (present day Gandak river). Its southern limits terminated with *Sarpika* or *Sayandika,* identified by some as present day Sai river. The fortunes of Kosala later became intertwined with the Magadh empire, and thereafter in the domain of the Kushans. Historians lament that this ancient period is almost barren as neither any literary nor archaeological sources available have anything to report.

The *pargana* of Lucknow is named after the city of Lucknow; the origin of the name "Lucknow" is definitely not traceable, and according to the *District Gazetteers*, (the official document of the UP Government), whatever traditions are available, are of extremely doubtful historical authenticity (Sharma, 1959). The origin of Lucknow city is itself shrouded in mystery; mythology, religion, fantasy, oral tradition as well as history, which often get mixed up with outright falsehoods and urban legends, whenever any discussion of the city's origins is taken up. There is a tradition that the settlement was named in honour of Lakshman, brother of Lord Ram of Ayodhya and that Lucknow's original name was *Lakshsmanpuri* or *Lakshmanavati*, which was later corrupted as *Lukhnau*, and later to its present designation, *Lucknow*. In the north-west part of the town, a hillock called *Lakshman Teela* did exist, which had an orifice, where people used to throw water and flowers as offerings to the serpent deity, *Sheshnag* who supposedly resided under the hillock. It is also interesting to note that Lakshman is believed to be an *avatar* or an incarnation in human form of this very serpent deity in the Hindu pantheon of Gods. No doubt the hillock still exists, but it is now crowned by the *Alamgir Masjid*, dedicated to Aurangzeb, the Mughal king. Ironically, the mosque is better known as *Teele Wali Masjid*.

It has been tentatively suggested that Mohanlalganj on the outskirts of Lucknow is the place mentioned by Hiuen Tsang as *Kia-shi-pu-lo* (Kashipur) and that Mahona may possibly be the *Pi-so-kia* mentioned by the same author. The Gurjara-Pratiharas ruled over the region during the 8th to 11th century AD, extending from present day Varanasi in the east to Gwalior in the west. The region did not have the flat topography we see today, but even then, the Gomti river was the lifeline of the settlement, much like the Saryu or Ghagra river, which wound its way in what would later be known as *Bangla* or Faizabad. Geological data, as well as artworks and historical references indicate unequivocally that ancient Lucknow's undulating layout resulted in the formation of streams and water bodies in the area (especially after the monsoon rains), some of them so vast, that they had to be traversed by boat. Hence, another possibility for the origin of Lucknow's name could be due to the presence of *lakhs* (hundreds of thousands) of *naus* (boats) in the area. Although it is doubtful that the meagre population of Lucknow of old would require such a multitude of boats, such suppositions no doubt add charm to the mythos of the city's origins.

If we go by oral tradition, the nucleus of the *Macchi Bhavan* citadel of Lucknow (Sarkar, 2021) appears to have been laid when the area was thus inhabited by indigenous tribes, with their own small principalities. The *Pasis* dominated the area of modern Hardoi, Malihabad and Lucknow, whereas *Bhars* established themselves in Mohanlalganj. *Kurmis* were dominant in Mahona and all of them were said to possess strong mud forts and hold positions of authority in their respective areas of settlement. That the Pasi King Karkotak established *Kakori*, Kansraj founded *Kasmandi*, Malraj founded *Malihabad* and Salliraj founded *Sandila*. Bijli Pasi established *Bijnor* (or *Bijnaur*).

The first notable incident in the post-Pratihara period was the invasion of Saiyyad Salar Masud, sent by Mahmud of Ghazni to subjugate the region, during 1031 - 1033 AD. Ironically, his *dargah* (shrine built over a grave or tomb) in Bahraich is a place of reverence for Muslims and Hindus alike. Built by Firoz Shah Tughlaq, it is believed that people taking a bath in the water of this *dargah* are cured of all skin ailments. Masud had made Satrikh (in Bara Banki district) his headquarters, from where he sent out expeditions in every direction. Tradition also says that Salar Masud's route lay through the *pargana* of Malihabad, where he drove out Kansa, the ruler of Kasmanda. From Malihabad, he proceeded to *pargana* Bijnor. Later, the Rajputs around Delhi and Kannauj made significant inroads into the territories of these tribes. Amalgamation of different communities also took place. According to local legend, the Pasi community desired to have a marriage alliance with a Brahmin girl, for one of their sons. The Brahmin community received help from Jai Chand of Kannauj and Bijnor was laid waste. It may not be possible to describe the Rajput invasions chronologically (Neville, 1904, 1922), but it is certain that with time, the Bais of Baiswara established suzerainty over Nigohan, Sissaindi and Bijnor. Similarly, the Panwars, Solankis and Chauhans drove out the Pasis, Bhars together with other local feudal chieftains and settled themselves in various demarcated areas. The first sustained Muslim movement in the area appears to have been during Mohammad Bakhtiyar Khilji in 1202, and what started as a trickle became a regular influx over a period of time. With the advent of the Mughals, Muslim occupation of the territory became the norm, although the Rajputs continued to hold sway in some areas.

The Shaikhs of Kasmandi Kalan were among the first Muslim arrivals in the area, although they were purported to be converted Hindus. The Kidwai Shaikhs arrived from Satrikh, in around 1200 AD. *Circa* 1256 AD is the date assigned to the advent of the Bijnor Muslims, under the leadership of one Qazi Adam, from whom the famous Shaikhs of Lucknow had descended. The Muslim clans who settled in the area of Lucknow and its neighbourhood included the Shaikhs of Salempur, Aman Zai Pathans, Bayazid Khel Pathans, Qandharis of Khalispur and the Afridis of Rohilkhand. But these families played practically no important role in the general history of the district, confining their attention to their own estates, giving rise to petty squabbles and conflicts.

The area in and around *Lakshman Teela* (discussed earlier) was initially populated by Hindu Brahmins and Kayasthas. The Shaikhs of Bijnor (see above) asserted their claim over the region, likely owing to its strategic location and the relatively low impact of periodic flooding. Other Muslim clans who flourished in the area were the Pathans of Ramnagar and the Nimbhara Shaikhs. The Shaikhs' fortification, *Qila Lakhna*, the pre-cursor of *Macchi Bhavan* citadel, attributed to a certain Lakhna Ahir, was established on a point of eminence next to the river Gomti. In all probability, it would have been a mud fort, but situated on a commanding position. Did his name *Lakhna* give rise to the name Lucknow, as this now flourishing settlement, *Lakhnau* took the place of the old *Lakshsmanpuri* or *Lakshmanavati*? It seems improbable, however, because the term, *Alakhnau*, had existed during the times of Mohammad Bin Tuglaq, as per traveller, Ibn Batuta, who had arrived in India during 1334 AD. According to him, *Alakhnau* had supplied large quantities of grain to Mohammad Bin Tuglaq during the famine of 1338 - 1341. The Governor of Awadh, Ain-ul-Mulk, who later revolted with his brothers, had been appointed by Mohammad Bin Tuglaq himself; however the Sultan had great difficulty in suppressing this revolt, as Awadh, due to its prosperity, had become a hot-bed of sedition and revolt.

Lucknow (and Awadh) remained under the Sharqi dyansty of Jaunpur from the year 1394 onwards, till Bahlol Lodhi annexed it and assigned Azam Humayun as its Governor in 1487 - 88. Azam was succeeded by Ahmad Khan and then Saeed Khan. The Lodhis faced the same problem faced by the Tuglaqs earlier, due to the general atmosphere of rebellion in the area. With the advent of the Mughals in 1526, Lucknow was occupied by Humayun for a brief period, after which it came under the control of the *Sūr* Afghans. Babur, however, re-occupied Lucknow in March 1528. Humayun again retreated briefly to Lucknow in 1539, after his defeat at the hands of Sher Shah Suri, where he was assisted by the Shaikhs. Sher Shah appointed Isa Khan as administrator of the area, with Qadir Shah in charge of Lucknow. Silver and copper mints were also established in Lucknow during this period. Under the *Sūr* (Afghan) rule, Lucknow began to rise in importance, and during the reign of Akbar, it was the chief town of a *sarkar* (administrative division of Awadh *suba*). Several *mohallas* started flourishing in the area, with the Brahmin and Kayastha community among the Hindus retaining their eminence.

The early Mughal governors included Husain Khan Tukriya, Mehndi Kasim Khan, Iskandar Khan, Kwaja Amin-ud-Din and Jawahar Khan, to name a few. The *Naib* (deputy) of Jawahar Khan, Qasim Mahmud built Mahmudnagar and Shahganj to the right and left of the now densely populated Chowk area, with the *Akbari Darwaza* at the southern end, as an honour to the Mughal Emperor.

Due to the administrative reforms of Akbar in 1590, the Mughal empire was divided into 12 *subas* (provinces), which later increased to 15 during his lifetime (Jahangir increased the number of *subas* to 17 during his reign, which increased to 22 under Shah Jahan). Under the Mughals, the head of administration in the *suba* was the *Sipahsalar* or Commander although later, the term *Subadar* or Provincial Governor began to be used. Other officials who assisted the *Subadar* in the *suba* included the *Diwan* (Head of Revenue administration) *Bakhshi* (Pay Master), *Sadr-e-Qazi* (Head of Judicial Affairs as per Islamic Law), *Amil* (Revenue Collector / Assessor), *Kotwal* (Police Superintendent), *Morbahr* (Superintendent of Rivers and Ports) and the *Waqia-Navis* (News Writer). *Suba Awadh* had five *sarkars*: Awadh, Lucknow, Bahraich, Khairabad and Gorakhpur. Akbar appointed Shaikh Abdur Rahim of Moradabad as Governor of Awadh *suba*; the latter built residences for himself and his five sons in the area previously occupied by the *Qila Lakhna.* Subsequently, this Five Palace complex came to be known as *Panch Mahalla*, with its imposing gateway facing the west, known as the *Shaikhan Darwaza.* One of the earliest descriptions of Lucknow's landscape and the elevations of the *Panch Mahalla* complex can be gleaned from the writings of Joseph Tieffenthaler, *Description Indiœ* and *Cursus Gangœ*. Tieffenthaler had stayed in Lucknow for five years, beginning 1766 and had attempted to describe not only the cartographic details

Figure 1: Palais Quintuple (Panch Mahalla)
palace complex of Lucknow, Tieffenthaler (1786).

of *Lacnau* or *Laknao* (Lucknow) and its rivers, *Goumati* (Gomti) and *Cocràl* (Kukrail) but also the *Palais Quintuple* (*Panch Mahalla*) palace complex of the *Shaikhzadas,* then a prominent structure (or principal edifice) of the city, which would later metamorphose into the *Macchi Bhavan* citadel under Nawabi rule. Descendants of Shaikh Abdur Rahim, referred to as the *Shaikhzadas*, held sway over Lucknow till the arrival of Burhan-ul-Mulk in 1722.

The development of Lucknow continued during the reign of Jahangir, who founded the *Mirza Mandi* area, west of the *Panch Mahalla.* Joannes De Laet was a geographer by profession and one of the Directors of the Dutch East India Company. His book *De Imperio Magni Mogolis sive India vera Commentarius ex variis auctoribus congestus* was published in 1631 in Latin. The following excerpt from its English translation by Hoyland and Bannerjee (1928) stated that: "From Cannove (Kannauj) to Lacanouw (Lucknow) is 30 cos (*kos*): this is a great trading centre: thence to Oudee (Ayodhya) - an ancient city, once the seat of Pathan Kings, but now almost deserted, 50 cos. Not far from this city may be seen the ruins of the fort and palace of

Ramchand, whom the Indians regard as God Most High: they say that he took on him human flesh that he might see the great *tamasha* of the world .." Chronologically, his travelogue coincides with Jahangir's rule. We can therefore conclude that Lucknow had already become a place of some prominence, *a great trading centre*, while neighbouring Ayodhya was in ruins during the times of Jahangir.

Sultan Ali Shah Quli Khan was Subadar of Awadh during the reign of Shahjahan. Quli Khan's two sons, Mirza Fazil and Mansur founded *Fazil Nagar* and *Mansur Nagar*. Mohammad Sharif, who succeeded Quli Khan "built magnificent buildings in his fief of Lucknow, and laid the foundation of the *serai* (inn) and the quarters of *Ashrāfabād.* He also laid out a garden which was a public resort. The date of its laying - engraved on the gate was - Bōstān-*i-Dōstān* - The Garden of Friends (1040 AH, 1630 - 31 AD). He lived in retirement in this garden till he went to the Garden of Eternity (Beveridge & Prashad, 1941)". His brother founded *Mushārrāfābād* or *Naubasta,* adjoining *Ashrāfabād.* Pir Khan, another Mughal noble established *Garhi Pir Khan*, on the west of the city. Lucknow's old copper mint continued to function during Shahjahan's reign. By this time, Europeans were successfully carrying out various trades in Lucknow, which included sugar, indigo and bleached cloth. As was his wont, Aurangzeb visited the now bustling city of Lucknow and the Alamgir mosque (discussed earlier) was built on Lucknow's most vantage and revered spot - the *Lakhsman Teela*, thus, sowing the seeds for religious confrontations which continue in present times. Fortunately, the later Safavid Nawabi rulers ignored any such religious schisms between the Hindu and Muslim communities of Lucknow, actively pursuing a policy of inclusiveness and communal harmony, as a result of which, the city remained free from communal disturbances throughout history till present times. However, the same cannot be said of other cities, where old wounds continue to fester till today, due to the shenanigans of Aurangzeb and his zealous generals. The *Firangi Mahal* property, established by European traders on a year-long lease during the reign of Jahangir was confiscated by the Mughal Emperor, and handed over (*madad-i-ma'ash*) to a renowned Islamic scholar, Mulla Qutub-ud-Din of Bara Banki. The descendents of Qutub-ud-Din founded a center of learning within the premises of the *Firangi Mahal*. Ironically, over the next two and half centuries, the *Firangi Mahal* was to become a renowned center for Islamic theology, its influence spreading far and wide beyond the city of Lucknow.

Other Mughal Governors during this period were Irij Khan and Jamal Khan. The *suba* also got a Hindu Governor, Raja Girdhar Nagar, the nephew of Chabila Ram Nagar, the governor of Allahabad. His wife founded *Rani Katra*, east of *Daulatganj*. Lucknow was now a bustling town, with localities like *Shivpuri, Ramnagar, Shyamnagar, Rooppur, Devpur, Ramganj, Mohinipur, Murlipur, Pitambar Kheda, Madhopur, Surajkund, Gau Ghat* and *Pipra Ghat.* Also, scattered areas like *Kanhai Kheda, Nat Kheda, Chabili Kheda, Bahadur Kheda, Mangal Kheda, Baldev Kheda, Kesri Kheda, Durga Kheda, Devi Kheda, Sardari Kheda*, were among the pre-Nawabi Hindu localities, mostly based on the livelihood of its inhabitants. The *yagya* (sacrificial rite) of the Vajpayee Brahmins during the time of Akbar had led to the establishment of *Vajpayee Tola, Katari Tola, Sondhi Tola, Banjari Tola* and *Ahiri Tola.* Other localities included *Asamau, Bhaptamau, Kesar Mau, Murau Mau, Chiraunda Purwa, Medhai Purwa, Changa Baba Purwa, Lodhan Purwa, Bhran Purwa, Rani ka Tila* and *Belwala Tola*.

In addition to the above Hindu and Muslim localities, the influx of holy men or *peers* during Islamic rule resulted in areas such as *Peer Jalil, Peer Bukhara, Rauza Bagh* (in present day Rajendranagar), *Takia Angara Shah, Takia Tara Shah, Qutubpur, Ghausnagar* and *Subhanagar.* The reader may refer to Table 1 for the significance of various terms used in the context of naming Lucknow's localities.

The Nawabi phase of Lucknow started with the arrival of Sa'adat Khan Burhan-ul-Mulk at Lucknow as successor of Raja Girdhar Nagar in 1722. He entered the territory of the ruling *Shaikhzadas* through stealth and local alliances and managed to subdue them. Sa'adat Khan put an end to the lawlessness prevalent in the *parganas* of Lucknow, Bijnor and Kursi. His contribution to the evolution of Lucknow city included assuming control of the *Panch Mahalla* which would later metamorphose as the Nawabi citadel of *Macchi*

Table 1: Significance of various colloquial terms used in the context of naming Lucknow's localities

Colloquial Term	Significance
Abad (आबाद)	Suffix after city founder's or patron's name, or simply indicating prosperity
Adda (अड्डा)	Starting / meeting point
Ahata (अहाता)	Compound
Bagh (बाग)	Garden, orchard
Basti (बस्ती)	Settlement
Deodi; dyodhi (ड्योढ़ी)	Vestibule; entry by way of a porch
Gali (गली)	Street; lane
Ganj (गंज)	Grain market
Garhi (गढ़ी)	Fortified building, small fort
Ghat (घाट)	Steps leading to river; river bank; area near river bank
Jheel (झील)	Lake
Khurd and Kalan (खुर्द and कलाँ)	Administrative designations used to indicate the smaller (*Khurd)* and larger (*Kalan*) segments of a town, village or settlement.
Katra (कटरा)	Caravan *serai* (inn)
Kheda (खेड़ा)	A small village or dwelling, typically belonging to farmers
Koocha (कूचा)	Narrow lane; by lane
Kuan (कुआँ)	Well, area near a well
Kund (कुण्ड)	Small reservoir, having sacred water / divine connotations
Mandi (मंडी)	Wholesale market
Mau (मऊ)	Camp
Mohalla (मोहल्ला)	Locality
Nagar (नगर)	Township
Naka (नाका)	Check post
Phatak (फाटक)	Gate, gateway
Pur, Pura (पुर, पुरा)	Township
Purwa (पुरवा)	Hamlet
Serai (सेराई)	Inn
Takia (टकया)	Mint, area near a mint
Talaab (तालाब)	Pond
Teela, Tila (टीला)	Mound, hillock
Tola (टोला)	Hamlet, typically occupied by members of same community or profession

Bhavan palace complex, under Safdar Jang, his son-in-law and successor from 1739 onwards. The emergence of localities such as *Katra Saiyad Hussain Khan, Katra Abu-Turab Khan, Bagh*

Figure 2: Vintage Painting Depicting the Rulers of Awadh, by Unidentified Artist. Strangely, the caption states: "Oudh Kings" which is not correct, since all the rulers were not kings. The painting also depicts "Diwan-i-Am" and "Diwan-i-Khas", obviously inspired by Mughal architecture, but these never existed in Lucknow.

Mahnarain in present day Chowk; *Katra Khudayar Khan, Katra Bazan Beg Khan* in present day Sa'adatganj, *Katra Muhammad Ali Khan and Serai Mali Khan* in Daulatganj and of Ismailganj, since demolished, to the east of the *Shaikhzadas*' citadel are attributed to the times of Burhan-ul-Mulk.

Safdar Jang held the dual charge of *Wazir* of the Mughal empire and *Nawab* (Naib) of Awadh, referred to as *Nawab Wazir*. Although based mostly at Delhi, he was responsible for several developments in and around Lucknow. The *Nawab Wazir* was instrumental in obtaining ownership and transforming of the *Panch Mahalla* complex into the *Macchi Bhavan* citadel; the evicted Shaikhs were given 700 acres of land in *Dugawan* or *Do Gaon* / two villages (located north of present day *Charbagh*) in exchange for the *Panch Mahalla*. The twin fish symbol began appearing as the heraldry of Awadh from his times onwards (Sarkar, 2021). The construction of the *Nawabi* or *Shahi Pul* across the Gomti River, also referred to as "Asaf-ud-Daula's Stone Bridge" by western authors, commenced during his regime, by Newal Rai, his *Naib* or deputy. For a long time, this bridge would be the only permanent one across the river, providing connectivity to Sitapur and trans-Gomti districts. To counter the Bais Rajputs of Baiswara, Safdar Jang fortified and strengthened an old fort in the eastern part of the city, renaming it as *Jalalabad Fort* - the original structure possibly being one of Bijli Pasi's 12 forts. It is surmised that the fort may have been renamed as *Jalalabad* in honour of his son, Shuja-ud-Daula, whose name was Jalal-ud-Din Haider. Only *Safdarbagh* (possibly *Sundarbagh* of today) locality is attributed to Safdar Jang in Lucknow.

On October 11, 1754, Alamgir II appointed Shuja as the successor of Safdar Jang. However, the *Wizarat* of Delhi still eluded Shuja, and the title was conferred to him on December 24, 1759. He assumed control of the *Macchi Bhavan* and converted it into a palace complex, so much so that western writers and artists started referring to it as Shuja-ud-Daula's palace in Lucknow. The *Bayasi ki Masjid* at Lucknow is attributed to Shuja-ud-Daula. Baba Hazara, a Nanak Shahi saint arrived at Lucknow in the rule of Shuja-ud-Daula and settled down at *Ahata Surat Mal* near *Garhi Pir Khan* for his abode.

The compound would later be known as *Bagh Baba Hazara.* The typical tripolia gateways with their accoutrements and other hybrid architectural features of Nawabi structures emerged at Faizabad, under the guidance of Shuja-ud-Daula's French advisors (Sarkar, 2021, 2023), which continued at Lucknow till the last days of Wajid Ali Shah's rule.

The contribution of Asaf-ud-Daula, son of Shuja-ud-Daula, towards the development of Lucknow, after he shifted the capital from Faizabad to Lucknow in 1775 was highly significant. He is credited for building the *Daulat Khana* palace complex with the *Asafi Kothi*, *Aina Khana / Gend Khana*, *Sheesh Mahal*, *Zenana (Sheesh Mahal) Talab*, *Pathar Wali Masjid*, *Asafi (Bada) Imambara*, *Asafi Masjid*, *Rumi Darwaza*, *Bibiapur Kothi*, *Asafi Kothi* (Chinhat), *Tope Darwaza* and *Sunheri Burj* palace - the last being Bahu Begum's residence at Lucknow. The localities attributed to Asaf-ud-Daula's times are *Astabal* (stables) at *Yahyaganj, Musabagh, Aishbagh, Moti Jheel, Charbagh, Wazirganj* (in honour of his son, Wazir Ali), *Amaniganj, Rakabganj, Nakkhas, Daulataganj, Begumganj, Nawabganj*, *Tirmaniganj, Tikri, Chaoni Hasan-ud-Din Khan, Bhawaniganj, Balakganj*, *Niwazganj, Ambarganj, Mehboobganj, Khayaliganj, Khansama ka Ahata, Nawazganj, Thakurganj, Khudaganj, Mohammad Bagh, Husnbagh* and *Hussain Bagh*.

Sa'adat Ali Khan succeeded Asaf-ud-Daula in 1798, (after an interim period of 6 months' rule by Wazir Ali, who was later deposed). The British Residency, *Tehri Kothi, Lal Baradari (Qasr-us-Sultan), Dilaram Kothi* (demolished during colonial rule), *Dilkusha, Kankar Wali Kothi* (demolished; site of Halwasiya complex), *Aine Wali Kothi* (present day Hindi Sansthan), *Khurshid Manzil* (now La Martiniere College for Girls), *Jarnail Kothi, Badshah Manzil, Chaupar Astabal* (stables), *Musabagh Kothi*, *Moti Mahal, Maqbara Janab-e-Alia, Kothi Singhara* and *Dargah Hazrat Abbas* are attributed to Sa'adat Ali. Among the localities including markets, Sa'adat Ali is credited for *Sa'adatganj, Rakabganj, Jangliganj, Maqboolganj, Golaganj, Maulviganj, Rastogi Mohalla, Barood Khana, Chiria Jhil, Chikmandi* and *Mashakganj*. The direct road cutting across the city from the Residency to the *Dilkusha Kothi* was also the creation of this Nawab.

This arterial road would later have many *avatars*, and a section of it would become the famed Hazratganj later on. Fateh Ali Khan, also known as Zafar-ud-Daula, was a close confidante of Sa'adat Ali Khan. He is believed to have built the Maqbara called *Masjid Kaptan*, at *Mohini Purwa,* near *Hussainabad*, where he was interred after his death. He was also responsible for the *Kaptan ka Kuan* near *Gol Darwaza*, Chowk, and a *talaab* near Charbagh. A market near present day Aminabad is also named as *Fatehganj* in his honour.

During the rule of Asaf-ud-Daula and Sa'adat Ali Khan, Hony. Maj. General to the ECI, Claude Martin made Lucknow his home and contributed to a number of striking edifices to the city, including his *Town House* (later *Farhat Baksh*), *Lakhi Pera / Constantia* (later La Martiniere Boys' School), *Old Martin Kothi / Gori Bibi ki Kothi* (present day *Kakori Kothi*), *Gori Bibi ka Maqbara* and *Gori Bibi ki Masjid.* The areas of *Martin Purwa*, *Gori Bibi ka Ahata*, *Captain Bazar* (presently occupied by the Martyr's Memorial), *Martingarh* and *Biposi* (Najafgarh, near Unnao) are also attributed to Martin. Both the *Town House* and *Constantia* had a kind of striking architecture, which is talked about even in present times.

Figure 3: Shahi Pul or Asaf-ud-Daula's Stone Bridge, 1870, Daroga Ubbas Ali.

Figure 4: Dilkusha, 1860, Robert & Harriet Tytler.

Figure 5: Durbar scene painted by unidentified artist, depicting Wajid Ali Shah embracing Lord Hardinge, then Governor General, during the latter's visit to Lucknow in November 1847. Despite the bonhomie and embrace, the British would unceremoniously depose the King in February 1856, paving the way for Colonial Rule in Lucknow (Awadh).

It need not be reiterated that by this time, Lucknow city had started to reach the peak of its glorious days, being second only to Delhi in north India. Foreign travellers, including writers and artists had started to throng the Awadh court, either on brief visits or looking for easy pickings. Their reaction to this oriental city was generally of awe, coupled with derision. Roads were non-existent or narrow, full of ordure. People went around with weapons of all kinds, but appeared receptive, especially to foreign visitors; there is not a single account of any foreigner being ill-treated or looted by the local populace. The buildings with their tall spires and domes were awe-inspiring from a distance, especially during sunset, yet presented a not-so-impressive look from close quarters; there was no marble or stone, but brick and stucco. The glittering domes were actually gilded, not layered with gold. The ornamentation was tawdry and defied convention. European visitors were invariably flummoxed on seeing statues of every shape, design and mythological origin, including those of animals, female figures and other decorative motifs and imagery, not normally associated with a Islamic city. These travellers marvelled at the gumption of the Nawabi rulers for erecting palaces which looked impressive from afar, but proved to be rather cheap imitations at close quarters. They could not accept the fact that the classical Greek orders of architecture could be so casually applied and also contaminated by this random and irrational pick-and-choose technique, exhibited by Lucknow's Nawabi-era builders. During his journeys covering Calcutta, Benaras, Allahabad, Cawnpore and Lucknow, Rev. William Tennant (1803), Chaplain with the East India Company, had the following derogatory comments for Lucknow:

"I yesterday went to view this Capital, which is said to contain millions of souls. Happening *(sic)* to enter the town at the west end, and contains the poor mechanics and labourers of every sort, I never witnessed so many forms of wretchedness, filth and vice. The street which leads to the palace is upwards of five miles long, more than one-half of which you wade through mire and filth. During the lapse of time the streets sink from clearing or by blowing away of dust while dry, so that they are fallen in the middle to the depth of ten or twelve feet, and are so narrow that two hackeries cannot pass, nor, indeed, any carriage however small. My palankeen (*sic*) was frequently stopped by small asses which were passing along loaded with bricks. This animal here is so slender that a stout porter could have no difficulty in literally carrying both the beast and its burden. Solomon must have employed an immense number in carrying the material of the temple, if his asses were not of a superior breed to these of Lucknow.

The concourse of a great number of people perhaps does not anywhere improve their morals; vice and poverty are the only qualities that this people uniformly display. Some saunter, others lie down in a kind of dubious state between existence and annihilation; others still are intoxicating themselves with the *hookah*; a few only labour at their professions. The show of rich shops and merchandize is remarkably small, though it supplies to the luxury of the court, or rather the palace; for here there is little affluence beyond the narrow circle of the prince's family."

Prince Alexis Soltykoff, grandson of Prince Nikolay Soltykoff, was an artist and traveller, who, during his visit to Lucknow in 1841, remarked that the surrounding country was completely wild like a sandy desert without a road (*desert sablonneux tout à fait sauvage et sens route*) but as an European, he respected the city for being unique (*le respect qu'on porte sociaux Europeens est vraiment unique*).

However, despite criticisms and encomiums, Lucknow continued to grow and prosper, for whatever good or bad it represented in terms of architecture and city planning, and its laid-back citizens.

Ghazi-ud-Din Haider was *Nawab Wazir* from 1814 - 1818; following which, under British instigation, he severed ties from the Mughal court and declared himself as an independent ruler, holding the reigns of Awadh from 1818 - 1827. He was responsible for building the *Shahnajaf, Bada, Chattar Manzil, Maqbara Sa'adat Ali Khan, Maqbara Khurshid Zadi, Mubarak Manzil, Shah Manzil, Qadam Rasul, Sher Darwaza, Matba-e-Sultani* (printing press) and the *Sultan Manzil*. The *Badshah Bagh,* (present Lucknow University), *Badshah*

Nagar, Hazaribagh, Mehndiganj, Hussainganj, Haiderabad, Chini Bazar and *Vilayati Bagh* also came up during his rule.

Nasir-ud-Din Haider, son and successor of Ghazi-ud-Din Haider ruled from 1827 - 1837. He was responsible for creating the *Choti (Khurd) Chattar Manzil, Darshan Bilas Kothi, Gulistan-e-Iram Kothi, Tara Wali Kothi, Iradatganj Karbala, Ghazi-ud-Din Haider Canal, Dar-ul-Shifa, Chakkar Wali Kothi* (King's Race Course), *Shahi Shifa Khana* (King's Hospital), *Khairat Khana* (Poor House) and *Banarsi Bagh* (present day Zoo). The areas of *Pasand Bagh, Ganeshganj, Chandbagh* (present day Chandganj and IT College campus) and *Chakkar Purwa* are also attributed to Nasir-ud-Din Haider.

Mohammad Ali Shah, who succeeded Nasir-ud-Din Haider is credited for adding several prominent edifices to Lucknow, including the *Chota Imambara, Sat Khanda, Hussainabad tank, Baradari* (present Picture Gallery), and the unfinished *Jama Masjid.* The area of *Hussainabad* came up during his rule, where originally, the *Jamunia Bagh* was extant, due to the presence of orchards of black plum (colloquial: *jamun*) - deforestation under administrative orders being the accepted norm then, as it is today.

Amjad Ali Shah "Hazrat", the father of Wajid Ali Shah ruled during 1842 - 1847. *Begum Kothi, Malka Geti Phatak, Shahi Kothi* and *Malka Geti Imambara* are attributed to him. The Iron (Rennie's) bridge had been imported from England by Sa'adat Ali Khan and the sections of the bridge had been delivered in 1816; however, Sa'adat Ali was dead by that time and his son, Ghazi-ud-Din Haider was opposed to the whole idea, since the bridge would directly connect the British Madiaon cantonment with the city. Company officials made attempts to persuade successive Nawabs to erect the bridge in 1823 and again in 1828. The sections lay on the banks of the river for more than thirty years, when finally, in 1845, it was erected by Col. Fraser of the Bengal Engineers during the reign of Amjad Ali Shah. The famous market of Hazratganj also got its name from the king, who was buried in the *Sibtainabad Imambara* built by him, in an area known as *Medu Khan ki Chaoni.*

The last ruler of Awadh, Wajid Ali Shah (1847 - 1856) contributed significantly to the now magnificence of Lucknow. The *Kaiserbagh* palace complex, including *Safed Baradari (Qasr-us-Aza), Pari Khana* (demolished and replaced by Canning College/ present Bhatkhande Music University), *Lanka* (demolished and replaced by present Amir-ud-Daula Public Library), *Hazratbagh, Chinibagh, Naginewali Baradari* (relocated to the Wingfield Park / Zoo), *Khas Muqam, Chandiwali Baradari, Shahanshah Manzil, Badshah Manzil, Ishq Manzil, Istrahat Manzil, Vaqar Manzil*, *Afsar Manzil, Shikoh Manzil, Haziri Manzil, Rahas Manzil, Gulzar Manzil, Aram Manzil, Hayat Manzil, Rahat Manzil, Zard Kothi, Qasr-ul-Khakan, Qasr-ul-Baizavi, Makan-e-Dilpasand, Dil Afza, Kabootar Khana, Makan-e-Chogobiya, Makan-e-Khas, Falak Sair, Bait-ul-Sarur, Jahan Numa, Makan-e-Chaupahlu, Kunj-e-Gulshan, Taskin Baksh, Indrasan, Shah Burj*; also *Kabootar Wali Kothi*, (present Oel House), *Sikchewali Kothi, Dilkusha Astabal* and *Jinnaton ka Masjid* were the contributions of Wajid Ali Shah before he was deposed in February 1856. He is also credited for establishing *Sikandar Bagh*, *Jarnailganj*, *Sarfarazganj* and *Sundarbagh* in Lucknow.

Other than the rulers, a number of localities and markets were established and edifices erected in and around Lucknow, by begums, noblemen, menial officials and even concubines belonging the Nawabi court. For example, Tikait Rai, a *Diwan* of Awadh (1791 - 1796) was responsible for building the *Tikait Rai ka Talaab, Tikait Rai ka Pul and Shiv Mandir, Shitla Mata Mandir, Masjid, Tikait Rai ki Haveli, Imambara, Baradari* (Bithoor), *Patthar Ghat* (Bithoor) and *Takia Sharif* (Kakori). He also established *Tikaitganj, Bazar Tikait Rai / Raja Bazar, Nishatbagh, Tikait Nagar* (Bara Banki) and *Tikait Ganj* (Rae Bareilly). Agha Mir, *Wazir* during the reign of Ghazi-ud-Din Haider, built the *Imambara Agha Mir* (present day Jubilee College), *Nur Baksh Kothi* (present residence of District Magistrate), *Zahur Baksh Kothi* and *Imambara* (demolished; site for present Epiphany / *Zahur Baksh* Church), *Karbala* (presently houses Masonic Lodge), *Kothi Malika-e-Jahan* (now demolished). He was also responsible for building / creating *Dyodhi Agha Mir*, *Serai Agha Mir*, *Wazir Bagh* and *Buland Bagh.* A bridge built by Jhau Lal, a courtier in the Nawabi court called *Jhau Lal ka Pul* in Aminabad area, an Imambara (*Shia Bait-ul-Mal*) in Thakurganj area, as well as a market named *Bazar Jhau Lal* are still extant in Lucknow. *Hasanganj* was founded on the north side of the river by Hasan Raza Khan, Chief Minister in the Nawabi court.

By 1856, Lucknow was already known as a city of gardens and palaces. There is evidence of at least thirty four gardens (Tandan, 2001) in and around the environs of Lucknow, having been commissioned during the Nawabi period. Out of these, twenty four had been apparently established during the 18th century and eleven in the 19th. With time and changing fortunes, many such Nawabi gardens underwent changes (Sinha, 2009) in usage patterns, although the names persisted, like *Sundar Bagh, Almas Bagh, Khurshid Bagh, Chand Bagh, Chiraya Bagh, Bagh Sher Jung, Ram Bagh, Lotan Bagh, Dali Bagh, Phool Bagh, Lalbagh, Wazir Bagh, Teli Bagh, Mausam Bagh, Nazar Bagh, Buland Bagh, Lotan Bagh, Mehtab Bagh, Mehdi Bagh, Sajjad Bag, Charbagh, Aishbagh, Badhshah Bagh*, *Alambagh, Bandariya Bagh, Banarasi Bagh* and many others.

After the annexation of Lucknow by the EIC in 1856, not much construction activity was evident - the primary focus being on the loot of Nawabi assets and appropriation of Nawabi palaces and gardens for self-use. However, all this was about to change, when a cataclysm hit Lucknow and its environs in 1857 and the ire of the British turned against the city and its people. Now it was the turn of cutting large swathes through the city to facilitate easy movement of troops; this was achieved under the directions of Col. Robert Napier, which will be discussed in detail in another Chapter. With time, as passions cooled down and the colonial masters realised the folly of their own actions against a former bustling city, efforts were made once more to revive Lucknow once more. A survey of the city was ordered by the Chief Commissioner, which commenced in July 1867. By the time the records and the maps were filed in the Deputy Commissioner's office, it was already June 1869. In this exercise, as expected, the survey of *nazul* lands proved to be of greatest difficulty. At that point of time, the city covered an area of thirteen square miles, containing a population of 27,326 inhabitants.

The chief thoroughfares of Colonial Lucknow were: (1) the Outram Road, which led upto Hazratganj and crossing it, continued by the Abbot Road, (2) the Aminabad Road which passed through the most crowded parts of the city to the south of Kaiserbagh and (3) the Canning Road, which ran south-west from the open ground round the *Macchi Bhavan*. Three roads from the Iron Bridge, by which the traffic for Sitapur was conveyed, from the old Stone Bridge and from the *pargana* town of Malihabad also led to the *Macchi Bhavan*. At their point of conjunction, the Victoria Road ran southwards, joining the Cawnpore Road. The city communicated with the Cantonment by: (1) the Strand Road, which ran parallel to the river side from the *Macchi Bhavan*, continued by the Hazratganj Road, passed the Civil Lines (Christ) Church, going by the Chief Commissioner's House (*Kothi Hayat Baksh*, now Governor's House), (2) by Major Banks' Road, which passed from the back of Kaiserbagh and joined the 1st Road above and (3) by the Cantonment Road which started from the Aminabad Road, commencing at the same point at the back of Kaiserbagh and Banks Road, crossing the Abbot Road, leading into the *Sudder (Sadar) Bazar* of the Cantonment. Three imperial

Figure 6: Panoramic view of Lucknow, after Napier's cleaning operations of the city, 1860, Robert Bourne.

Figure 7: Panoramic view of Lucknow, after Napier's cleaning operations of the city, 1870, Robert and Harriet Tytler.

Figure 8: Europeans enjoying a hockey match near the tombs of Sa'adat Ali Khan and Khurshid Zadi, Unidentified Photographer.

Figure 9: Ramparts of Macchi Bhavan, 1860, Robert & Harriet Tytler.

metalled roads from Lucknow branched out to Cawnpore (Kanpur), Fyzabad (Faizabad) and Seetapore (Sitapur). Local roads branched out to Kursi, Dewa, Sultanpur, Rae Bareilly, Mohán and Malihabad. A *kaccha* (un-metalled) road led to Bijnaur (Bijnore). The railway was in its nascent stages, with the Oudh & Rohilkhand Railways (O & RR) branching out in three directions: East, South-West and North-East.

Butts (1871) thus presented a rosy picture of colonial rule, "Quieter times, if less congenial to the native spirit - have come for it with the introduction of British rule, roads have been carefully laid out and well kept; streets have been widened, bazars have been made, in which the comfort and convenience of tradesmen and their customers have been studied; stringent cleanliness is enforced; and local Government introduced in a municipality, in which the native wishes are consulted by the appointment of native members, whom their fellow townsmen may themselves elect. Dispensaries, schools and other public buildings have been established, nor should mention be omitted of the magnificent hospital in the course of erection, which is due to the munificence of Maharaja Drigbije Singh of Balrampur..."

In addition to maintaining a tight control over the native population and revenue collection, the focus of the colonial administration was now on sanitation, water supply, creation of memorial parks and markets, re-aligning of old roads and creating new ones, laying of railway lines, construction of bridges as well as hospitals for controlling communicable diseases, enhancing agricultural production, promoting education and religious conversions, encouraging local industry and creation of job opportunities. By the turn of the 20th century, and the creation of the Lucknow Improvement Trust in 1909, significant efforts were made by the agency to improve the city of Lucknow through several "Schemes." Some of these Schemes will be discussed in Chapters IV and V. The Trust also successfully constructed several arterial roads in the city, including Hewett Road (between Abbott Road and the La Touche Road), Sri Ram Road (between La Touche Road and Aminabad Road) and Ganga Pershad Road from Aminabad Road to Rakabganj Bridge *via* Canning Street.

The Municipality of Lucknow was divided into eight wards known respectively as "the Chauk (*sic*) ward, the Yahiaganj (*sic*) ward, the Ganeshganj ward, the Hazratganj ward, the Wazirganj ward, the Saadatganj ward, the Daulatganj ward and the Hassanganj ward. The Wazirganj, the Saadatganj, the Daulatganj and Hassanganj wards were conterminous (sharing common boundary) within the limits of the municipality with the police circles whose names they bore. The limits of the Chauk (*sic*) and Yahiaganj wards were co-extensive with those of the Chauk (*sic*) police circle and separated from each other by the line of the road commencing from the Hardinge bridge, passing the Medical College and hospital on the west, over to the Qasaiwala (Kasiwala) bridge and thence along Victoria Street to its junction with Aishbagh Road, the eastern portion being the Yahiaganj (*sic*) ward and the western portion the Chauk (*sic*) ward.

East of Wazirganj and divided from the new Hazratganj ward (one of the most important in Lucknow) was by a line drawn from Bruce Bridge along the Mall down Quinton Road to Capper Road, along Capper Road to Forsyth Road, thence to Abbott Road and from this junction to the Naka Hindola lay the Ganeshganj ward. It was traversed by the Cantonment Road, Banks Road and had a good communication in the La Touche Road."

The reader may refer to Annexure II for an indicative list of roads and areas in Colonial Lucknow.

However, it ought to be pointed out that the developmental and welfare activities in Colonial Lucknow were mostly targeted towards the Europeans residents of the city, with native Indians providing a passive support system, as menial clerks, coolies, gardeners, peons and pursuing other petty jobs / vocations. It was extremely difficult, if not impossible for any Indian (other than few favoured elites and British sympathisers) to rise up in the hierarchy and occupy a position of some substance. This colonial model of development would gradually change with time, as WW II loomed in the horizon and the Indian Freedom Movement gathered momentum once again.

Chapter - II

Up For Grabs I

European Claims and Counter Claims

"But the British Government will ever insist on rewarding the undeserving and neglecting the deserving. Such a policy, if it be a policy is by no means calculated to preserve the integrity of the British subject. Before distributing favours, the first question to be asked is, "Is the recipient deserving?" If not, rather let the favour be cast into the sea, than be the means of creating discontent, bickering jealousies and ever-lasting heart-burnings."

- George Yeoward,
An Episode of the Rebellion and Mutiny of 1857 and 1858 (1876)

Post 1857, Awadh as a whole and Lucknow in particular, had become a popular hunting ground of those searching for freebies, including land grants, confiscated properties, perpetual pensionary benefits or simply monetary compensations. It is true that many Europeans had lost their assets (including ill-gotten gains), which they had managed to amass during their brief stay in the city of Lucknow and elsewhere, prior to the Uprising. No doubt, their "properties" had been looted and vandalised by the Indian revolutionaries and their business establishments reduced to rubble. But then, this was to be expected as an occupational hazard - when one entered another country under the garb of trade and then tried to take over the role of the ruler. The colonial administration opened a channel for redressal of grievances through a "Compensation Commissioner" for such "victims" of the Uprising, although, as we shall later see, there was no hard and fast rule or common yardstick for processing such claims and the eventual settlement, if any, was a very, very tough task indeed. The Compensation Commissioner at Lucknow was Lt. Col. Lousada Barrow, who would later officiate as Commissioner of Lucknow during 1860 – 61 and be Chief Commissioner during January - April 1871.

Since it was not very clear to the claimant or "memorialist" as to where the claim would have to be submitted, i.e. at Lucknow or Calcutta, memorialists often submitted their claims to the highest office available - that of the Chief Commissioner at Lucknow or the Governor General at Calcutta, from where it would be re-routed to the Compensation Commissioner at Lucknow. This entailed delays and several claims got misplaced in the process. The last date for registration of such claims, which was December 1, 1858, was not widely known, and many claimants were totally unaware of such a time limit imposed by the government. The heirs of even Henry Lawrence, idolised as the "Hero of Lucknow" had to face queries as to "why his heirs and executors failed to register their claim within the appointed time." The claim (1860) was allowed only after the personal intervention of the Governor General at Calcutta (File #2315).

The demarcating line between the claims of military officials and those from civilians was also blurred. Further, as we shall see, many of the claimants including "war widows" had left Indian shores soon after the Uprising and were unable to personally pursue their cases back in India. Such claimants took the help of "military agents" e.g. M/s Thacker Spink & Co., to pursue their files. Inflated claims and petty claims were also common, as many people rushed to grab property or corner monetary benefits during the chaos that ensued after 1857 - 58. Claims, if found proper after initial scrutiny, would be "registered." Often, the same would be investigated; sometimes the claimants would be asked to submit further clarifications. Ultimately, the claims would be categorised as "Passed", "Doubtful" or "Inadmissible."

We shall now outline some cases of "claim" below, for the knowledge (and occasional mirth) of the reader.

- One Brevet Major Kaye's claim (1858) faced considerable bureaucratic delay due to the circumstances in which he had faced losses - his property at Lucknow had been looted when he had been in Delhi on sick leave (baggage @ Rs 1890/- and two horses @ Rs 1316/-). Apparently, his claim was liable to be decided by the civil administration and not military authorities as he had been on leave and not on duty at his place of posting. Later, it came to be known that several military officials were caught in the same situation, and a policy matter decision was urgently required as to whether such claims were to be decided by the civil administration or the military authorities. Fortunately, the government later decided that Major Kaye and all similarly situated officers "would be entitled to all the benefits accorded to the military, under the rules." (File #790)
- The claim of Major L Barrow (1858) was more interesting; he had provided a list of damages, including dishes, salt cellars, hanging lamps, a clock, 6 pictures of his children and books, which totalled to Rs 3436/-. The typical bureaucratic response to this claim was to ask for vouchers regarding the payments made for the household articles, and "a declaration to the effect that the amount of property lost has not been overestimated." He was also asked to explain how he had put a value (Rs 300/-) on the pictures of his children? (File #780)
- The case of one Mr Green was curiouser (1858). He was employed in the Department of Public Works, Oudh and drawing a salary of Rs 100/- per mensem. He died *before* the actual siege commenced at Lucknow and left behind his widow and three young children (Robert, age 6 years, Susan, age 4 years and an infant). Was he entitled to a pension similar to other Europeans who had died *during* the siege? As he had been an artillery volunteer and a former soldier of the 1st Bengal Fusiliers, the colonial government proved to be surprisingly generous in this particular instance, and sanctioned a pension of Rs 80/- per month for the family.

The calculation was interesting: Rs 32/- for the wife and Rs 16/- x 3 for the children, totalling to Rs 80/- per month, which was 80% of the original monthly salary which the deceased officer had drawn during his lifetime, thus setting off an encouraging precedent for future claims (File #597).

- An application of one JS Smith (1858) who was employed as a clerk in the post office on a meagre salary of Rs 50/- per month was granted succour money of Rs 50/- after much correspondence and bureaucratic delays (File #1204).
- J. Johannes prayed (1858) that certain houses and gardens which belonged to him in the city of Lucknow may be protected from destruction after the recapture of the town. Describing himself as a "poor and ruined man", who was then staying in Allahabad, he queried if it was possible to prevent the demolition of the houses and gardens in the list and place them in the care of someone, so that he could take possession of them when he returned. This "poor and ruined man" had been formerly a serving Lieutenant in the army of the ex-King. A pensioner, he later submitted a huge claim for Rs 1,53,180/- for properties destroyed by the revolutionaries and Rs 3,200/- against property destroyed by the British Engineers. Johannes got a total sum of Rs 1450/- for his efforts, "as per the rank of Lieutenant in the Hon'ble Company's service." The rest of his claims were rejected on the ground that "the house in question has been deserted by you; and that though destroyed by our Engineers, it was not destroyed until it had been made uninhabitable by the works of the enemy." Some doubt was also expressed on Johannes' loyalty during the siege at Lucknow (File #2278).
- John Bensley Thornhill, of the Bengal Civil Service and Assistant Commissioner of Oudh, had been staying in the Residency. He had volunteered to go out and bring in the wounded when General Outram and Havelock had forced their way into the Residency on the previous evening. Thornhill was familiar with the area and collected as many

injured as possible in *doolies,* but lost his way while returning, as a result of which, the long train of *doolies* reached the *Khas Bazar* area, near the *Sher Darwaza*. Here, they were set upon by the Indian freedom fighters and put to death. Thornhill himself was wounded and his right arm had to be amputated; he died later on October 12, 1857. Against her application (1858), Mrs. Thornhill, widow of the deceased was granted a pension of Rs 70/- per month and gratuity of Rs 186/-, "being the pension and gratuity to which a widow of a Captain would under similar circumstances had been entitled." (File #738)

- John Barker had been employed as a musician in the court of the ex-King of Awadh, and was in receipt of a pension @ Rs 20/- per month. His son, Edward's claim was for the continuation of this allowance (1858). When the siege commenced, the young lad and his elder brother succeeded in getting into Baillie Guard, but the father and other brothers reached late and could not get admittance. They remained concealed in the city for about a month after which, they were discovered and killed. The elder brother in the Residency deserted and was also killed. Edward, only 8 years of age, was supported by his brother's wife, "who herself was in very poor circumstance and earned a livelihood has a seamstress." The petition was moved by the widow of John Barker, but she could get no succour; the minor child was awarded a pension of Rs 5/- p.m. by the Chief Commissioner, to be paid till the child attained the age of 18. The colonial authorities were unusually harsh in this case - the case of desertion preying heavy on their minds (File #2061). It must be noted that in this particular instance, Martin Gubbins's book, *An Account of the Mutinies of Awadh and the Siege of the Lucknow Residency*, which had described the desertion in some detail, was used as reference material. Gubbins, the Financial Commissioner was *persona non grata* in the eyes of the colonial administration - his book and version of the Mutiny were generally ignored. But in this particular case, it was expedient to quote his writings for denying a measly pension to a widow (File #2061).

- The petition of one Thomas Baptist (1859) was rejected, although he had stated that he was no revolutionary - he had merely been the Band Leader in the services of the former King of Oudh (File #382).
- Mrs. Elizabeth Peter submitted a claim (1859) against losses during the mutiny. She was asked to submit reason for late submission of claim, but her reasons were not found to be satisfactory and her claim was rejected. Also it was discovered that, "she had not accompanied her husband in the Baillie Guard and offered no sufficient reason, either for not having done so, or for having failed to prefer her claim at the proper time." (File #2238).
- Surgeon Wells of the 48th Regiment Native Infantry (1859) was conscious of his entitlements. In his petition, he stated that, "Some natives and Christians have already received houses of equal value to those destroyed by the insurgents; I beg to add that I am willing to be similarly compensated and I do not consider myself less entitled to the consideration of local authorities than any of those who have been remunerated." The claim was denied (File #266).
- The claim of J Carbery (1859) for grant of land in consideration of his services during the mutiny was denied (File #1338).
- A sum of Rs 700/- was sanctioned (1859) to Mr Forbes, Deputy Commissioner "on account of an elephant plundered by the rebels." (File #2712)
- GI Christian was killed with his wife and family and all his property destroyed at Sitapur. The sister, Miss Christian applied (1860) for compensation and was sanctioned a lump sum amount of Rs 4000/- and a monthly pension of Rs 80/- per month (File #2515).

- George Bayley submitted a petition (1859) for compensation against the loss of four of his father's houses, which had been destroyed by British army engineers (and not by the rebels). The rude response of the colonial administration to this was, "the house known as Khan Ally Khan's was selected and accepted in full compensation...... it was valued at rupees 2000/- but said to be undervalued. Mr Bayley, a person deserves no consideration whatsoever. A house was promised him, selected by his agent and accepted by him in full demand at a time when there was little hope of compensation being sanctioned by the government for losses. Mr. Bayley has changed his mind since the government has resolved to compensate. Mr. Bayley is found guilty of colluding with a rebel of notorious character, is it to such a person that such indulgence can be extended?" In all this brouhaha, no one spared a thought for the unfortunate "Khan Ally Khan" and his whereabouts, once the mutiny was over (File #392, 69).

- As an "exceptional case" HD Chick, editor of the *Oudh Gazette* and Co-Editor of *The Central Star* was successful (1859) in getting a grant of Rs 1000/- against his original claim for Rs 3200/- as a "consequence of the Mutiny and Award for services in the Garrison." (File #690)

- Mrs. Sago, a school teacher lived in a small house within the Residency premises, although it was not part of the Resident's establishment. During the siege, it was fortified with cannons under the command of the 32nd Regiment and referred to as "Sago's Post." After the siege was over, Mrs. Sago submitted an exhaustive list of 64 items (not for the house, which was in ruins) but for household goods, including a piano, furniture, Chinaware, glassware and even curtains, totalling to Rs 2500/-. Unfortunately, her claim (1859) got misplaced but a copy of her claim was allowed to be registered as "a special case." In fact, she got paid a little over and above of what she had claimed for in the first place, which made her case indeed "special." (Files #1153, 1576)

- The claim of Major James (1859) for Rs 4000/- which was on account of his "house in the cavalry cantonment which was burnt down and plundered by the mutineers." His claim also included a list of forks, knives, cooking pots, saddles and bridles. The claim itself came late as he arrived in India on January 2, 1859 (File #374).
- One Mr. DJ Blenman (1859) submitted a claim for compensation of property lost in the Lucknow Garrison. The claim was registered but no further information was available on file regarding its admissibility (File #406).
- The petition was GW Lenaine (1859) for grant of a *batta* (allowance) on account of his son, who was shot dead in the Lucknow Garrison (Residency) and compensation for himself on account was a wound was denied (File #78).
- Mrs. Fareen Ragheline was the widow of Stephen Ragheline who "had suffered by the mutineers, a loss of his cash and properties worth a sum of Rs 25000/-." She was assured a sum of Rs 4941/- but "the poor petitioner, whose husband was dead received a note of Rs 500/- only." On protesting. she received a terse reply that, "You can get nothing more than the Rs 500/-, already given to you as compensation for your losses" (File #52).
- The case of Jane Donovan (1859), wife of late Sgt. Major M. Keogh was tragic. She had initially resided in the Madiaon cantonment but had proceeded to the Residency on May 24, 1857, where her husband and 9 year old child were shot dead during the siege. Her bungalow and all her household property had been burnt down in the Madiaon cantonment on May 30, 1857. Her claim was a mere Rs 867/- for the loss of her buggy, horse, tents, tables carpets, trunk and bedstead. The claim was passed for payment (File #405).
- The mortal remains of 19 year old Lt. Charles Keith Dashwood lie in eternal peace in the grounds of the *Dilkusha*. He had died a horrible death inside a *doolie* in the Field

Hospital on November 22, 1857, having both his legs blown off earlier, during the siege of the Residency. However, the compensation claim on his behalf (1859) was declared "inadmissible" as it as not "backed by sufficient testimony of its justness." (File #85).

- Edward Barker applied for relief (1860) in the form of a house in lieu of three destroyed at Ismael Ganj, opposite the Kukrail Bridge (one *pucca* masonry and two *kutcha*) worth Rs 2000/-. These houses had been destroyed by the British themselves after the re-occupation of Lucknow and not by the mutineers. Barker's claim was rejected at first instance, as it was past the due date (discussed above) for submission of such claims. When he applied again, his petition was transferred to the Chief Commissioner at Lucknow, who dismissed it on the grounds that, "he was in receipt of Rs 5/- per month and his sister-in-law of Rs 8/-, as an act of grace. The father of the applicant was a deserter from the Baillie Guard during the siege." I am sure that the reader will find this example of colonial idiosyncrasy as hilarious as the author does (File #458).
- Lieutenant AH Bruce, Executive Engineer, Futtehgur (Fatehghar) Division managed to get a compensation (1860) of Rs 350/- against the loss of his bungalow during the mutiny (File #1536).
- Miss Martindale (1860) prayed that the term of her minor brother's pension be extended to the age of 20 years; furthermore, two villages - the properties of her deceased father (killed by rebels) be granted to her in compensation for her losses due to the Mutiny. She got a typical bureaucratic response, "the Chief Commissioner cannot entertain the claim to prolong the term of her brother's pension. As for the villages, the petitioner is requested to state where they are situated and how her father came to own them." The lady provided a copy of the sale deed of the villages, which seemed to satisfy the colonial authorities; a pension of Rs 10/- was

sanctioned to her, and her brother's pension extended to his attaining 20 years of age. Rs 7000/- was granted as lump sum for the loss of her father's villages (File #2246).

- A petition came up from one B Kendall (1860), concerning his losses in Secora, Oudh during the mutiny. Strangely, Kendall had submitted 2 blank forms together with a schedule of losses in Secora, requesting the Chief Commissioner to "fill up the forms and sign on the blank certificates if the claim was considered just." As expected, the Secretary to the CC replied to the petition on February 8, 1860, denying the claim (File #155).
- A claim of Mrs. Mary Jane Cameron (1860) was allowed, providing her pension @ Rs 64/- per month and Rs 22/- per month for her son, even though her claim had detailed how her husband, Robert Cameron had died in the house of Martin Gubbins (Financial Commissioner, Lucknow Residency) and "his gold watch was stolen from the table when he was in hospital at Lucknow." In this case, even police verification was carried out, and it was stated that Mrs Cameron had a house in Secora valued at Rs 2000/-; the small amount of personal property had already been auctioned publicly in the Residency after the death of her husband. Although "the case of Mrs Cameron was not a satisfactory one" a sum of Rs 1000/- was further allowed as 50% value of her property in Secora (File #157).
- The petition of Mr. Garrett (1860), a postmaster in Calcutta requested for the "grant of a *zumeendaree* (ownership of land with revenue collection rights) of confiscated land in Oude on the ground that applications from several parties have been liberally attended to." Garrett continued with a long list of his achievements, both in military and civil services and also the fact that the wife of Captain JP Orr (discussed elsewhere in this book) had been brought up from infancy by his (Garrett's) family. Garrett's arguments left the authorities at Calcutta unimpressed and denial was swift

on the grounds that it may constitute a precedent to submit similar claims. Thus, the Calcutta postmaster's dream of becoming a *zumeendar* in Oude came to naught (File #154).

- Monsieur Duprat (T. Depratz) was a French merchant, with leanings towards the British. He was wounded during the siege of the Residency and died soon afterwards. A claim for Rs 50,000/- was submitted (1860) on his behalf, for damaged property and in respect of certain items and stores that he had thrown "into the *Macchi Bhavan* fort at the express request of late Henry Lawrence." The claim was rejected by the colonial authorities, although the ruins of Duprat's House was there for all to see, in the Residency premises (File #1724).
- Maria Block, widow of Adam Henry Block of the Bengal Civil Service in Oudh represented (1860) to the Secretary, Govt of India, that she was based in the United Kingdom, and although she had been writing to the India offices for her claim of £ 855.00, she never received any replies. The Lucknow office armed with the now repetitive set of objections, introduced a new one this time - the last location of the deceased official could not be ascertained; Whether it was Durriabad (Dariyabad in present day Bara Banki) or Sultanpore (Sultanpur). Ultimately, Rs 2983/- was sanctioned to her, that too as a "special case." (File #1933)
- Mrs. Mary Hare, describing herself as "a poor widow with a large family to support, who lost her two houses near Jhao Lal's Bazar" asked (1861) for "some remuneration for her razed house." Her claim was denied without assigning any reason (File #451).
- A memorial of Col. CG Barlowe (1861), soliciting grant of a *jagir* (land grant), in lieu of his military pension was considered as "manifestly frivolous" and denied (File #36).
- One Captain Aitkins (1861) was blessed in getting a substantial payment of Rs 350/- as compensation for

his losses, in addition to the amount awarded by the Compensation Commissioner. It is possible that this was the same Robert Hope Moncrieff Aitken, in whose honour, a defensive post in the Residency was named as Aitkin's Post (File #2207).

- The long-drawn-out, dogged campaign of two years by Monsieur Campagnae (pun intended) to rightly get his dues from the colonial government at Lucknow is an eye-opener. In this particular instance, the Governor General at Calcutta had to personally intervene not once, but twice, issuing directions to the Chief Commissioner at Lucknow, whose office tried to deny the claim on petty grounds and personal biases, rather than on the basis of settled law or administrative norms and procedures. The gentleman, residing in Calcutta, submitted a claim (1859) against properties destroyed by the military authorities at Lucknow, drew forth the usual set of objections that his claims ought to have been directed to the local authorities, instead of the Chief Commissioner. When asked for documents by the Chief Commissioner to buttress his claim, Campagnae enquired as to what documents, of judicial character, had the government provided to him, as owner, before demolishing his houses? That the destruction of property was the issue, resulting in losses to the owner, and whether it was destroyed by rebels or the government was immaterial. This acrimonious debate reached the Governor General who issued directions to the CC to re-examine the case. The CC's office perversely informed Campagnae that his claim had been rejected. On being petitioned again, the Governor General was constrained to remark that, "the case of an European having his houses half destroyed by the rebels and finally razed by our own engineers, appears to His Excellency in Council, to be a hard one." Campagnae finally received a compensation of Rs 9000/- having brought the office of the CC to its knees at Lucknow (File #1936).
- Major R Troupe submitted a bill (1861) for property destroyed at Lucknow on May 31, 1857, which was rejected

since he had not been present in Lucknow at that time and his claim was chargeable not to civil but to military authorities. He persisted in his claim, this time asking for the house of Beechey in the old Madiaon cantonment, which was a property of the military authorities. George Duncan Beechey, we will recall, was the court painter during the reign of Nasir-ud-Din Haider and Mohammad Ali Shah. His house, reputed to be haunted, had been later occupied by Rev. Polehampton, the Chaplain of Lucknow. Major Troupe, who was subsequently promoted as Brigadier and posted as Commandant in the Agra cantonment, got a measly amount of Rs 3666/- as compensation against his claim above (File #2543).

- A petition from JC Beadon (1862), requesting permission to buy certain villages in "Roy Bareilly" to restart an indigo factory which had been lying defunct for the last 30 years was allowed, since it was as per government policy to encourage European settlers (File #1548).
- Mr. Fieldbrave's petition (1862) pleaded for a pension and the grant of a village, hilariously claiming that, "When I was a fighting man in the Lucknow Garrison during the mutiny, I had sore ears by the reports of the guns. One (ear) was cured, the other one was so bad that it was left uncured." To cut a long litany short, including the presence of "small small worms" in his ears, Fieldbrave bravely concluded (pun intended) that "his disease became incurable and he was not fit for any work." Since he had "got the disease in the Garrison, on government work and the bravery of his fighting and hard work was well known to all the peoples in the Garrison", he asked for a small pension of Rs 500/- to support his wife and four children; he also asked for 500 *bighas* of *muaffee* land in a village called Babookhaira (present day Babu Khera) in the district of Mooradabad (present day Moradabad). The Chief Commissioner regretted that he could not recommend the grant because the petitioner had not submitted any relevant materials as proof of his services, which are required unless

those services had been very great. Furthermore, the land applied for was not in the province of Oudh (File #877).

- Major Anderson of Bengal Engineers, Oudh died at the Residency and a claim (1862) of Rs 20,000/- was subsequently submitted. Ordinarily, a sum of Rs 5000/- would have been allowed - the maximum allowance for "personality" (personal loss), but owing to the departure of Major Anderson's widow for England, the required information required to substantiate the claim could not proceed, and it was consequently disallowed. In a strongly worded observation, the Chief Commissioner wrote that, "The estate suffers from not being properly represented; the widow should at least get Rs 2813/-, being the amount of succour money according to her husband's rank as a Major in the Engineers." (File #2469)
- The beautifully hand-written petition of George Elliot and his brother Alexander Elliott (1863) narrated a long tragic story, which would have an equally tragic conclusion. The brothers had been unable to enter the Residency timely as advised by Henry Lawrence, and by the time they reached the Baillie Guard, the Indian freedom fighters had already laid siege to the place. They preferred to seek refuge in rural Oudh, with George disguised as *fakeer* (mendicant), but both brothers were captured by the natives and handed over to Raja Devi Bux. In the meantime, their families had dispersed in the villages and were never found again. The brothers managed to escape the Raja's custody and ultimately meet the Collector of Gorakhpur, giving him information regarding the enemies' position. Back in Lucknow, they found that their properties had been plundered and houses razed to the ground. George was appointed as *Thanedar* of Kakoree (Kakori) and Nawab Gunge (Nawabganj) and Alexander was appointed as *Naib Thanedar* (see Annexure II for explanations on terminology and nomenclatures used).

The Deputy Commissioner ordered the *Nazul Daroga vide* order dated February 15, 1859 to allot a *nazul* house situated in Junglee Gunge (present day Jangali Ganj) contiguous to Ameenabad (present day Aminabad). But after 4 years, the *nazul* department demanded rent for the same. The colonial administration also demanded that the brothers re-submit their petition on stamped court paper of appropriate value, which the brothers did. They also argued that they were in possession of the ownership papers of the aforesaid house, and they had spent a lot on refurbishing it to make it liveable. The counter argument of the government was that the *nazul* office had no legal right to transfer the ownership of a *nazul* property to the brothers in the first place; that the brothers were actually tenants and not owners. The Elliotts countered this by stating that they had not received any compensation for the damages to their property in Lucknow, although some people had received compensation upto 1861, long after the Compensation Court was closed.

However, the colonial administration remained strangely intransigent in this particular instance. The Elliott brothers got no relief and a question was even raised about the appropriate value of the stamp paper on which they had re-submitted their petition (File #1204).

- Thomas Henry Kavanagh, an assistant field engineer, had volunteered to slip out of the Lucknow Residency on the night of November 9, 1857 to make contact with Colin Campbell's relief force and guide it back through the city for the final assault. Although a civilian, he had earlier gained a reputation for courage in the underground battles during the siege and his offer was accepted by Outram. Crudely disguised as a native Indian, and hopeful that the darkness would provide as an effective camouflage, he managed to make contact with a British picket outside the *Alambagh* camp, from where he was escorted to Campbell. Kavanagh was recognised as a hero by the British and awarded the

Victoria Cross, being one of only five civilians to have ever been awarded the VC. This part of his story is well known.

What is generally not known is that after the British regained control of Lucknow and Kavanagh was appointed as Assistant Commissioner for his war efforts, (including the rounding up of scattered mutineers), he moved an application (1864) for the grant of four confiscated villages in Meerut district. For this, he was prepared to return (in instalments) the cash award given to him earlier. The villages in question were Baolee, Mulakpoor and Loen in Tehsil Baghpat (modern day Baoli, Malakpur and Loni) and Daha in Tehsil Sardhana. To buttress his claim, he put forth a long list of justifications, including the argument that "many estates were bestowed in Oudh and elsewhere on Europeans and natives for meritorious services during 1857." He claimed to have "always endeavoured to serve honestly and fearlessly in peace and war and humbly hoped to be treated liberally as other good servants of the state who did well when it was in difficulties." Kavanagh VC also stated that the "residence of thirty three years in India, unsparing exposure to sun and rain and unusual hardships during the whole of the war impaired his health" and "made him dangerously ill from overexertion to the sun which would compel him to seek retirement and forfeit his pension, causing difficulties in maintaining his large family." His petition was referred to the Governor General at Calcutta who tersely responded that he "cannot reopen the Kavanagh case or give him any further rewards as he had already been sufficiently rewarded for his services." It was indeed an irony that this highly decorated British hero of 1857 should beg for small mercies and weaken his case by stating that his stay in India had impaired his health, and in the same voice ask for land grants to further stay in the rural India instead of returning to England and its perceived comforts (File #385).

Kavanagh died in Gibraltar on November 13, 1882, and was buried there in the North Front Cemetery. His Victoria

> Cross, on its own, without the Indian Mutiny Medal, was auctioned in London on September 14, 2022, fetching a price of £750,000 from an unnamed bidder.

We shall end this Chapter with the woes of a certain Mr George Yeoward, Head Clerk in the Province of Oudh, who had been imprisoned for some time by the rebels, but was lucky enough to gain freedom as the British finally emerged victorious in their campaigns. "After tranquillity had been restored throughout the province of Oudh, I expected some recognition of some of my services would be evinced by Government. But nothing was said." Yeoward proceeded to Benaras and then to the establishment of Col. Willoughby Osborne, the British Resident at Rewa. The latter had the case thoroughly investigated, and being convinced of Yeoward's genuineness, sent a letter to Cecil Beadon, the Secretary to the Govt. of India at Fort William, espousing the clerk's case and recommending a personal allowance for the latter. On being asked by Calcutta "as to what reward he expected", Yeoward requested that two of his children may be admitted free into the Martiniere schools at Calcutta. The reply was to the effect that "such a request could not be granted as the children were not residents of Calcutta. As regards Col. Osborne's recommendation for a personal allowance, the state of finances, at that time, would not admit it."

As a last resort, Col. Osborne applied for the salary of Yeoward to be increased from Rs 180/- to Rs 250/- per mensem. This too was rejected by the benevolent colonial government. The dejection of Yeoward grew as Col. Osborne later became seriously ill and had to leave India. The office of the Political Agent at Rewa was abolished and the unfortunate clerk became unemployed once again. He eventually returned to Lucknow and managed to get his daughter admitted to the La Martiniere Girls' School. His son was not so lucky.

While the hardships faced by Yeoward may or may not interest the reader, an anecdote related by the gentleman in his memoirs (1876) would surely appeal to the reader's sense of humour. This anecdote concerns the activities of Raja Man Singh, whose activities and intentions during 1857 - 58 had confounded both the British and the rebel freedom fighters alike. To quote Yeoward *verbatim*:

"Man Singh obtained an interview with Huzrut Mahil (*sic*), the rebel Queen and mother of the notorious Bridjis Kudr (*sic*) the rebel prince and heir apparent to the rebel throne, and offered to drive back the British, if her Majesty would grant him a Commission and give him command of troops. Huzrut Mahil (*sic*) granted his request, but she had no troops to spare, except the Gwalior contingent and there was over three months pay due to them. Man Singh offered to arrange for their pay, he wanted nothing but Her Majesty's commission. Armed with this document he sounded the assembly, read the terms to the rebels and gave them twelve hours to prepare and march in company with his own trusty retainers. In the interim he snatched from their peaceful homes by force some ten or a dozen native Christians who were living in the city in the character of Hindoos and Mahomedans. At the same time he committed a little plundering by which he lightened a few mutineers of the wealth which they had accumulated and marched with the whole force, not to meet the British, but to his own stronghold in the district of Fyzabad. Arrived at the Fort (*sic*), the contingent was ordered to encamp outside, while Man Singh and his men with native Christian prisoners went inside.

By next morning a *sowar*, with a portentous looking letter left the Fort at full gallop. The letter that the *sowar* was despatched with was addressed to Mr Wingfield, who was then scouring the districts at the head of the Flying Column; its contents purported to give urgent information to the effect that Man Singh was besieged in his Fort by a large force of rebels; that he had a number of Christians under his protection and he couldn't hold out much longer. This was urgent indeed! Mr Wingfield started his force to the rescue as fast as they could tear. Arrived on the ground, appearances were decidedly in favour of the truth of the contents of the letter. Charge!! screamed out the ringing voice of Wingfield, and in fifteen minutes the ground was covered with dead and dying; the gates were thrown open; Wingfield and his force entered in triumph, "Where are the Christians?" demanded the conqueror. After some demur the ten or twelve wretched looking native Christians were produced. Is this all, said Wingfield. “I didn’t think they were of this sort,” he retired with his staff laughing heartily. One of the party, a Mrs Duhan is still living in Lucknow and is well known; but even she does not really know why Man Singh took her to his Fort.”

We shall come across Man Singh again elsewhere in this book.

Chapter - III

Up for Grabs II

Native Claims and Counter Claims

If the fledgling colonial government was deluged with European claimants after 1857 as we saw in the previous Chapter, it also had to deal with claims in a dissimilar vein from native Indians. From a perusal of such claims, it would become evident that while the European claims were against losses suffered *during* the events of 1857, as well as some frivolous, greedy and petty submissions, the Indian claims were much more complex, and genuine, although not altogether devoid of greed. The Indians had suffered in 1857 and *post 1857 also* (which was not so in case of the Europeans), as the colonial administration selectively destroyed or confiscated their properties, or summarily claimed their holdings as *nazul*. Besides, some of the native claims were mired in ancestry and complex legacies, which also involved sibling rivalries. The native Indian petitioner had to walk on a tightrope: first and foremost, he had to conclusively prove that he had not been on the side of the revolutionaries or "rebels"; secondly, he had to produce documents to support his claim - documents which could have been destroyed during the earlier mayhem. Thirdly, it cannot be denied that although the old Nawabi order had been demolished, a sense of entitlement existed among the nobility and even in their minions and this sense of entitlement was not in consonance with the current political scenario. Fourthly, the sense of alienation was complete, when the British brought in from the hinterlands of Awadh, the landed barons or *ta'aluqdars* who had been loyal to the British cause and attempted to settle them in Lucknow, together with land grants of confiscated properties belonging to those who had sided with the revolutionaries. The landed barons had never been very comfortable with the Nawabi court at Lucknow, and now here they were - the British sympathisers, although relatively few in number, cornering benefits while a majority, who had shed blood for their motherland were now penniless and being deprived from their estates. There were also mavericks like Man Singh, who cornered benefits from both sides with aplomb. This tragic situation made the case of Indian claimants' cases very complex and as we shall see, most faced rejection.

- Moomtaz (Mumtaz) Mahal, widow of Nasir-ud-Din Haider, second king of Awadh submitted a claim (1858) for Rs 8000/-, stating that her house Sheesh Mahal (looking glass palace) inside the Macchi Bhavan fort had been taken over by Henry Lawrence, Resident, before the siege had commenced. This had been done to strengthen the defensive position of the British and Lawrence had promised her a sum of Rs 8000/- as compensation. Although sympathetic to her cause, the colonial authorities queried as to whether the lady would accept a house or garden instead of the money. When the lady refused, it was noted that if the "claimant could show any service of loyalty rendered during the rebellion, it may be entertained, otherwise it is superfluous." Ultimately the British capitulated and Rs 8000/- sanctioned to her (File #2290).
- The petition of another Mumtaz Mahal (1858), fourth wife of Ghazi-ud-Din Haider, the first king of Awadh was approved and she was granted a political pension of Rs 13,200/- per annum (File #2349).
- Mallika Jahan, widow of late Mohammad Ali Shah, the third king was Awadh was more fortunate (1859). It may be recalled that she had managed to carry on the partial completion work of the Jami Masjid at Hussainabad in

Lucknow by 1845, after its builder, the king had died in 1842. The dowager Queen's allowances were restored (they had been stopped after 1857) and paid with arrears (File #258).

- Nawab Dulhan Begum submitted a petition (1859) for grant of a pension @ Rs 500/- per month. Interestingly, this venerable lady, also known as Birati Khanum, was the daughter of James Martin, adopted son of General Claude Martin; she was also the mother of Alam Ara Begum, the *Khas Mahal* of Wajid Ali Shah. The pension claim was rejected by the British on the grounds that the name of the claimant had not been entered in the Royal Pension List, and hence she was not entitled to any relief (File #520).

- The petition (1860) of Mumtaz un-Nisa Khanum, the sixth wife of Amjad Ali Shah outlined her travails and amply illustrated the pitiable conditions of junior (*khurd*) begums in Nawabi court, particularly so when the husband (ruler) had died. The tragic situation was compounded after the annexation of Awadh. The begum had been in receipt of Rs 500/- per month as stipend, which was reduced to Rs 100/- per month after her husband's demise. She lived in the Chattar Manzil palace, with the family and children of Mirza Sikandar Hashmat (younger brother of Wajid Ali Shah). The Chattar Manzil was stormed by the British and the petitioner, with her two sons were imprisoned in the Residency during the siege. Subsequently, she was shifted to Alambagh Kothi, and finally handed over to Daroga Mir Wajid Ali Shah's custody.

  Thankfully, her claim was verified by the British and approved, which was no mean achievement (File #2662).

- A query was raised by the colonial administration (1860) on recognising the grants in perpetuity given by the ex-King to singers, dancers and musicians. "It seemed absurd to perpetuate these grants and recognise them for life" although the British were bound to respect the *sanads* of the ex-King. It was clarified that the war had changed the scenario, and the British would only recognise those grants, if the present occupant was the original grantee, other things being extraneous. Thus, by inserting this *post-facto* clause, the British could now renegade on the responsibility of recognising the estates granted by Wajid Ali Shah during his rule (File #15).

- Mallika Dauran, the sister of Wajid Ali Shah, submitted a claim (1861) for the possession of certain *nazul* houses in Lucknow. The colonial administration's response to this was hilarious - her claim being rejected on the ground that "she was with the rebel begum in the Chowlakhee (*sic*) Palace. She fled with the begum and remained with the Raja of Nanpara until the arrival of our columns.... she had justly fortified her estates and refused to restore them." (Files #397, 1929, 1932) The same lady would later be entrusted with the care of Sibtainabad Imambara in Hazratganj (discussed elsewhere in this book).
- Some junior wives of Nasir-ud-Din Haider and Mohammad Ali Shah petitioned the Governor General (1860 - 1862), stating that they had been in receipt of pensions till the time of Wajid Ali Shah, which was then discontinued. It was prayed that since they had no means of subsistence, the pensions may be restored. The Governor General returned the petition, asking the petitioners to submit their grievances to the Chief Commissioner. The CC, after receiving the petition, once again returned it to the petitioners, asking them to re-submit, after affixing seals on the document. When the directions of the CC were complied with, the petition was rejected on the grounds that there was no previous record of the ladies having received pensions earlier. All this rigmarole took two years, and yet there was no fruitful conclusion - which was another example of British sense of fair play and justice (File #1241).
- Ali Naqi Khan, erstwhile Prime Minister of Awadh continued to send petitions (1860 - 1863) for succour from the British,

most of which were rejected. Apparently, he had lost Rs 72 lakhs in cash, gold and jewellery before the city was captured in 1858 (Llewellyn-Jones, 2014). Khan claimed the ownership of a Nawabi *bagh* (garden) and certain houses which were refused (File #1289). Referred to as Ally Nukkee Khan or Alee Nuckee Khan by the British, he did not enjoy their confidence, although it is widely accepted by historians that it was he who had unauthorisedly affixed the royal seal of Wajid Ali Shah on the Proclamation and Treaty of Annexation which was basically an Instrument of Accession - authorising the East India Company to take over the administration of Awadh. Ali Naqi Khan also requested the British to pay him the stipend, which was being paid earlier to his sister Kubra Begum (now deceased), for the maintenance of her tomb and the support of her children, composed of 3 nephews and 7 nieces. The claim was promptly denied, after investigations revealed that the "dependants" were actually adults who had not been supported by the Begum when she was alive (File #1176).

- The ex-Prime Minister also laid claim for "houses destroyed for the requirements of the state and the restoration of other property said to have been given away to other parties." The claim was rejected tersely because, "it has always been held that the city when taken by storm fell as prize of war. And that government is at liberty to do what it pleases with all the houses in it." (File #2165) Ali Naqi Khan had one house in Lucknow released in his name on January 1860. His claim for rent in respect to the houses claimed but not released was refused (File # 1563).

- Mohammad Mustafa Ali Haider, born in 1819, was the elder half-brother of Wajid Ali Shah. Although the eldest son of Amjad Ali Shah, he was repudiated by his father in 1838, deprived of his titles and even imprisoned for sometime. The reason behind Mustafa Ali's conflict with Amjad Ali Shah appears to have been his propensity to complain to Mohammad Ali Shah (the king and his grandfather), against his own father, about day-to-day events in the court. Historians have also surmised that Mustafa was *persona non grata* for another reason: he was not the son of *Khas Mahal*, Mallika Kishwar. But this is open to question. On February 5, 1861, he submitted a petition to the British government to reconsider his claim for continuation of a pension @ Rs 15/- a month, which had been included in the relevant register, by the Captain Fletcher Hayes (Military Secretary to Henry Lawrence) but was never paid, as the mutiny broke out soon afterwards. Mustafa claimed that the pension had been admissible to him from the times of Ghazi-ud-Din Haider. (which could be chronologically true). However, his pleas fell on deaf ears, and even this measly sum was denied to him (File #752).

- Another prayer of Mustafa Ali (1861) for a suitable house was rejected by the colonial government (File #2345).
- A number of ladies from the harem of Nasir-ud-Din Haider, second king of Awadh (1861) submitted a joint petition for restoration of their pensions, but they were advised to submit their prayers individually, on stamp paper. The petitioners were Bee Chutro, Bee Kazima, Bee Moonnee, Bee Ruttan (*sic*) and others. It is impossible to decipher their anglicized names at this point of time. The petitions were submitted in English on stamp paper of requisite value, through their Agent. All the petitions mentioned that they had been on a pilgrimage, and after their return to Lucknow in 1859, they had been aggrieved to note that their pensions, which had been granted by Mohammad Ali Shah, the third king of Awadh, had been discontinued. Surprisingly, all the petitions had a common error: that *Badshah Begum, wife of late Nasir-ud-Din Haider, imprisoned in Chunar Fort with Munna Jan continued to receive the pension sanctioned by Mohammad Ali Shah, while the claimants had been deprived of their pensions* (emphasis by author). Badshah Begum was the widow of Ghazi-ud-Din Haider, not Nasir-ud-Din. Also, she had died way back in 1846 at Chunar. Yet the present claim,

dated 1861 stated otherwise. Come what way, the aggrieved ladies could not get any relief as their petitions were rejected by the colonial government (File #1731).

- Nawab Mallika Jahan, widow of Mohammad Ali Shah, submitted a petition (1861) that "on the construction of several roads and by-roads, several of my *pucca* houses have been knocked down, the details and numbers of which have been inserted below. I therefore most humbly beg the favour of your Lordship favouring me with a number of houses in any part of the city which may compensate for the loss I have suffered." She submitted a list of 3 *pucca* houses and 32 *pucca* shops valued at Rs 63,300/- which had been demolished by the British. Her petition was rejected without giving any reason or further correspondence (File #2387).

- Mallika Geti or Gaiti was the junior (*khurd*) begum of Amjad Ali Shah, the fourth King of Awadh. On January 13, 1861, she received an extortion note from one Sgt. Thomas Lambert, informing her that he had in his possession, three promissory notes valued at Rs 55,000/-, which he had obtained during the re-capture of Lucknow in March 1958, during a time that plunder was allowed by the Commander-in-Chief (obvious reference to Colin Campbell). The rogue sergeant expected a "handsome reward" for restoring them to the begum. In case she did not give her consent, he would send the notes to England and "enforce a right to the entire amount." In case the begum wished to contest his claim, she would have to spend a considerable amount of expense. He also cautioned the begum not to waste her time in arranging for duplicates since the originals were in existence.

  A similar extortion note was received by Dara Sitwat Mirza, the son of Mallika Geti, informing him about five notes worth Rs 11,00,00/-, together with accompanying threats and demands.

  The royal family preferred to appeal to the colonial administration, which although apparently sympathetic to the formers' cause, preferred to wash its hands off the entire unsavoury affair. The British admitted that the sergeant had no right to encash the notes even in England, even though they were blank endorsements. The administration conceded the fact that the extortionist could be "compelled to deliver them to the owners" but advised the royal family to come to a settlement by paying a "moderate amount" to the sergeant, although the option to institute proceedings against the sergeant was also a possibility (File #422).

- The petition of Bandé Ali Khan (1862) for the payment of pension as a legacy was also unsuccessful. He was the adopted son of Mirza Ali Khan from the family of Tafazzul Hussain Khan, the latter also known as "Khan-è-Allama", who had been appointed as the tutor of Sa'adat Ali Khan by Shuja-ud-Daula. He had remained a close associate of Sa'adat Ali for some time, but ultimately became a British sympathizer, being quite supportive of Warren Hastings, and later, Lord Cornwallis. He contributed behind the scenes to get Sa'adat Ali Khan anointed as Nawab of Awadh by John Shore. Tafazzul extended his services to Haider Beg also, but could not get the support of Tikait Rai or Hasan Raza in the Nawabi court. There is no doubt that he was a well-lettered, learned person, respected by scholars, but his blind support for the British undermined his own importance in the Nawabi court as Jhau Lal's successor. In the present case, the petitioner's plea was that by convention, "the pensioner appoints his or her heir in his or her life time and such nominations being duly attested and confirmed by the government to receive or draw the pension legacy" did not cut much ice with the British authorities, who perversely summoned all the family members to court, simply to ascertain the truth and put on record the names of all such the pensioners in the extended family. Even after this lengthy exercise, Bandé Ali's petition was ultimately rejected (File #1310).

- A claim for possession of Sikandar Bagh and its adjoining areas was submitted (1862) by one Iqbal Mahal (wrongly written as Ikleel Mahal), also known as Badshah Begum (no relation to the dowager queen of Ghazi-ud-Din Haider, also known as Badshah Begum). The garden had been built for Sikandar Mahal, one of the wives of Wajid Ali Shah and given to her as a *jagir*. On her death, it passed on to Sultanat Mahal and then to Iqbal Mahal, in whose possession it remained for 7 years, till the annexation of Awadh. The typical colonial response was that the "site had been already developed as Horticultural Society's Garden. The place was associated with the exploits of the Commander-in-Chief's army on the 2nd Relief of Lucknow. This trophy of war cannot be returned as it has constantly been on the *nazul* list." (File #1658)

- Mallika Ahad, wife of late Amjad Ali Shah (father of Wajid Ali Shah) submitted a petition through her Agent, Mr Hollingbeiry (1862), claiming compensation for Mahomed Bagh (Muhammad Bagh) and Soleyman (Suleiman) Bagh, valued at Rs 16,600/-. The claim was denied with a note that, "these estates were undoubtedly confiscated under the Outram Proclamation. The claimant joined the rebels and did not return within the period proclaimed by General Outram and consequently, her houses and gardens were forfeited to government. The houses were duly reported and sanctioned *nazool* confiscation by the Chief Commissioner. The gardens declared so by the Deputy Commissioner but not reported for sanction as they should have been. The award of houses to the lady was not in compensation, but as a residence for life out of commiseration. She being one of the Royal Family, consideration was shown to her. The estates have been taken up for public purpose *viz.* that of a military cantonment and their appears to me no ground on which to recommend that government should grant compensation." (File #2485)

- Mariam Begum's plea (1863) that her stipend of Rs 220/-, which had been discontinued, should be allowed to continue was rejected by the colonial authorities (File #1165).

- The life of Prince Hamid Ali, heir designate (*Wali Ahad)* of Wajid Ali Shah was full of misfortunes for no fault of his. He was reduced to a prince without a realm after 1856, when Awadh was annexed; he was superseded as the rightful heir of Wajid Ali when his half brother, young Birjis Qadar, was anointed successor at Lucknow by the freedom fighters on June 5, 1857. Earlier, Hamid's long journey to London and back to petition Queen Victoria in favour of his father, had not yielded any success. Later, his relations with his father at Calcutta also become estranged, but that was no surprise; the ex-king did not seem to enjoy the company and support of his immediate family members in his last days. Regrettably, Hamid passed away before his father; his unfortunate death in 1874 (Wajid Ali died in 1887) brought forth a strange claim, from the ex-king himself, in which he requested (1874) the British authorities to take over the *jagir* (estate) of the late prince and have it managed by the Deputy Commissioner or any other officer selected by them for the purpose. Lt. Col Mowbray Thomson, Agent to the Governor General with the King of Oudh informed that "His Majesty has begged me to add that he agrees to pay all charges of management..... the profit of the *jageer* (*jagir*) be kept in deposit with you till sent for through this office" and that the prince himself, sometime before the death "wrote to say that the *sunnad* (deed) had not been received by him." The *jagir* had been granted in perpetuity to Hamid Ali in 1849, by Wajid Ali himself and consisted of 7002 villages spread over seven *talukas*.

- A third angle to this conundrum was added by petitioners Haji Hussain Quli Khan and Jaffar Quli Khan, residents of Khayaliganj, Lucknow, who appealed to the C authorities, requesting the Chief Commissioner, Oudh, to protect their interests as caretaker of the *jagir* and "prevent them from involving into troubles and difficulties." Enquiries revealed that the *sanad* had been given earlier to a Jacob Johannes, representative of the prince. The colonial administration did not seem keen to oblige the ex-king and his proposal as "it did not seen advisable that the Deputy Commissioner should take charge of the estate." (File #467)

From the point of view of Wajid Ali Shah, it had seemed to be a viable option, as he was in dire need of funds to meet his burgeoning financial obligations in *Metia Burz*, including the expenses of his ever expanding menagerie. He still had faith in British sense of fair play (despite his own miserable situation) and felt that late son's estate would be safer their hands, instead of being in the hands of his immediate family members in Lucknow. We shall come back to Wajid Ali Shah's petitions later in this Chapter.

- Mashuq Mahal (Pyari Sahib) was the fourth wife of Wajid Ali Shah, having married the prince in around 1842. In 1861, she filed a petition for a pension which was rejected. She then filed a petition in 1863 regarding her *jagir*, held by the government in perpetuity. Her claim (1874 - 76) for succour money @ Rs 223/- was, however, granted (Files # 2700, #1863, #2129).
- Mirza Jahan Qadr, son of Sikandar Hashmat (younger brother of Wajid Ali Shah) had been in receipt of a pension @ Rs 600/- during the years: 1860 - 1861. The pension was thereafter stopped, and not drawn during 1861 - 1864. The British acknowledged this fact but objected that the payment of pension arrears beyond 12 months needed special sanction; here it exceeded two years. The records available on file have no further information as to what happened to Mirza in this particular case (File #2506).
- Payment of pension arrears of one Hussain Ara Begum against her petition (1866) was approved (File #652).

Our favourite deposed King, Wajid Ali Shah, also submitted a litany of complaints, claims (and protests) to the colonial authorities after 1856. The King's file on record at the UP State Archives, Lucknow is the most voluminous of all, and it can serve as the source material for a separate book in itself. For example, on December 1, 1858, the ex-king submitted a petition to the colonial authorities in Calcutta, stating that government securities in the form of promissory notes, bearing the seal of his mother had been in the possession of his mother (Mallika Kishwar), who was now dead. These notes were now with person(s) who had been with her. He urged the administration to secure these promissory notes, which were not transferable, claiming an interest of Rs 5 lakhs (till April 1857), which would be payable to him. He also informed that properties belonging to his sister, Afsar Bahu Begum (discussed elsewhere in this book) were being sold in Lucknow unauthorised. (File #917).

With deference to his status as ex-King, Wajid Ali did not petition the colonial government directly, but through officials provided to him for the purpose, who also kept a close eye on his affairs. These officials held the title of "Agent of the Governor General with the King of Oudh" (note the term, *King* and not *ex-King*). The first Agent was Major Charles Hebert; Lt. Col. William Francis Prideaux was the last. These officials would forward the communications received not only from the ex-King, but also from his sons and begums, to Fort William, with their own recommendations. Often accused of bias, many of these Agents were prominent persona in the own right. For example, George Bruce Malleson, the third Agent was the well known author of *History of The Indian Mutiny* which is referred to, even today. Lt. Col Mowbray Thomson was one of the few survivors of General Wheeler's entrenchment at Cawnpore (Kanpur) and subsequent massacre at Sati Chaura Ghat. Prideaux was a highly accomplished author of books related to archaeology and numismatics.

The ex-King continued to submit petitions all through the three decades of his stay in Calcutta. Many were granted, many more rejected and a few ignored. But all were considered with due diligence, so characteristic of the colonial administration. However, we shall be shirking from our duty, if at the end of this Chapter, we do not discuss a petition dated June 2, 1877, submitted by Begum Hazrat Mahal, and her son Birjis Qadr, then a fugitive in Nepal under the protectorate of the Rana, addressed to the Governor General, seeking permission to visit India for the purpose of arranging marriages for the children of Birjis Qadr (Mirza Mahomed Wahid Ali, Mirza Mahomed Akram Ali, and two unnamed daughters, aged 11 and 12 years). A strongly-worded response from the Secretary to Government, North-Western Provinces and Oudh dated July 16, 1877, stated that, "His Honor the Lieutenant-Governor and Chief Commissioner directs me to say that at the present time while affairs are in an unsettled state in a great part of Asia and Europe, he is of opinion that Birjis Kadar (*sic*) and his mother, *who is, or was, a very clever and designing woman* (italics by author) should not be allowed to visit British India. And under no circumstances would His Honor recommend that Birjis Kadar (*sic*) be allowed to reside in Oudh, at any rate for some years to come. His Honor does not think that Birjis Kadar (*sic*) deserves any support from the British Government; and were he to reside in Lucknow as a pauper, he would naturally obtain the sympathy of many of his fellow-countrymen, and might do much to foster any ill-feeling among those who are discontented with our rule, and in a large city like Lucknow, with more than two hundred thousand inhabitants, many of whom have been reduced from affluence to poverty by the removal of the Court, it would be absurd to hope that there are not a number of disaffected persons who would be glad of any change."

Further, the colonial administration in a letter dated August 6, 1877, also requested the Nepal government to "discourage any request which may be made on behalf of Birjis Kadar (*sic*) or his mother to visit British India." This stance of the colonial government gave a new lease of life to Birjis Qadr, who was poisoned to death on August 14, 1893, during his visit to Calcutta, British India.

Chapter - IV

Colonial Development of Lucknow I

The Major Projects

Historical Background

The buildings erected by the British in Lucknow after 1857, reflected their immediate needs, *i.e.* places of worship, the railway station, hospital and the new cantonment. The churches were invariably Gothic, while the new cantonment did not boast of any architectural style; it was populated by soulless barracks and bungalows, the latter inspired by native, thatch-roofed *banglas*. The colonial administration

Figure 10: Vintage View of Gol Darwaza, Chowk, Unidentified Photographer.

insisted on arcades for all its major commercial spaces, including Hazratganj, Lalbagh, Kaiserbagh and Chowk (Gol Darwaza). While some contemporary writers attribute the present day Gol Darwaza (or whatever remains of it) to Nawab Asaf-ud-Daula, it needs to be emphasised that the British carried out two extensive makeovers in the Chowk area - one was the development of Victoria Park in the heart of Lucknow's old city (possibly to serve as a constant reminder of their superiority and that they were the new rulers of the country), and another was the Gol Darwaza commercial area, "to improve the surroundings of the Gol Darwaza by the demolition of buildings on either side and their reconstruction in a semi-circular form" and also provide a "direct route to Circular Road (present day RK Tandon Road) across Patanala to the Gol Darwaza, by realignment of portions of Crommelin Road (present day Nimbu Park Road) and will allow construction of a broad arcade in front of the buildings to the south of the road." This was supposed to be financed by the Mohammad Ali Shah's Hussainabad and Allied Trust, then under the control of the British themselves. Realignment of roads on scientific principles was a constant endeavour of the colonial government, even though the exercise resulted in acquisition of private properties and their demolition as well as extensive landscaping, which was a costly affair. In the makeover of Hazratganj or Queensway or Civil Lines (which was part of Strand Road, see Annexure II), diversions of Lalbagh Road, Shahnajaf Road, Forsyth Road (present day Dayanidhan Park Road), Church Corner Road and Park Road were carried out. The year 1900 saw the laying of the Foundation Stone for the Judicial Commissioner's Court building, which would later become the premises for the Lucknow Bench of the Allahabad High Court. The "style of architecture was Muhammadan made to suit the requirements of such a building", drawn up by WG Wood, Executive Engineer and PA to the Chief Engineer, NWP and Oudh.

The Indo-Saracenic style now proliferated rapidly in Lucknow in the early 20th century, with the Victoria Memorial designed by Swinton Jacob (1904), King George's Medical College (Swinton Jacob, 1906) at Macchi Bhavan, the Kotwalis at Hazratganj and Chowk (Lebanti, 1909), the new campus of Lucknow University (Swinton Jacob &

Tika Ram, 1911) at Badshah Bagh, the new Railway Station (JH Horniman, 1914) at Charbagh and the Government Arts College (S. Crookshank, 1917). Some non-governmental buildings in Lucknow also adopted the style, e.g. Lucknow Christian College, Colvin Taluqdar's College, Butler Palace, Rifa-e-Am Club, Amir-ud-Daula Public Library and Carlton Hotel - the latter described as "a very fine hotel facing Clyde Road; largely Saracenic in design and one of the handsomest buildings erected of late years in Lucknow." Marris Market in Kaiserbagh, envisaged as a modern, hygienic market for Europeans went a step further: it sported the twin fish motif at its entrance - a symbol of the erstwhile Nawabi rulers!

However, not all buildings adopted the Indo-Saracenic architectural style. Isabella Thoburn College in Chand Bagh (Martin & Company, 1922) was totally European in character, its architecture unabashedly inspired by the Parthenon (Greece). A renewed interest in Renaissance and Baroque styles could be seen in buildings of a more "serious nature" such as the Council Chamber (Lanchester

Figure 11: Vintage View of Post Master General's Office, Lucknow, Unidentified Photographer.

Figure 12: : Vintage View of Imperial Post & Telegraph Office at Lucknow, Unidentified Photographer.

Figure 13: Wingfield Park with its Nawabi Baradaris, Lucknow, 1863, Samuel Bourne.

& Rodick, 1928) / present day Vidhan Sabha, which resembled the Central Hall of Westminster in its conception. The Nawabi Begum Kothi (now demolished, in present day Janpath Market area) had functioned as a Post Office for quite some time. It was eventually replaced by the Imperial Post & Telegraph Office (now GPO) building, with its lofty tower was also designed by Lanchester and Rodick (1929 - 32), in consultation with Geoffrey Clark, the Post Master General. To dispel another urban legend of Lucknow, it needs to be clarified that the present GPO was not the former Ring Theatre (*sic*). The area on which the Lucknow Council Chamber and the Imperial Post Office were constructed was mostly open space. Additional space was acquisitioned *vide* executive resolution of the colonial government dated March 9, 1920, for taking over the nearby *Rink Theatre* and the YWCA, after paying appropriate compensation, together with parts of Darul Shafa, (which was already government property and no compensation needed to be paid). Earlier, the Post Master General's office had been designed on a typical European template by J Begg (1917), described as "a fine new building erected on a site south and slightly to the east of the Bank of Bengal fronting on the Mall to accommodate the office of the Post Master General of the new Post Telegraph department of the United Provinces. The postal administrative and kindred offices of the Lucknow Postal Division will also be located in this building."

Two colonial parks, dedicated to Queen Victoria came up in Lucknow, post 1857. One was in Chowk, the old quarter of Lucknow, for which land was retrieved after demolishing scores of Nawabi era structures. Another was a small area, roughly corresponding to the earlier Nawabi Payn Bagh, in which a marble canopy over a red sandstone plinth was erected to house the statue of Queen Victoria as a "Victoria Memorial."

A significant exercise of the colonial government was the creation of the Wingfield Park encompassing the old Banarsi Bagh of Nasir-ud-Din Haider and also portions of the vast grounds of Agha Mir's *karbala* in 1860. On February 17, 1860, a resolution was moved *vide* letter no. 470, to convert the old Nawabi garden into "a public garden, ornamental and horticultural @ Rs 12,000/-. The consent of the

Chief Commissioner arrived soon enough on May 17, 1860, *vide* letter no. 1918, with the rider that the proposed park was to be called Wingfield Gardens or Park. The Nagine Wali Baradari was translocated in its entirety from Kaiserbagh to the middle of the Wingfield Park. Other small marble kiosks were also erected in the premises. The reason for the Nagine Wali Baradari being removed from Kaiserbagh and reconstructed at Wingfield Park has an interesting back story. Wajid Ali Shah, during the heydays of Kaiserbagh, used to dress up as a *jogi* (mendicant / ascetic) during the annual *Jogiya Mela* and participate in elaborate dance dramas in the premises. The citizens of Lucknow had an intense emotional connect with their deposed King and the venue of his dramatic performances would be a point of gathering for the public, which had to be avoided at all costs - so felt Lucknow's neo-colonial masters. Wingfield Park was originally laid out by one Reginald Berkeley, whose plans were later modified by M/s Morrison and Hodges, under the supervision of Charles Wingfield, Chief Commissioner of Lucknow and Lousada Barrow, his successor. It later metamorphosed into the Prince of Wales Zoological Gardens in 1926 (See Annexure V). Presently, its most recent *avatar* is as Nawab Wajid Ali Shah Zoological Garden (although Wajid Ali Shah was not a Nawab). During the time of writing of this book, the Zoo was in the news for less fortunate reasons - including its impending closure, and possible concretisation of the vast green belt, which incensed concerned citizens of Lucknow, resulting in protests and dissent.

The Major Projects

The Hussainabad Clock Tower

In 1881, Richard Roskell Bayne was commissioned by the British to design a 68-meter tall clock tower in Lucknow. Many writers have tried to analyze the motives behind this decision. After bringing the uprising under control, it became imperative for them to prove their superiority and omniscience. And what could be better than to erect an edifice, which would not only rise above all other 'native' structures in the vicinity, but would also remind everyone of the new order, through a gong that resonated periodically?

The Hussainabad clock tower was built at a cost of Rs 1,17,000, funded by the Hussainabad Endowment Trust, which had been set up earlier by Mohammed Ali Shah, the third king of Awadh, for the upkeep of his *Imambara* and other works. Lt. Col. Norman Horsford of the Bengal Staff Corps & Lucknow City Magistrate initiated the process, to ostensibly honor Sir George EW Couper, the first Lieutenant Governor of the North-Western Provinces & Chief Commissioner of Oudh (1877 – 1882), "during whose administration and auspices, the management was reformed and improved." Bayne

Figure 14: Vintage View of Hussainabad Clock Tower, Lucknow, Unidentified Photographer.

had already designed several 'Raj' buildings, across the country. At Lucknow, he designed a structure nearly as tall as the Qutub Minar in Delhi. His clock tower borrowed nothing from traditional Islamic architecture in India; instead, its square plan, horseshoe-shaped arches, and broad band of relief columns with intersecting decorative arches appeared to be of Moorish design - most notably inspired by the La Giralda minaret of Seville (Spain). The clock tower would be 221 feet high and 20 feet square. A Moorish dome on top of the tower was apparently covered with a metallic sheet and equipped with a wind vane.

The clockwork, made entirely of bell metal, was imported from JW Benson of Ludgate Hill, London. Each of the four clocks on the four sides was 13 feet in diameter, with the dials being flower-shaped, each petal being 3 feet in diameter. The minute hand was 6 feet long and the hour hand was 4.5 ft in length. Since the clock tower was installed before the advent of electricity, above the clock-room were eight copper lanterns, two for each dial, having plate glass-fronts and silver-plated 'holophotal' reflectors. From these, a powerful stream of light shone upon an exterior reflector placed so that light would be projected on the centre of the dials. The outside reflectors were movable, all four being extended, or withdrawn, at the same time, by an arrangement of wheels and cogs. The striking part had the hammer being raised by the great wheel, by means of which, a heavier blow and more sound was obtained. The system used was the rack-repeating type, which was the easiest in its action, safest in its locking and the most modern in its time.

Immediately above the dials was the bell-chamber with the bells mounted on a teak frame, as to produce the greatest volume of sound. These five bells, especially cast for this clock, were of the finest bell-metal, and their tones were extremely clear and musical. The hammers were mounted in frames and fitted with steel counter-springs to prevent 'chattering'. Despite its advanced features, "the clock gave so much trouble that after several tries by engineers; it was put up by a mechanic of the Oudh & Rohilkhand Railways named Mr. Mutloe." In a recent make-over of the Hussainabad area, the clock was made functional through private enterprise. But it continues to function only sporadically at the time of writing this book.

The Cantonments

"They represented the first stage in the physical separation of the rulers and ruled which characterised the Raj; a phenomenon which at its best promoted an aloof, incorruptible government and at its worst, arrogant ideas of racial superiority. Insulated from the teeming bazaars of the native quarters, cushioned from the chaos and squalor of native life, the British created a wholly separated existence which bore little relation to the real India. Thus, the growth of the cantonment marks a parting of the ways between European and Indian societies (Davies, 1987)."

Historically, cantonments were places where the army of the colonial government had to be exclusively quartered in an effort to keep the armed forces totally insulated from the ruled. After Asaf-ud-Daula shifted his capital from Faizabad to Lucknow in 1755, a fledging Garrison of British troops was stationed beyond the north bank of Gomti river, almost opposite to the Nawab's *Daulat Khana* palace complex. However, the first formal British army cantonment of Lucknow came into physical existence during the reign of Sa'adat Ali Khan. Situated in today's Aliganj area, it stretched from Sitapur Road (Mohibullapur) to present day Chandganj. The area was known as *Madiaon* (Mariaon), possibly after an ascetic, Mandal Rikh who had dwelt in the forest there (discussed earlier), before the cantonment came up. The wily Nawab wanted British troops to be stationed away from the Capital and accordingly, imposed strict conditions on the day-to-day activities of the soldiers stationed there, including a clause that: "No delinquents were to be given sanctuary within the premises, and any criminals who tried to hide there would be handed over to the Nawab."

The first available description of this cantonment or *Paltan Gaon* or *Murriaon*, was by Thomas Lumsden in 1819, who described bungalows built in cottage-style, each having a garden with out-offices, stables and servant quarters. Trying to emulate the English countryside, visitors were "astonished but delighted at the sight of a herd of English cattle which Mordaunt Ricketts, the then Resident had arranged for." The settlement initially consisted of Lines for Infantry Regiments, a Battery of European Horse Artillery and a Bullock Battery of Regular Native Artillery. A race course, cricket matches at the *Gend Ghar*, a ball room and a theatre provided entertainment. At least two European shops sold imported goodies. In the evenings, the band stand would be a congregating point for families. A small church catered to the religious requirements of the inhabitants. Its graveyard was a grim reminder of the harsh realities of colonial service, as the British, especially the children, suffered high mortality rates.

On the night of May 30, 1857, the 71st Native Infantry at *Madiaon* rose in rebellion, killing Brigadier Hanscombe, Lt. Grant and wounding Lt. Hardinge. The 32nd Regiment remained loyal and assisted their British officers in defending their posts, but not before the bungalows of the cantonment had been torched and reduced to rubble. On June 29, 1857, Madiaon was finally abandoned. In 1860, it was decided to retain the old cantonment as a separate *mauza,* called

Figure 15: Old Military Bungalow in Lucknow Cantonment, 1865, Unidentified Photographer.

Chownee Murriaon, to be ultimately handed over to the civilian authorities, by selling it off to the highest bidder, provided the burial ground, cordoned off by a boundary wall erected by the PWD, was retained. Today, only the graveyard partially remains, containing obelisks and mouldy tombstones.

1862 saw the establishment of the new cantonment, this time in the *Dilkusha* wooded park of Sa'adat Ali Khan, "the high ground at the rear of the Dilkoosha (*sic*), extending by the Beebiapore (*sic*) park and overlooking the windings of the Goomtee (*sic*), seems to offer every convenience for a military station, and it is far enough from the more dangerous parts of the city to keep the men out of temptation in the summer."

Approximately 7000 acres of forest land was appropriated by the British authorities to construct residential areas (consisting mainly of bungalows for officers and barracks for the less fortunate), commercial areas, places of worship, and the actual military area which occupied approximately 90% of the entire premises. Dilkusha Kothi was occupied by the Commander, Lucknow Division for quite some time, after which it was partially dismantled due to reasons unknown, leaving it as a ruinous, ghostly structure (Figure 4). The roads and "lines" of the new cantonment were named after the British "heroes", who had played a significant role in the uprising of 1857. Regrettably, some of these names continue till this day, like Neil Lines, named after Brigadier General James Neil, whose sobriquet as a butcher is well accepted, even in British circles. A number of churches and schools also came up in the cantonment, details of which are discussed in Chapters VI and VII of this book). With time, the Lucknow cantonment military cemetery (listed as "Christian Graveyard) housed 106 graves of Indian soldiers martyred during WW I. It is presently looked after by the Commonwealth War Graves Commission. The former Mohammad Bagh or "Prophet's Garden" was razed, gardened (as per colonial norms), bisected with a broad mall, shaded with mangoes and soft sand on ether side. It now housed an elite club for defence service officers, called Cantonment Club (later Mahomed Bagh Club or MB Club), which boasted of a theatre, cricket ground and bandstand, among flower-beds and pergolas sheltering palms and ferns. Asaf-ud-Daula's Bibiapur Kothi also came under the control of the army and used as an adjunct to the military dairy facility for some time, before being declared as a protected site in 1917. The Lucknow Cantonment Board was governed by the Cantonment Act. Among the official members were the Health Officer of the Cantonment, the Garrison Engineer and a representative of the District Magistrate, usually the City Magistrate, and 3 military officers nominated by the Officers Commanding the Station. The Station Commander was *ex-officio* President of the Board while the Vice-president was appointed by election.

Balrampur Hospital

Balrampur Hospital, designed by Sydney Crookshank (1869) was a sprawling complex, functional but devoid of aesthetics. However, its very location came under controversy, with a reprimanding note dated August 23, 1869 from the Governor General himself, that "in selecting the site chosen for the hospital, the local administration completely overlooked the explicit resolution of the Government of

Figure 16: Vintage view of Balrampur Hospital, Lucknow, 1872, Unidentified photographer.

India that the space in question (clear ground adjoining the Residency) should be kept clear of buildings of any kind. But as the action of the local government has proceeded so far and has been attended by a considerable degree of public ceremony, the Government and the Military Department consider it would be inexpedient to offer any opposition to the construction of the hospital on the site chosen for it." The Chief Commissioner at Lucknow was cautioned that "no other part of the ground referred to in the Military Department Proceedings dated 1st March 1864 is to be made use of for any sort of building without a previous reference to the Government of India and the Military Department."

Charbagh and the Railways

The first railway constructed in the district was the broad-gauge line from Cawnpore (Kanpur) to Lucknow, passing through Bijnaur *pargana* and entering *pargana* Lucknow, terminating at the main railway station at Charbagh, close to Rae Bareilly road. It was opened on April 23, 1867. On January 1, 1872, a continuation of this line

Figure 17: Vintage View of Old Railway Station of Lucknow, Unidentified Photographer.

to Bara Banki and Faizabad became operational. February 1, 1872 saw another line from Charbagh to Bareilly, via Sandila and Hardoi, which formed part of the Oudh and Rohilkhand Railways. On the eastern side, the same main line looped around Dilkusha and Vilayati Bagh, leading to Rai Bareilly and Mughal Serai, offering direct connectivity to Howrah/Calcutta. At Lucknow, credit must be given to the Oudh and Rohilkhand Railways for displaying an unusual sensitivity during the land acquisition process. For example, a letter of the Oudh and Rohilkhand Railways dated February 5, 1891, in connection with land acquisition in Mawaiya for construction of a station yard informed that "the trees on the land which is being taken up at Lucknow may be left standing and the owner of the mosque may be paid such compensation to free the property from all claims on his part in the future." The original railway station of Lucknow had been described as *"a low, unimposing, barrack-like structure of red brick, quite devoid of any architectural feature of note.*

Access to the platform was gained through the booking hall – a gloomy, cheerless chamber, and with its iron railings, more

Figure 18: Boarding a Train at old Lucknow Railway Station, Unidentified Photographer.

Figure 19: Front Elevation of Charbagh Railway Station, Lucknow.

Figure 20: Charbagh Railway Station (BG) Under Construction, 1921, UP State Archives, Lucknow.

suggestive of a prison than a railway station." The spacious new railway station (designed by JH Horniman, 1914) was ready by 1923, the stakeholders of the new station being the O & RR, Rohilkund and Kumaon Railway, the Military Authorities and the Lucknow Improvement Trust. 237.74 acres of land was transferred from the cantonment to the O & RR, not only for the new railway station but also for the development of the adjoining areas, including road

Figure 21: Construction of Charbagh Railway Station Concourse, 1921, UP State Archives, Lucknow.

Figure 22: North view of Rohilkund and Kumaon Railway (MG) Station, Lucknow, 1921, UP State Archives, Lucknow.

Figure 23: Team involved in Construction of Charbagh Railway Station, Lucknow: R Marriot, JC Banerjee, BN Bhattacharjee and Others, 1921, UP State Archives, Lucknow.

diversions. The Executive Engineer of the project was R. Marriot, with BN Bhattacharjee and JC Banerjee, being the Works Manager and Contractor respectively. It is not that the project did not face initial hiccups, with the observation that, "the meter gauge line set apart from the broad gauge, meaning that the passenger who has to change trains must of necessity carry his goods and chattels outside the premises of the station before he can enter the other. This appears to be unusual." Obviously no one took heed of this genuine observation and the anomaly continues till today. From Lucknow's Aishbagh, the railways also covered Daliganj, Mahona, with stations at Madiaon, Bakshi ka Talab and Itaunja, portions being covered by meter gauge railways also.

Narhai

After Lucknow became the state capital of the United Provinces in 1921, the Lucknow Improvement Trust floated several "Schemes" to improve the city's sanitation, road network, prominent markets and residential areas, thereby trying to introduce a semblance of order and planning in the old Nawabi capital. Due to its occasional ham-handed ways, it also faced criticism like, "the Improvement Trust is said to have been created for the improvement and edification of the city in which it exists, but it has been frequently noticed that its proceedings do affect the people in a way quite opposite to what they were meant to be."

Earlier, other than building a new army cantonment, the British had merely built bungalows for self-occupation on *nazul* land and appropriated Nawabi properties for official and residential use. But now, many of these old properties were in dire need of periodic maintenance, with many of them showing their age. Major development projects of Hazratganj, Kaiserbagh, Lalbagh, Charbagh and Chowk (Gol Darwaza) apart, a hilarious situation occurred when the colonial administration tried to develop Narhi (or Narhai) - a rather insignificant, densely populated, market-cum-residential area adjacent to Hazratganj. It appears that the local inhabitants of Narhi were not in favour of their traditional *bazaar* being uprooted under the guise of "improvement." Among a flurry of petitions to the authorities and letters to the newspapers, about 400 - 500 people congregated in the premises of Narhai Municipal School on August 23, 1921 to protest against the high-handedness of the LIT officials, who had been behaving "in a most arbitrary manner as regards the so-called "Narhai Improvement Scheme." An evocative poem was also published in a National Daily, an extract from which goes as follows:

Narhai Bazaar

Before

The eager buyers at the flush of dawn
Hie onwards to the city's busy mart
Where still bazaars die waiting for the morn
In Lucknow daily life so play their part
Thronged are the streets the bartering once more
Of those who buy and sells fill the air
The villager repletes his scanty store
Then learns the gossip of the city there..

After

What silence this that hangs like heavy pall
O'er Narhai's lanes where now the living stream
Of erstwhile buyers, where are the sellers?
All have vanished like the passing of a dream..

Although the protests and particularly the poem above did not go down well with the colonial administration, discretion being the better part of valour, the plan to drastically improve Narhi was rescinded, and only a few shops here and there were relocated, as a face-saving measure, together with the laying of an improved drainage system.

Hazratganj / Huzrutgunge

We shall observe the wavering fortunes of Amjad Ali Shah's final resting place (which continued for a long time, even after 1947) in the next Chapter; however, we must not lose track of Hazratganj as a whole. The development of Hazratganj as a commercial area had several phases. Firstly, a road was had been developed across the city, from the Residency to the Dilkusha, which was not a straight road but at least a direct approach, during the times of Sa'adat Ali Khan. This road was lined by *kothis* like Nur Baksh Kothi, Aine Wali Kothi, Kankar Wali Kothi to Kothi Hayat Baksh. These were occupied by family members of Sa'adat Ali. There are indications that this area might have been referred to as Munawwar Baksh, but it is not substantiated. The second phase commenced with the building of the Begum Kothi of Mallika Ahad, a junior or *khurd* begum Amjad Ali Shah "Hazrat", and also the building of the Sibtainabad Imambara in the area known as Mendu Khan ka Ahata or Mendu Khan ki Chaoni. The *Imambara* became the final resting place of Amjad Ali Shah and the area derived its name from *Hazrat* and a *Ganj* or native market existing in the area, which the British later demolished to build the police station and other buildings. Earlier, after the British had taken over the city in 1858, they had cut large swathes across the city, smashing through palaces, gateways and natives' quarters alike, under the supervision of Colonel Robert Napier of the Bengal Engineers, who had earlier carried out a similar exercise in Old

Delhi. Palaces, kothis, even royal gardens, or 'enemy property' were declared as *nazul,* and taken over by the colonial government for themselves, or simply sold / auctioned off at throwaway prices to British sympathizers.

In the Hazratganj area, the ire of the British was naturally directed against the Begum Kothi, where they had faced significant casualties (including the death of their poster boy, Major William Hodson). The boundary walls of the *kothi* were demolished; the main building of the *kothi* started functioning as a post office and the Kothi Inayat Sultan within the complex, was bought by Munshi Newal Kishore for establishing the offices of his publishing empire. Newal Kishore also built his own house in main Hazratganj. This building, with a clock tower, now houses the premises of the Central Bank of India. The premises of Kothi Jafar Ali and Kothi Zarur-ud-Daula, west of Begum Kothi were demolished during colonial rule to make way for the offices of the Oudh & Rohilkhand Railway (present day office of the Divisional Railway Manager, Northern Railways). The eastern and western wings of Sa'adat Ali Khan's cruciform Chaupar stables

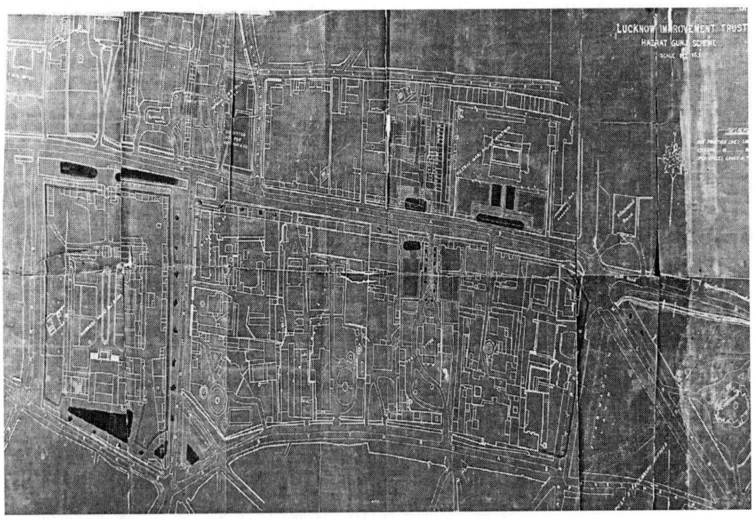

Figure 24: Blue-print of Hazratganj Scheme by Lucknow Improvement Trust, UP State Archives, Lucknow.

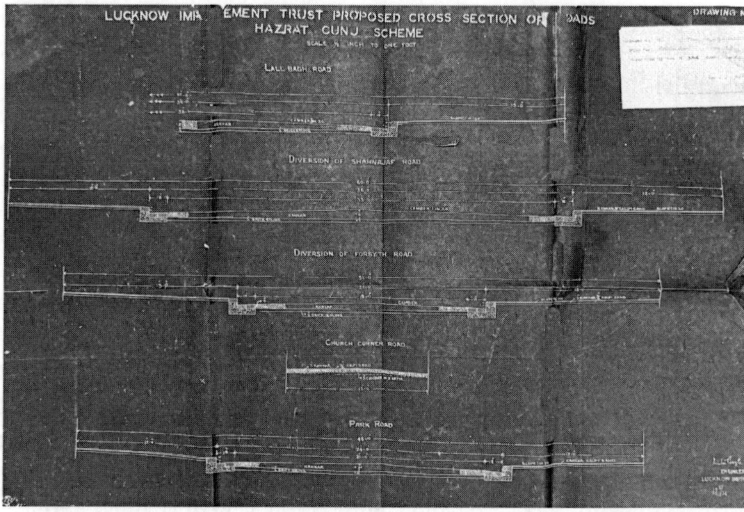

Figure 25: Blue-print for Re-alignment of Roads under Hazratganj Scheme by Lucknow Improvement Trust, UP State Archives, Lucknow.

were demolished, to make way for low-cost housing for Anglo-Indians, together with the main building (Lawrence Terrace). One (southern) wing of the Chaupar, however, survived as the Lucknow (Residency) or Union Club. Both Lawrence Terrace and Lucknow Club shall be discussed separately. A new road started from the Gomti, cutting across Sikandar Bagh (now part of NBRI). This road, christened as Outram Road (now Ashok Marg), continued as Abbot Road (now Vidhan Sabha Marg), which cut across the Begum Kothi compound. New roads *viz.* the Lawrence Road (now Newal Kishore Road) and Oliver Road (now Sapru Marg) were laid parallel to main Hazratganj, which was itself christened as Queensway or Civil Lines or the Mall.

The nucleus of colonial *Huzrutgunge* emerged from the Meeting of the "Local Agency" comprising of Colonel SA Abbot, Major Hutchinson, P. Carnegie, WC Wood and Captain Rawlins, held on July 6, 1859 which proposed "a plan for turning the square and *serai* in the Huzrutgunge.... into a fine *pukka* Gunj, much in the plan of the two corner shops called Colonel's Abbot's shops. A number of

Bunneahs and squatters had come forward to say they will build the shops if we give them the sites." The plan was put into action, with the Secretary taking measures to give effect to the resolution at once. In 1871, the Commissioner circulated a blueprint for the design and layout future shops to be built in Huzrutgunge, which was being gradually converted in the form of a Civil Lines. Such were the humble beginnings of the Hazratganj we know today.

Colonial Huzrutgunge was to be a commercial hub, on the ruins and remnants of old *kothis* and palaces, which had earlier lined the road. In effect, the British had actually revived the arterial road laid earlier by Sa'adat Ali Khan. Huzrutgunge or The Mall was part of the greater Mall Road, which according to Beg (1911) was "one of the longest, best kept and most frequented roads,.. it makes a start near Hussainabad Imambara, goes along by the side of the Residency, between the public Courts and Chutter (*sic*) Manzil (United Services Club) through Hazrutgange (*sic*), passes by the Roman Catholic and Christ Churches (Protestant), the Exchange Cottage, another range of buildings where large European and native shops are, then by Government House North Gate, over Canal, by the Loretto (*sic*) Convent through the Cantonments and finally ends at the Race Course, a distance of 6 to 7 miles."

Perhaps this was the heyday of Huzrutgunge (officially called Queensway), when it became a centre of fashion, much merry-making, and a true commercial hub. The Prince of Wales Theatre (later Prince Cinema) was the first cinema hall of Huzrutgunge, which traced its origin from the Prince of Wales' visit in 1876. In 1934, the Plaza (then Regal, then Filmistan, and present-day Sahu PVR cinema), came up in the parking space in front of Prince Cinema. Capitol opened in 1937, all three halls serving the purpose of cinema as well as theatre performances. 1939 saw the inauguration of the Mayfair building, with the Mayfair cinema, a bar and a ballroom. The Ambassador Restaurant and Dance Hall came up subsequently, In the '30s, Royal Café, then situated in the Halwasiya Court was famous for its live band. Valerio's Tea Room and dance floor functioned from the present premises of the Gandhi

Ashram!! above it (present day Soochna Kendra) was a guesthouse for soldiers called Soldier's Home. An English departmental store, Whiteaway, Laidlaw & Co. existed where the present LIC building now stands. Other prominent British shops included AN James & Co. (pharmacy), Murray & Co. (general merchants), SH Clarke & Co. (provisions and wines) and Anderson's (tailors). Among the Parsee outlets, Sohrabjee (wine merchants), Minoo & Dinshaw (watches, cutlery) and Taraporewala (sewing machines) were the most well known. For a more detailed listing of commercial establishments in colonial Huzrutgunje, the reader may refer to Annexure IV of this book. The erstwhile Begum Kothi was now the Post Office for a long time (till the Imperial Post Office came up discussed elsewhere); diagonally opposite to this old Begum Kothi Post Office was a *Ganj*, which was basically a grain market. This *Ganj,* described as having "dilapidated and squalid native shops" was razed to the ground and the Hazratganj Police Station came up in its place (similar to Chowk Police Station), together with large, commodious double storied buildings, designed by Lebanti (whose contributions to Lucknow's colonial era architecture are indeed impressive). The Police Station, built in 1909 resembled a medieval castle, complete with turrets and a portcullis (a heavy grating that can be lowered down grooves on each side of a gateway to block it). Unfortunately, the Police Station was demolished in 2009, to make way for a multi-level parking lot during the recent makeover of Hazratganj. The "large, commodious buildings on either side" remain today with a variety of commercial outlets, a south Indian style restaurant, the Gandhi Ashram and the State Information Center (Soochna Kendra)."

Drinking, dancing, seeing risqué live shows, enjoying (authentic) Chinese dinners, buying the latest trousseaus imported from London – colonial Huzrutgunge had it all. It was truly the place to be at that point of time. Perhaps modern day Hazratganj will never see such Bohemian, carefree days again. Post 1947, the market saw several make-overs and facelifts over the next century and a half, but a descriptive analysis of those would be beyond the scope of this book, which is dedicated to Colonial Lucknow.

Kaiserbagh and Lalbagh

The Lalbagh and Kaiserbagh Circles or roundabouts we see today, (or whatever remains of them) were constructed through extensive planning and landscaping, with the Kaiserbagh complex being bigger and more elaborate than the Lalbagh counterpart. Kaiserbagh circle was carved out from a portion of the erstwhile Kaiserbagh palace garden complex of Wajid Ali Shah, whereas the Lalbagh circle was developed from Shah Bihari Lal's vast estate. Lal was an affluent merchant from the times of Ghazi-ud-Din Haider and the term *Lalbagh* emerged in his honour and not due to the presence of any buried treasure or red rubies in the premises (Sarkar, 2021).

Interestingly, the buildings at Kaiserbagh circus, with their arcades were built by different owners as per the plan provided by the Lucknow Improvement Trust. Land at the junction of Cantonment Road and La Touche Road was sold to a Mr. Madan, who agreed to erect the buildings according to the plan of the LIT. The Trust would build the market on the land between La Touche Road and Aminabad Road. Land between Aminabad Road and Circular Road was purchased by Dr. RK Tandon, who agreed to construct the building in accordance with the scheme. LIT also planned a housing scheme for the vendors who would have their shops in the market, meant exclusively for Europeans *viz* Marris Market and Saunder's Market. Charles JG Saunders was the Bishop of Lucknow (why name a meat market in honour of a priest?) during 1928 - 1938 and William Sinclair Marris was of course, the Lt. Governor of the United Provinces during 1922 - 1928. The new market was "a single storeyed place of large dimensions with gauze wire netting to keep out the flies, this is another of Mr Butler's conceptions and is a very striking edifice, in it are marble slabs to help the butchers keeping the place clean. It has several skylights to it, allowing plenty of fresh air to get in, there are four entrances to it and it has a Bazaar Sergeant to see that the place is kept clean and in order. The market opened with a garden party under the auspices of H.H. Sir James Prescott Hewett L.G. of the UP of A and Oudh and the elite of the station; all other shops have been abolished and only the market will be used as the place for sale of both beef and mutton along with fish."

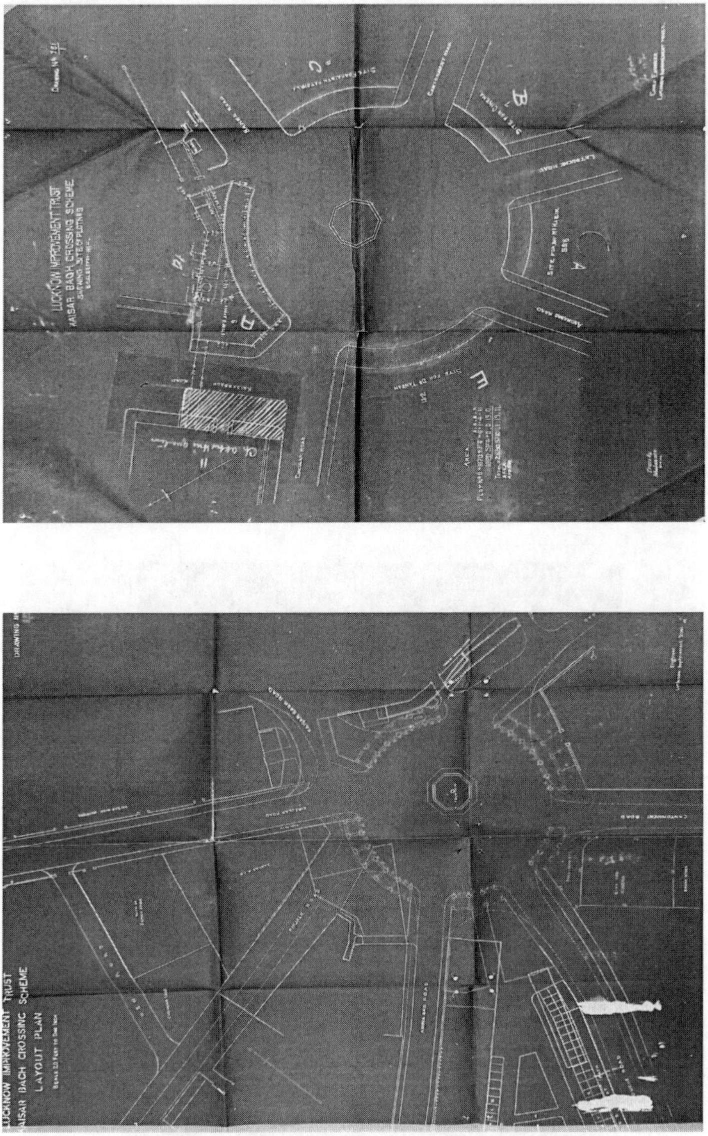

Figure 26 : Blueprints of Kaiserbagh Crossing Scheme by Lucknow Improvement Trust, UP State Archives, Lucknow.

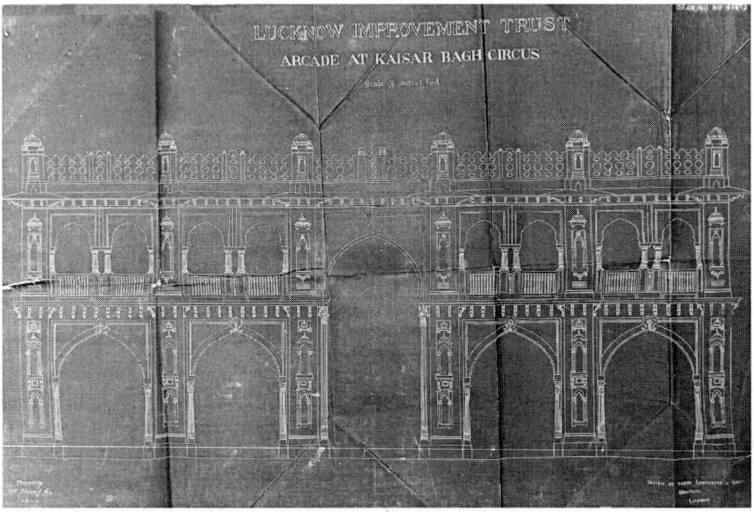

Figure 27: Blueprint of Arcades at Kaiserbagh Circus
by Lucknow Improvement Trust, UP State Archives, Lucknow.

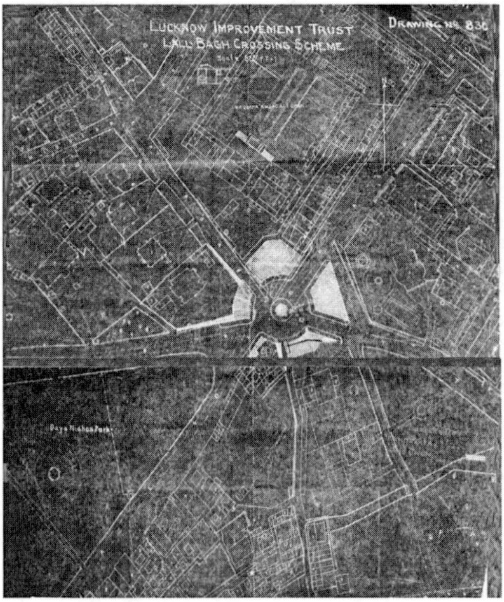

Figure 28: Blueprint of Lalbagh Crossing Scheme by
Lucknow Improvement Trust, UP State Archives, Lucknow.

One building in the Kaiserbagh circus was reserved for a cinema, where the Eliphinstone came up (later Anand Cinema).

Aminabad Park

This Scheme was initiated by Rai Ganga Pershad Verma Bahadur. An "extremely dirty and unsightly quarter was removed and the present park constructed at no extra cost to the tax-payer, as the scheme was self-supporting. The Park possesses a fine clock tower and fountains and is thronged with people every evening. The buildings surrounding it are double-storeyed as in the cloth market having shops below, connected by means of a continuance colonnade and residential quarters above. These shops are now the acknowledged business centre of the Indian merchants in the eastern part of the city. The opening of the Aminabad Park distributed mercantile interests to a certain extent and Hazratganj has not the monopoly it had in the past. It is still however, the chief centre for European shops." According to Beg (1911), it was "a market place where all kinds of imported, both English and foreign goods are sold, along with country manufacture also. The different Banks have a branch in it also, and there is a branch post office. It has derived its name through the ground on which it stands, being a portion of Aminabad bazaar, the old houses having been demolished and new shops erected on a more elaborate style in a quadrangle of three sides with a lawn thrown out in the centre. This is light (*sic*) by Kiston lights, has a fountain and a clock tower. The entrance being from all sides. This has also added to the thinning of the population, making it more sanitory (*sic*) and thus staving off a deal of sickness which year by year would have come about. This along with other places mentioned thereafter was planned out by Mr Butler one of our most energetic Deputy Commissioners who has since received a promotion and gone to the Government of India as Secretary to Government Foreign office."

The Council House / Council Chamber

Although the Indo-Saracenic style dominated Colonial Lucknow's skyline for quite sometime, a renewed interest in Renaissance and Baroque styles could be seen in buildings of a more "serious nature" such as the Council House / Chamber (present day Vidhan Sabha / Vidhan Bhawan), which resembled the Central Hall of Westminster in its conception. The construction of the Council House at Lucknow was decided by the Legislative Council on August 1, 1921. Its Foundation Stone was laid by Harcourt Butler in December 1922, who was then the first Governor of the United Provinces of Agra and Oudh, having earlier served as Lt. Governor during 1918 - 1921. The building was to be constructed by M/s Martin & Co. (no relation to Claude Martin) for civil works and M/s Jessop & Co. as the electrical contractor, from the design prepared by Architect, HV Lanchester. Before finalisation of the design, Maj. General Crookshank had provided the ground plans of the Delhi Council Chamber for reference. At Lucknow, Crookshank, who worked as an Executive Engineer in Lucknow also planned and constructed the King George's Medical College and Hospital, the Canning College, the Arabic College, School of Design and Balrampur Hospital.

The actual construction of the Council Chamber started from August 23, 1922, with a deadline of 5 years for completion. Work, however, was stopped in June 1923 and resumed in September 1925

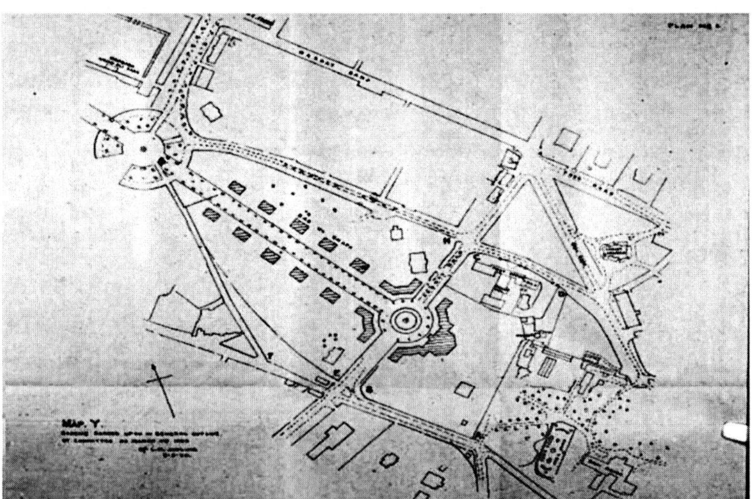

Figure 29: Plan of New Council Chamber, Lucknow, UP State Archives, Lucknow.

Figure 30: New Council Chamber Building, Lucknow, February 28, 1928, Unidentified Photographer.

due to administrative delays, as well as shortfall in supply of stone. In April 1927, Lanchester intimated that the Central Block would be ready by October 1927. The building was finally completed in July, 1928 although it had been officially opened by Alexander Muddiman, then Governor, on February 21, 1928. The project cost the colonial government a tidy sum of Rs 26,33,000/-. The accompanying delays also caused problems for the timely inauguration of the building.

By 1935, the requirement for increased accommodation, a Press Gallery, the Secretariat, as well as provision for joint sitting for both Lower and Upper Houses came up. Till that time, the Camp Office Secretariat and "Old Council Chamber" in Kaiserbagh, in the former Canning College premises had been functioning (discussed later), albeit with some difficulty. Members of the Legislative Council from Allahabad who arrived at Lucknow stayed at the Imperial Hotel and Burlington Hotel. Hence, there was also a proposal to take over Imperial Hotel itself to provide accommodation for the legislators - "in any case, the hotel was not doing too well." This time, the Consulting Architect for the extension work was AL Mortimor of

Leeds, England. Lanchester, the original architect was also involved in the work, which included the "preparation of sketch designs, drawings and specifications for proper execution of the work." M/s Ford & Macdonald and M/s Sen & Sanyal would be the contractors for civil and electrical works respectively. The extension of the Council Chamber cost the government a sum of Rs 35,00,000/- against a budget estimate of Rs 45,00,000/-

Figure 31: Sketch of Canning College Building, Tika Ram.

Canning College and Marris College

The Foundation Stone of the Canning College building (present day Bhatkhande Music University) at Kaiserbagh was laid by the Viceroy, Sir John Lawrence, on November 13, 1867. The design first accepted in 1866 was subsequently rejected. The construction was completed in 1879, after several delays. This building was built on the grounds of the erstwhile *Parikhana* - a significant part of Wajid Ali Shah's Kaiserbagh palace complex (Sarkar, 2022), which had been demolished post 1857. According to a paper read at the Royal Institute of British Architects, by the Executive Engineer,

JA Willmore, "the soil on which the building was erected was found to consist of 2 feet of rubbish, remains of former old buildings and below that, of sand." The architectural plans and elevations of the Canning College building (now housing the Bhatkhande Music University) are available on record (Brandreth, 1879). The building's design which was ultimately selected was by Tika Ram (1881), Head Draftsman in the Office of the Engineer-in-Chief, Rajputana State Railway. Swinton Jacob, who was also stationed as Chief Engineer in Jaipur, later designed Lalgarh Palace, Bikaner (1902 – 1926), which was architecturally inspired by the Canning College building. The latter, an ambitious project of the colonial government, was unabashedly based on Nawabi and Rajasthani elements (comprising of *chabutras* / platforms, *chajjas* / balconies, *chattris* / pavilions, *jalis* / lattice work and *jharokhas* / bay windows) combined with European architectural styles in one package - an early example of the so-called Indo-Saracenic architecture, which would later proliferate rapidly, but then, it faced criticism. *The Builder* (1881), a prominent London-based journal devoted to architecture and related subjects like engineering and construction works noted that, "The general effect of the exterior must be regarded as very poor. The style, as the designer stated, is in harmony with the surrounding buildings of the Kaiser Bagh - a bad standard." Polished brass finials were provided for the turrets, minarets and the projecting windows of corner towers. There was no woodwork in the whole building except the doors, *chowkhats* (door frames) and library skylights. The total cost of the building was Rs 1,73,299/- and construction time was 2 years.

After Canning College vacated the premises and shifted to its Badshah Bagh campus, the building was then used by the government to house the Provincial Museum, which was shifted from the Lal Baradari to the old Canning College building in 1884 (Annexure VI). The Canning College building also served as the venue of the temporary Council Chamber and Camp Secretariat, till such time the new Council Chamber and its extension came up (see above).

The Marris College of Hindustani Music was established in 1926, due to the efforts of Pt. Vishnu Narayan Bhatkhande, Rai Umanath Bali, Rai Rajeshwar Bali and other patrons of music. Inaugurated by the then Governor of Awadh, Sir William Marris - it was named in his honour, and housed in the Canning College building discussed above. In view of its unique requirements, a separate building had been proposed for the same, with "special focus on sound proofing so voice / music of one room may not penetrate into the other." Building plans were obtained from Asit Kr. Haldar and Kalyan Singh of Govt. School of Arts and Crafts, but the new building could not materialise. The financial grant for the building sanctioned in 1926 was returned to the government in 1928, and the music college continued to occupy the premises of the old building of Canning College. Of late, this has given rise to fake claims and statements from certain quarters that the colonial Marris (now Bhatkhande Sanskriti Vishwavidyalaya) College of Music was established in the premises of the erstwhile *Parikhana* - a song, dance and drama instructional school for young and not so young women during the reign of Wajid Ali Shah. This falsehood needs to be repudiated and rejected.

Marris College, in the first year of its existence, had 7 teachers, 13 students, one *tanpura*, one *sitar* and a *tabla* set. As per a noting on file, "there was not a single shop in Lucknow dealing with musical instruments and the same had to be procured from Calcutta." This statement must be taken with a pinch of salt since Lucknow had been intimately associated with music and dance for the past one and half centuries, long before a colonial school for music had come into existence. Possibly, these shops and their owners had met their sad end during the events of 1857.

Architects from the West

Patrick Geddes, an eminent Scottish town planner had visited Lucknow in 1914 and had been appalled at the town planning which had been imposed on the old quarter of Lucknow, half a century ago after 1857, at the behest of Robert Napier, a military engineer. Napier's plan to create spaces by demolishing native buildings left and right, thereby creating wide open swathes, had been accepted and implemented by the colonial government with alacrity. The creation of Victoria Street in Chowk area was a result of this massive exercise, which had effectively resulted in the razing of 70% of old Lucknow.

Geddes returned to Lucknow in 1916, and proposed the rectification of Victoria Street, by introducing green belts and more significantly, arcades for the commercial areas, which would benefit both the owners of the aforesaid buildings, due to additional floor space, as well as the public, who would be sheltered from the natural elements, while going about their daily pursuits. Some of these proposals and architectural plans were implemented in due course of time, but the character of the old city was essentially gone. Napier had succeeded in re-constructing Lucknow, based on military considerations, (like most war torn cities all over the world of that era), whereas the contribution of Geddes, with his noble ideas of 'real re-construction' coupled with the renewal of social life, were too little and came too late.

Walter Burley Griffin, an American architect from Chicago, who had earlier designed the Australian capital city of Canberra arrived at Lucknow in 1935, having won a commission to design the Tagore Library of Lucknow University. Although his design never saw the light of the day due to administrative complications and financial issues (contrary to popular belief, the Tagore Library we see today was designed by Mr Narwekar, an Indian architect and not by Griffin), the American architect was inundated with new

Figure 32: Arcaded Building in Victoria Street, Chowk, Geddes, Unidentified Photographer.

Figure 33: Architectural Design for Pioneer Press Building, Griffin, Unidentified Photographer.

commissions including the Lucknow University Student Union building, a library and museum for the Raja of Mahmoodabad, a *zenana* (women's quarters) for the Raja of Jahangirabad, the Pioneer Press Office and Works, municipal offices, several private homes, the stadium, numerous pavilions, rotundas, arcades and towers for the 95 acre site for the United Provinces Industrial and Agricultural Exhibition held in December 1936. Griffin designed the site plan of the numerous temporary pavilions using a variation of the local building method of bamboo and plaster. Of his private assignments, the Bir Bhan Bhatia house at Lucknow, has been widely appreciated, as well as the Pioneer Press Building. Griffin is also credited for designing the canopy for the statue of King George V, opposite the GPO (presently housing the statue of Mahatma Gandhi), and the Capitol theatre opposite to the canopy.

Chapter - V

Colonial Development of Lucknow II
The Minor Projects

Historical Background

Due to the trauma faced by the British during 1857 - 58, including the galling fact that they had been unceremoniously ejected from Lucknow by the revolutionaries, soon after regaining control of the city, (aided by a ragtag bunch of mercenary Gurkha foot soldiers, led by notorious freebooter, Jang Bahadur), the post 1857 model of colonial "development" for Lucknow was guided by certain unwritten principles, which could be summarised as follows:

- To decimate the old Nawabi order, by way of coercion, subjugation and systemised loot of the nobility and their supporters / sympathisers.
- To physically "clean" Lucknow by cutting broad swathes across the city, demolishing palaces, private houses and religious places in the process; this would ensure quick movement of British troops in the event of any future uprising.
- To establish a new social order, by encouraging the *ta'aluqdars* or landed barons of Awadh, (confined to those who had supported the British during the uprising) to settle in Lucknow by offering them land and confiscated property

at Lucknow at rock bottom prices, thereby creating an effective buffer between the local populace and the colonial administration.

- To shock and awe the citizens of Lucknow, by way of building colonial edifices like clock towers, statues and memorial parks (often at the expense of older, Nawabi structures), which would serve as a constant reminder to the public about the new colonial regime.
- To maintain a tight control on the native population, with harsh deterrents and punishments in place, so that a repeat of 1857 did not occur.

In fact, with the passage of time, Lucknow had started to become a ghost town, having a sizeable military presence (due to obvious reasons) in the newly created cantonment carved out from the erstwhile Dilkusha hunting forest grounds of Nawab Sa'adat Ali Khan and the railways, carved out of Nawabi gardens like Charbagh, Aishbagh and Alambagh. Any colonial development in the city, be it the railways or water works or even a poor house for the destitute, was not aimed at the general native populace, but focussed on the benefits (and security) that they would offer to the military and civilian European population.

While a complete listing and descriptive analysis of such "developmental activities" would be beyond the scope of this book, having discussed the "major" projects in the previous Chapter, we shall now discuss some "minor" projects - quite a few being successful and some skewed, which would throw light on the prevailing circumstances in Lucknow during those troubled times. Although the narrative below might occasionally be a source of mirth to the reader, the undercurrent of tragedy in those dark days of Lucknow would also become evident.

The European officials stationed at Lucknow, particularly those belonging to the civil services, had their own peculiar problems. The military had built their new spacious cantonment with offices and living quarters as per entitlement. This was not so with civil service officials, who had to make do with old Nawabi properties, however commodious the latter might have been. In the highly bureaucratised and layered Victorian society of those times, there would be frequent comparisons and heartburns between the "stiff upper lip" officials of different departments as regards their rank, entitlements and benefits due.

Soon after the annexation of Awadh in 1856, the Kadam Rasul, an Islamic religious structure, was converted to a powder magazine, with scant regard to the sentiments of the local Muslim populace. Similarly, buildings such as Taaron Wali Kothi (Imperial Bank), Kothi Hayat Baksh (Residence of Lt. Governor / Chief Commissioner), Khurshid Manzil (La Martiniere School for Girls), the Chaupar stables (Lawrence Terrace) and many others were put to various uses as indicated in the parenthesis. The Daulat Khana in the Sheesh Mahal complex became the residence of Brigadier Gray, while the Sheesh Mahal itself was converted to army stores. Musa Bagh Kothi was occupied by the 4th and 7th Regiments of the Oudh Irregular Infantry. The General Commanding, Oudh Division occupied Dilkusha Kothi for many years, till it was declared "unsafe" and partially demolished, shortly after 1862.

Figure 34: Vintage View of Chattar Manzil Palace Complex, Unidentified Photographer.

Figure 35: Vintage View of Kothi Hayat Baksh, Claude Martin's arsenal, later Major Banks' House and lastly converted to Governor's House, Unidentified Photographer.

Figure 36: Vintage View of Tehri Kothi, Unidentified Photographer.

Figure 37: Dil Aram Kothi, 1870, Robert & Harriet Tytler.

Figure 38: Kothi Singhara, 1870, Robert & Harriet Tytler.

Figure 39 : Kothi Gulistan-e-Iram, 1870, Robert & Harriet Tytler.

Figure 40: Kothi Darshan Bilas, 1870, Robert & Harriet Tytler.

Figure 41 : Kankar Wali Kothi, 1870, Robert & Harriet Tytler.

Figure 42: Vintage View of Lal Baradari, 1905, Unidentified Photographer.

Figure 43: Vintage View of Roshan-ud-Daula Kothi, Unidentified Photographer.

Figure 44: Vintage View of Farhat Baksh in forefront with Chattar Manzil at the back, Unidentified Photographer.

Figure 45: "Meeting of the Generals", 1860, Thomas Barker Jones.

Post 1857, various prominent *nazul* (confiscated "enemy" property) buildings of Lucknow were earmarked for occupation by European civil servants. These included the Tehri Kothi (Judicial Commissioner and the District Superintendent of Police, Lucknow), Noor Baksh Kothi (Deputy Commissioner, Lucknow), Kankar Wali Kothi (District Judge, Lucknow) and an unspecified property named Barlow's Bungalow (City Magistrate, Lucknow). A measly rent was charged from the occupants on the logic that "these originally cost the Government nothing, and since rent was based on the cost of acquisition, it should be lower and not higher than usual for houses occupied of officers of similar rank." However, comparisons of rent, entitlements, predecessors and privileges of officers posted in different districts, other than Lucknow, as compared to those posted in Lucknow, continued to dog the colonial administration. One official requested the use of a vacant plot of land next to the Tehri Kothi (which was denied), while another official wanted remodelling of Tehri Kothi, including "removal of stains from outside to inside, and building of a chimney, the want of which made the house almost inhabitable in the cold weather, as no fire could be lit without filling the house with smoke." The administrative control and maintenance of various buildings also vacillated between the PWD, Nazul Office, Lucknow Improvement Trust and various individual departments. It was observed that the Noor Baksh Kothi was "superior to any house in Lucknow", while the Kankar Wali Kothi and Tehri Kothi, though occupied, "were not convenient houses." The Kothi Singhara remained unoccupied (possibly due to the severe damage faced by the building during the flooding of the Gomti). Lawrence Terrace (discussed later) managed to get 19 tenants from the subordinate services. Later the Kankar Wali Kothi was sold off for an amount of Rs 35,000/- and a new residence built for the District Judge. Earlier, a District Judge, then occupying Kankar Wali Kothi had petitioned the authorities that he had been on privileged leave during June - July 1917 and again during May - June 1918, and that he should not be liable to pay rent for the premises during the periods mentioned (although he had not vacated the property during the period of leave). For added convenience, it was also proposed that the various officials would have their offices and residences within the same property, but this did not find favour with the colonial government, as it would lead to lack of privacy for the families and result in the presence of domestic servants and orderlies lounging about the premises.

As regards the seraglio of the former Nawabs of Awadh, the occupancy of the Lal Baradari, former Coronation Hall of the Nawabi era, remained in a state of constant flux; while the extant Provincial Museum inside the premises was to be shifted to the Canning College building in the erstwhile Pari Khana area of Kaiserbagh, even the spacious basement or *tykhana* of Lal Baradari was earmarked to serve as a godown, The Chota Chattar Manzil would house the Department of Land Records, Cooperative & Credit Society and Civil Veterinary and Agriculture Departments. Kothi Gulistan-e-Iram was earmarked for the Inspector General of Hospitals and Sanitary Commissioner. The Office of the Sanitary Engineer would be housed in the Darshan Bilas. It would be later used by the PWD for offices and residential accommodation. Interestingly, the names of Chota Chattar Manzil, Gulistan-e-Iram and Darshan Bilas were used collectively by the colonial administration as Chota Chattar Manzil. Also, it was reported that the Government Quinine Factory had been relocated from Aligarh Jail, along with the Epidemic Stores Department to the Lal Baradari. But in actuality, the Baradari never housed these; possibly it was the Chota Chattar Manzil which accommodated all sorts of offices related to the medical and health departments, including the Malaria and Epidemiology Departments.

The Bada Chattar Manzil, would of course continue to house the elite United Services Club, whilst the Farhat Baksh Kothi would be given over to the Union Club (discussed later) and then used as a Station Library. Sikchewali Kothi became the District Judge's Court, while Imambara Amin-ud-daula was occupied by the Tehsil Office. Jarnail Kothi was used for housing local government offices, and parts of it used as residential quarters. Darul Shafa was used for residential purposes, while its compound would be subsumed in the new Council Chambers (discussed elsewhere). Kaiser Pasand (Roshan-ud-Daula Kothi) would become the Court of the Deputy Commissioner of Lucknow. The Central Jail (no longer extant), next to the new Cantonment, constructed in 1865 and was composed of "two blocks on the standard pattern." For the Lucknow Water Works, a proposal for acquiring 41 acres of land, 3 roads and 15 palaces in Aishbagh was submitted on August 2, 1893. Municipal water supply for Lucknow commenced operations in 1894, with thirty two miles of pipes laid for distributing water in the city. After intake from the Gomti river (an earlier plan to draw water from deep bore wells failed within two years), the water was pumped to tanks in Aishbagh, filtered, purified and supplied throughout the city, including the Civil Lines and cantonment area.

Few European enterprises also came up in Lucknow during this period. The most prominent among these was the Upper India Couper Paper Mills, which came into existence in 1879, soon becoming a flourishing concern. The distillery at Aishbagh was first opened in 1858, which was burnt down in 1869. The facility was revived in the same year on an adjoining site. M/s. E. Dyer & Co. brewery started in 1882, producing an impressive amount of beer annually. Rest all European liquor was imported. The ice manufacturing facility, together with its pits near the Farhat Baksh was closed down, and

M/s. John Ice Factory started operations in 1902. The only flour mill of the city, Sri Venkateshwar Flour Mills was established in 1921. Oil pressing was one of the lucrative industries during WW II, and there were four units in Lucknow which produced vegetable oils. Other than the oil and flour mills, the cotton ginning mills at Tal Kathura (present day Talkatora industrial area) deserve mention. M/s India Hume Pipe Co. Ltd. of Bombay established their branch factory in 1938, for the manufacture of cement processed products like hume pipes, poles and other related projects. The Agricultural Implements and General Engineering Works, engaged in the manufacture of agricultural implements and miscellaneous engineering goods like oil expellers, cane crushers, lathes etc. was first established in 1937 in Maulviganj, but shifted to the Aishbagh Industrial Area post-1947. M/s Northern India Iron Press Works was started in 1935, for the manufacture of wood screws, tower bolts, aldrops and tonga channels. The Newal Kishore Press & Iron Foundry, as well as Oudh & Rohilkhand Railways provided employment opportunities, giving rise to the demand for suitably qualified and trained youth, with technical skills. This will be discussed now in the next section of this Chapter, together with other "minor" not so successful projects.

The Minor Projects

An Industrial School

By and large, the colonial mindset did not approve of native Indians acquiring technical skills; the latter were more "suitable" for clerical and subordinate jobs. However, due to persistent demand, an Elementary Industrial School (also known as Railway Industrial School) came into existence in Lucknow on November 1892. It offered a mixed bag of education to the sons of railway employees, consisting of drawing, carpentry, vernacular languages, English and Arithmetic. The School was located in the western quadrangle of the Wingfield Manzil beyond Kaiserbagh, on rent-free accommodation provided by the British India Association. There was some correspondence as to who would pay the salary of the *chowkidar* (guard), but nonetheless, the admissions were later thrown open to the public and more subjects of "a practical nature" were introduced. This rosy picture, however, was shattered when the BIA asked for the return of its premises in 1895, for the "convenience and use of the Talukdars (*sic*) not having quarters in Kaiserbagh." With no alternative accommodation in sight, the BIA was requested for a reprieve, to which it acquiesced since "the Association was always prepared to obey the order of the government." Nevertheless, the BIA, vide letter dated January, 1897, persisted for a definite commitment for vacating its premises. More trouble was in store when the students of this school could not find gainful employment, primarily due to slow industrialisation in India and colour bias. For example, the European mill owners of Kanpur wanted Indian labourers under European supervision and not vice versa.

The dismal scenario above changed with World War II, when the colonial government was forced to formulate comprehensive plans for technical and vocational education on a country-wide basis. However, the discrimination against Indians continued, with all senior administrative and management posts being centred around the Europeans themselves. This would continue till India finally gained independence in 1947.

The Meeting of The Generals

"The Relief of Lucknow" or "The Meeting of The Generals", as it is popularly known was a painting by British painter Thomas Barker Jones (1813 - 1882), depicting Havelock, Outram, Inglis and others greeting Colin Campbell, against the backdrop of the Moti Mahal palace complex during the so-called Second Relief of Lucknow. Interestingly, the painting in stark relief showed details of the landscape and Nawabi buildings, many of which were subsequently removed by the colonial administration. The meeting actually took place on November 17, 1857, although the painting itself was completed in 1860. In March 1891, the Commander-in-Chief of the British Indian Army stationed at Calcutta, on a visit to Lucknow expressed the view that "a tablet be fixed on the wall of Moti Mahal near the gap through which Outram and Havelock rode their way to meet Colin Campbell when the relieved and the relieving forces joined hands on November 17, 1857. The tablet might be of marble as there were a lot of spare slabs in the Kaiserbagh on a little tower near the high road." The estimate was worked out to be Rs 50/-, the inscription being duly finalised and approved by the CIC on March 13, 1891, substituting the word "passed" for "rode" since both Havelock and Outram had been on foot at that time. Expectedly, there was some bureaucratic vacillation on whether the tablet would be made of iron or marble - the latter option being finally selected after some deliberation. The work was carried out by M/s Martin, Sculptor, supervised by the Executive Engineer of the PWD, NWP & Oudh. M/s Martin had no relation with Claude Martin as blindly conjectured by some writers.*

A Poor House for The Destitute

The concept of a poor house for European vagrants teeming in Lucknow actually originated from a letter dated July 18, 1878 from Col. J Reid, Commissioner, Lucknow Division addressed to the Secretary, Govt. of North Western Provinces & Oudh. Concern had been expressed regarding the helpless people of European and Eurasian origin, who had been thronging Lucknow of late. These included the blind and the lepers also. It was proposed that the "Strangers' Home" would run on charities and government grants, and the inmates would be provided with a small pension, railway passes and refreshments. The listed refreshments for the destitute appeared to be quite lavish (as per today's standards). These included the usual "*Chota Hazry* or early breakfast, consisting of bread and tea, and meals having steaks, chops, roast, soup, curries" etc. An additional condition was that "no person, while in the House, would be permitted to beg from house to house or write begging letters, and any person disobeying the rules would be expelled forthwith." The reader might smile at this conundrum, but November 1879 saw the Chaplain of Lucknow (who

* *M/s Martin had no relation with Claude Martin (who had died almost a century ago), as conjectured by some writers. CA Martin, with his assistant, A Gomes provided processional sculpting services from 1862 - 1906, from their establishment in Cantonment Road, Lucknow. Martin's inscriptions appear in several colonial-era tablets and tombstones, including one in the erstwhile Canning College at Badhshah Bagh.*

was also the Hony. Secretary of the Lucknow Poor House) writing to the Lt. Governor of NWP and Oudh, regarding the great influx of the destitute in Lucknow for various reasons, leading to the shortage of funds and problems of accommodation. At that point of time, the Poor House had been functioning in one block of the Wingfield Manzil, which the Maharaja of Balrampur had "willingly and gratuitously" acquiesced to provide, albeit temporarily.

As in the case of the Technical School discussed above, (which would later face the same problem), the Maharaja, on second thoughts, asked the Chaplain to look for alternative accommodation, although "Wingfield Manzil was very suitable for being adopted as a House of Refuge, both from the point of view of its spaciousness and location." In desperation, the Chaplain vacated the premises and rented "an old and dilapidated Emamburra (*sic*) for a monthly rental of Rs 22/-. The Secretary to the Govt. of NWP and Oudh, in a communication dated December 1879, addressed to the Commissioner, Lucknow Division, expressed regret at the unreasonable amount being spent on the inmates, and stated that in the present scenario, the inmates had no compulsion to look for work, and those who did find work, had no legitimate reason to remain in the Poor House.

In 1894, landed property for the Lucknow Poor House was finally acquired in Mohalla Hussainganj, from one Jeremiah Bailey. This deal, however, was not without controversy because a slew of petitions addressed to the Government, revealed that Jeremiah was not the sole owner of the property (consisting of a "Kottee" and grounds), being the son of (late) Isaac Bailey, the latter having other children in Calcutta named Wilson, Adolphus, Cornelius and Alice. Jeremiah had not only sold off the property without the consent of his brothers and sister, he had not even give the share of the proceeds obtained by sale of the property, to his siblings. No further records are available as regards the claims and counter-claims, but by June 1894, extensive repairs of the two storey building or "Kottee" commenced. Apparently, "the timbering of both upper and lower floor were absolutely unsafe and no amount of propping up would suffice as it was rotten through and through." Moreover, there were squatters in the building, who were asked to vacate the premises. The Poor House of Lucknow would finally have its day, but not for long.

A Nawabi Stable and a Colonial Club

As discussed earlier, the Rev. William Tennant (1803), a Chaplain of the East India Company had visited Lucknow during the times of Nawab Sa'adat Ali Khan in 1799 and had put forth the following description of the famed cruciform stable (Chaupar Astabal), which was based on the Panopticon model: "The stables of the Nawab consist of a large square court of buildings, supported on brick pillars, with a view to the admission of air: these consist of more than one range; that which I examined contained about four hundred stalls, almost all filled with excellent Persian horses. There are separate studs for mares; but breeding does not seem the favourite pursuit here."

Post 1857, the Chaupar stables were later converted to barracks for the 32nd regiment and its name changed to Lawrence Terrace. In 1861-62, Lord Canning made over the buildings of the Kaiserbagh to the *ta'aluqdars* of Awadh and Sir George Yule, then Chief Commissioner ordered the conversion of Lawrence Terrace into sets of quarters "to accommodate at a suitable rent, the government clerks, who had been removed from Kaiserbagh. Also, in 1861, the Bada Chattar Manzil had been provided, rent free, to the United Services Club, for covenanted officers. Simultaneously, the Union Club or Residency Club for uncovenanted and non-officials (non-gazetted in today's parlance) was provided accommodation in Farhat Baksh Kothi, adjacent to the Chattar Manzil. Both Clubs continued for a period of twenty years, after which, the "junior club" was allotted a portion of Lawrence Terrace on a lease of 23 years. The lease expired in 1910, but was not allowed to be renewed, although the Club had provided "social amusements to the community for about half a century." For several reasons, the colonial administration, by now, had developed an antipathy towards this Club, the first and foremost being that it had only fifty members on roll and secondly, it did not actually represent the Anglo-Indian / Eurasian community (which had expanded considerably in the preceding years but remained fractured), as claimed. Also the Club seemed to prefer members from the railways, who had its own Railway Club. Voluminous correspondences, proposals and appeals did not seem to work and the Club lost its government patronage. Even the desperate proposal to convert it into a "Volunteers' Club" was not agreed to, as "the history of Voluntary Clubs, with few notable exceptions, had been unfortunate and not worthy of encouraging."

In the meantime, a private builder, one WE Crawshaw put up a proposal of acquiring a part of land (which partially included the grounds of the Club) to build a range of quarters, two "coach houses" and two stables for the McConaghey Free School (present day Christ Church College, see Chapter VI). The quarters would provide "accommodation for the poorer classes of the domiciled and Anglo-Indian community, especially government pensioners, who with small pensions and large families were compelled to live in the slums of bazars (*sic*)." The Club management was not against the proposal in principle, but preferred the "new buildings being owned by the government and not by a private builder." The Club, by now was under an extended lease, under the Anglo-Indian Association of Allahabad.

Although the Lucknow (Residency) Club continued beyond India's Independence and exists even today, it is but a shadow of its former self, with no signs of the British or Anglo-Indians drinking and dancing the night away in its premises.

A Controversial Gateway

Kaiserbagh had been the palace complex and residence of the last King of Awadh, Wajid Ali Shah. Later, it became the stronghold of Begum Hazrat Mahal and her band of intrepid freedom fighters. It is generally accepted that the palace complex had many entry gateways, but the one on the north-east (opposite Taaron Wali Kothi) was the principle entrance, which led to a court and the Jilau Khana or triumphal arch. Between Taaro Wali Kothi and Kaiserbagh, a pyramidal colonial obelisk pays tribute to the refugees from Sitapur, including Mountstuart Jackson, Captain Orr and others, who had been imprisoned in the Kaiserbagh premises during 1857, but later done to death, presumably on the instructions of Raja Jai Lal Singh, a *ta'aluqdar* of Awadh. It is said that the Raja ascended a Kaiserbagh gate and witnessed the killing. Jai Lal Singh was later arrested and hanged to death in 1859, on the very spot where he had "committed the crime."

Around 1910, a question was raised by the colonial administration regarding a Kaiserbagh gateway known as China Bazar Gate,

Figure 46: North East Gateway of Kaiserbagh with the Colonial Obelisk, 1870, Robert & Harriet Tytler.

proposing its demolition, as it was "rickety and an obstruction to traffic, with practically no architectural interest." One Mr Olliver had previously claimed that this was the gate from where Raja Jai Lal Singh had supervised the murder of the Orr and Jackson party, whose obelisk now faced the gateway. Later it was clarified that the Raja did not sit on this gate, but on another, long since demolished. It was hilariously noted that "the only authentic historical event with this gate was that Olliver had sat on it in 1859, to witness the execution of Raja Jai Lal Singh." Who said that the British did not have a sense of humour? On a more serious note, it was concluded that "it was practically the only trace of the front of the Kaiserbagh palace and had been rightly or wrongly associated with the worst of the Mutiny tragedies."

Miraculously, the China Bazar gate was subsequently repaired and allowed to stay on; today it houses the UP Press Club and its compound is home to a slew of restaurants serving the famed Nawabi cuisine of Lucknow.

Bureaucracy and a Bridge

Post 1857, Sikandar Bagh was bisected into two parts, with Outram Road (present Ashok Marg) crossed the Gomti via the wooden Pile Bridge connecting Sikandar Bagh to Bruce Ganj (present-day Nishatganj), with the Lunatic Asylum on the left and Upper India Couper Paper Mills on the right. The bridge was extensively damaged during the flash floods of 1891, resulting to widespread loss of life and property.

A bureaucratic tussle soon broke out between the colonial municipal authorities and the PWD, regarding the jurisdiction and the source of funds for carrying out the repair work, or building a new bridge from scratch. A question was raised as to whether other existing bridges over the Gomti were not sufficient for public and troops? When it was reasonably justified that the new replacement bridge would benefit the eastern half of the city, including the Railway Station, Civil Lines, and the high road (=highway) to Bara Banki and Faizabad, as well as traffic for the Lunatic Asylum and the Civil Cemetery (=Nishatganj Cemetery), it was queried as to whether the remains of the old bridge had been removed? There was also some correspondence regarding the requirement of additional land from the Paper Mill, but this was offset by the fact that the sizeable movement of goods from the paper mill (both raw and finished) would be benefited.

The construction cost of the washed away Pile Bridge had been Rs 10,000/-. The estimate for the new bridge was Rs 25,000/-. But as the volume of official paperwork, consisting of queries and replies increased, the cost estimate also shot up accordingly. By 1899, the work on the bridge had still not commenced and the budget estimate was now Rs 1,15,000/-.

The bridge was finally rebuilt as its current avatar, the Nishatganj Bridge, being funded by the Government and Municipal Corporation of Lucknow. It was a purely utilitarian structure with no architectural merit whatsoever. But it did serve its purpose of "benefiting the eastern half of the city" for quite some time.

Mausoleum of "Hazrat" Amjad Ali Shah and Nawabi Hazratganj

The credit for laying the foundation of the Hazratganj commercial-cum-residential area we know today, goes to Sa'adat Ali Khan, the sixth Nawab of Awadh. The road from the British Residency and Nawabi Chattar Manzil Palace in the west to Dilkusha Kothi in the east, was laid during his rule. On either side of the road, impressive residential buildings for his family members came up, which included Noor Baksh Kothi (present day residence of the District Magistrate), Aine Wali Kothi (present day Hindi Sansthan), followed by the Kankar Wali Kothi (present day Halwasiya Court and adjoining areas). Adjacent to the new road were the cruciform Chaupar stables on the north side and the Shifa Khana (Darul Shafa) on the southern side. A little ahead was Kothi Hayat Baksh (present day Governor's House / Raj Bhavan). However, the area was primarily a residential one, occupied by nobility. During the reign of Amjad Ali Shah, the second king of Awadh, the massive Begum Kothi complex came up (present day Janpath Market). The establishment of a grain market (=*ganj*) in the area, was also due to Amjad Ali Shah, popularly addressed as Hazrat due to his pious nature (Incidentally, Amjad Ali's Chief Minister, Amin-ud-Daula, is credited for having founded the Aminabad market, which was later given a make-over by the colonial authorities discussed elsewhere).

After the death of the king in 1847, he was buried in his mausoleum called Sibtainabad in the western part of this area, called Chhavni Mendu Khan or Serai Mendu Khan - the entire stretch now being referred to as Hazratganj in his honour. Sibtainabad was modelled on the earlier Imambaras of Asaf-ud-Daula and Mohammad Ali Shah; it was smaller in size but no less ornate. Expectedly, as with other Nawabi structures, it faced damage during the events of 1857. After the final capture of the city in 1858 by the British, the building and its surrounding area was appropriated for religious (till the completion of the new Anglican Christ Church in 1860, built in the memory of British soldiers who had died in Lucknow during the Uprising.) and commercial use. Lord Canning even attended divine service in the Sibtainabad Imambara during his visit to Lucknow in 1859. The compound of the mausoleum was parcelled into small houses and shops for British and Eurasian families. The Imambara also functioned as temporary premises for the native students of La Martiniere School. The school was offered alternative accommodation in Lal Baradari, Darshan Bilas or Gulistan-e-Iram; however it preferred to eventually return to its original premises, the Constantia. By 1863, when the tricky question of long-term maintenance of Sibtainabad came up, the British first made an offer to Wajid Ali Shah, (then residing at Calcutta), as to whether he would be willing to maintain the mausoleum of his father (together with the shops and residences!), to which the deposed king naturally refused. It was then offered to the daughter, Afsar Begum or Ashraf un-Nisa, also known as Mallika-i-Dauran (sister of Wajid Ali Shah), in August, 1863, on the undertaking that the building would be kept clean and in good repair, and also the necessary religious observances would be followed - the structure being a Muslim tomb. However, during the handover of the premises, it was noted that 86 beams, 71 doors, 40 door frames, 40 patao (*sic)*, 500 yard of jhanp (*sic)* and parts of the roof of the mausoleum were missing. The gates and all the shops were leaking and the mahal serai or mahalsara (private apartments attached to the mausoleum) had fallen down on the west side.

After the death of Afsar Begum in Calcutta, her daughter, Choti Shahzadi took over the property without any protest or fresh deed from the colonial government. She in turn "gifted" it to her nephew, who allegedly planned to sell it off to the "Baniyas of Rastogi Tola." Later it came to notice that the property had been already mortgaged to the widow of a "well known Hindu Kathak dancer in September 1918" by Choti Shahzadi. As the possibility of a Muslim religious property falling in Hindu hands became a distinct reality, there was a hue and cry over the legal status of Afsar Begum and of the property itself. It was concluded that "the property had not been transferred to Afsar Begum, or granted to her for life and her heirs. She was actually a manageress to keep maqbara in a state of repair; on her death, her heirs had no title."

Monarchy Caught in Bureaucracy

King George V had been the Monarch of the United Kingdom, the British Dominions, and Emperor of India, from 1910 until his demise in 1936. Back in Lucknow, the colonial government, in a bid to commemorate the late King, submitted a proposal to erect his statues in Lucknow and Allahabad. The tentative budget for the project was

Figure 47: Ruins of Sikander Bagh during Colonial Rule, Unidentified Photographer.

Figure 48: Vintage View of Victoria Memorial, Lucknow, Unidentified Photographer.

an odd figure of Rs 63,000/-. And strangely, the government did not deem it fit to utilise its own resources for the purpose; instead it constituted a "King George V Provincial Memorial Fund," with CW Gwynne, Chief Secretary to the Government of the United Provinces, as President of the Memorial Committee. This Committee would collect contributions from wealthy individuals and business houses for funding the project. Ironically, the prominent persons and businesses so identified were mostly Indian and not European. Written appeals and reminders were sent to such people at Cawnpore (19 nos.), Allahabad (17 nos.) and Lucknow (15 nos.); those who had already contributed responded immediately while those who had not kept silent or tried to vacillate.

At Lucknow, the location of the proposed memorial statue also became the subject of a long and acrimonious bureaucratic debate. It was tentatively decided to locate the statue in front of the newly constructed Imperial Post Office, which was *nazul* land. In those days, almost 90% of Lucknow was *nazul* (confiscated), and it was easy for the colonial government to claim large chunks of these *nazul* lands or properties for various developmental activities, without any accountability or ownership disputes. The parcel of land in question was locally known as Prag Narain Lawns (after Prag Narain, nephew and adopted son of Munshi Newal Kishore), where it was proposed to place the statue on a pedestal, under a canopy. A question arose on the notional price of this *nazul* land, which was under the supervision of the Superintendent of Government Gardens. Although the price would be Rs 10,000/- per *bigha* (non standard measurement of land, ranging from 1 acre to 3 acres), the statue would hardly occupy 2 - 4 *bismil* (fraction of a bigha), which would not constitute much of loss in income for the owners. In fact, this parcel of land could be leased out to the Memorial Committee, as also "it would enhance the beauty of the locality." The reader might be amazed at the amount of bureaucratic delays over this small project concerning the late King, with the file moving from table to table - each learned official having something to add to the notings on the file; not one would simply countersign and forward the file to the next official in the hierarchy (a work culture which has percolated through the centuries and continues even today in Independent India). Accordingly, Mr Gwynne pointed out that the land need not be leased to the Memorial Committee, but be gifted to the government, as the Committee would cease to exist once its objective (of erecting the statue) had been achieved. By this time, 3 years had already passed since the initial proposal of the statue had been mooted.

Eventually, the late King's statue, sculpted in England was brought all the way to Lucknow (like many other colonial statues), to be installed under a canopy designed by American architect Walter Burley Griffin (discussed elsewhere). But it found no peace. By this time, the freedom movement in India had gained pace and one Babu Lal Rastogi, "a well known revolutionary attempted to desecrate the statue one night in December 1939, at 1.00 am." This deed set off a flurry of correspondences and bureaucratic notings once again, and it was decided that "in view of future possible attempts, proper lighting arrangements were to be made as done in the case of statue of Queen Victoria." A provision of Rs 680/- per annum was made for lighting the statue at Lucknow from 1940-41 onwards (although a query was raised as to how many other statues have a similar lighting arrangement). India's freedom in 1947 also brought freedom from many such commemorative colonial statues (but not all) and this particular statue was relocated to the grounds of the UP State Museum, where his Majesty has the company of other similar rulers, including Queen Victoria. The canopy and pedestal of King George are extant, on which the statue of Mahatma Gandhi stands today.

In fact, a bronze statue of "Queen of England, Empress of India" purchased in London in commemoration of her Majesty's Jubilee Year, had been placed on a granite pedestal and erected near the Gol Darwaza of Chowk as per the communications on file dated September 1892 between the Deputy Commissioner & Chairman, Municipal Board of Lucknow and the Commissioner, Lucknow Division. The work was carried out by the PWD free of charge, because it involved the Queen of England. Again, a small area, roughly corresponding to the earlier Nawabi Payn Bagh, in which a marble canopy over a red sandstone plinth was erected to house the statue of Queen Victoria as a "Victoria Memorial." From the discussion above, it appears that the colonial administration was not too keen on spending public money on commemorative statues of its rulers and preferred to either collect funds through donations or get the work carried out gratis. A signs of the times indeed.

The Elusive Tram Line

Tram lines were common enough in colonial cities of Calcutta, Bombay and Delhi, of India. Colonial Lucknow too would have got its own tram services, but unfortunately, the proposal got lost in a bureaucratic maze, unforeseen delays and logistical problems, and the proposal was ultimately shelved. Initially, the Lucknow tram line was envisaged to run from Hazratganj to Charbagh railway station, via the Cantonment area. The proposal was submitted in 1903 by M/s Marshall Sons & Co. of Calcutta, for constructing a tramway within the Municipal area of Lucknow, and also to provide electric traction lines for the same, under the Indian Electricity Act 1903. (Incidentally, similar proposals had also been floated for Cawnpore and Benaras). Subsequently, M/s Kincaid, Waller, Manville &

Dawson Co. a highly reputed engineering firm of London also came up with a similar proposal, and joined the fray. A comprehensive route gradually developed for Lucknow's proposed tram services, starting from Gol Darwaza, Chowk to Cantonment Road and Sudder Bazar (*sic*) via Circular Road. A branch line would loop off to the railway station at the crossing of Abbot Road. Another tram line from the Dy. Commissioner's Office at Kaiserbagh would connect to Cawnpore Road, via Aminabad. A loop line from Circular Road would pass through Hazratganj, via Lalbagh, to Cantonment Road. It was also proposed to cover the whole length of Victoria Street and Canning Street (please see Annexure II for demystifying road names in Colonial Lucknow vis-à-vis present day Lucknow). The gauge of the tram would be a uniform 3 feet, 6 inches, unless approved otherwise, with maximum speeds not exceeding 8 miles per hour. Also, the trams would have 2 classes of carriages.

The proposal immediately faced resistance from the army authorities who voiced security concerns. The trading community of Hazratganj, "the heart of the European trade in Lucknow" raised their alarm over the trams trundling in front of their commercial establishments, creating disturbance for customers. The Lucknow Municipal Board also objected to the proposal on the grounds that it would interfere with normal traffic on the road. Apprehensions were expressed about the Hazratganj street not being broad enough to accommodate a tram line. Although it was pointed out that "Hazratganj was a street of ample width, far better suited than many densely populated streets in European cities, where tramways worked without difficulty or inconvenience," an alternate route was proposed, which would run through Kaiserbagh. While all these debates were on, the then Oudh & Rohilkhand Railways (O&RR), which operated most of the trains in Lucknow section voiced their concern that the proposed tram line would cross the railway tracks of the O&RR on at least one point, so who would responsible for building and manning the railway gate at this point? The now frazzled colonial government rapped the knuckles of the O&RR, stating tersely that the railway company had been aware of the proposed Lucknow tram line since the latter's inception, and it was too late to raise such objections at this juncture. At one point of time, it also appeared that another company, M/s British Eastern Electric Power Co. of London would get the job order to work exclusively in the cantonment area.

Come what may, even after two decades of file movements, the routes could not be finalised and the work could not commence; the Lucknow tram line proposal (together with similar proposals for Cawnpore and Benaras) was ultimately shelved, although details are not available in the relevant files, regarding its final closure in around 1924. It would take more than a century of waiting for Lucknow to get its own mass rapid transport system between Hazratganj and Charbagh (and beyond) in the form of Lucknow Metro, which was formally inaugurated on March, 2019.

The Gomti Weir

A weir was constructed across the Gomti river, a little to the east of the Upper India Couper Paper Mills, in order "to raise the level of the water above the weir during the dry season on sanitary grounds and to give a better river frontage within the city." Essentially a small-scale dam or barrier built across the river to control and raise the water level slightly on the upstream side, it was completed in 1913 - 14, at a cost of Rs 1,31,953/-. It was 276 feet across (flank to flank), and consisted of 31 crest gates or shutters with a sluice against the right flank. 28 crest gates were 8 feet long and the remaining 3 were 8 ft.8 inches long; all were 5 ft. 9 inches high above the top of the crest wall which was about 2 ft. above the bed of the river, the sluice gate being 20 ft. long with a 6 ft. pier between the sluice gate and the last crest gate.

The sluice gate could be raised and lowered by an overhead crab and winch arrangement, and the crest gates could be raised by means of a travelling crane. Each gate was held in position by a strut fitted on the downstream face, which engaged a tumbler fixed in the floor of the weir. Each tumbler was connected with a lever, which, when depressed, automatically released the strut and so allowed the gate to fall. To provide the force required to depress the levers, they were arranged so that the lever of each gate was operated on by the preceding gate, which came in contact with, while falling. The gates were raised one by one, starting with the one nearest the left flank, the tumbler of which was kept locked in position by a hand operated lever fixed on the left flank wall. To drop the gates (which could only be satisfactorily done when the weir was full and the levers, downstream, were entirely above the downstream water level), the lever on the left flank was smartly pushed forward; this released the tumbler of the first gate, which immediately fell due to the pressure of the upstream water and in falling, depressed the lever, thereby releasing the tumbler of the second gate. The operation was thus repeated automatically till all the gates were down. When all the crest gates were up and the weir was full, the water level was raised by about 7 ft. 9 inches (at the weir) and this affected the level of the river to a distance of about fourteen miles upstream.

With time, spanning a century, and the construction of the Gomti barrage, the weir fell into disuse and faded from public memory. However, parts of it resurfaced during the draining of the river during the Gomti River Front Project work in 2016, throwing the public in a tizzy.

Wingfield Manzil

We shall conclude this Chapter with a short discussion on the elusive *Wingfield Manzil*, about which few are aware of. This building complex was not a colonial creation, but was inexplicably built by the *ta'aluqdars* of Awadh under the aegis of the British India Association on honour of Charles Wingfield, Chief Commissioner of Oudh, during February 15, 1859 - April 20, 1860. Those were troubled times, but it was Wingfield (and to a lesser extent, Robert Montgomery) who had convinced Lord Canning that a "clemency" policy would bear fruit, instead of further confrontation and conflict with the traditional landowners of Awadh. The latter responded by proposing to construct the Wingfield Manzil at Lucknow in his honour. The first *Lucknow Durbar* was held on October 26, 1859, during the tenure of Wingfield, in which Lord Canning announced his government's noble intentions towards the *ta'aluqdars* of Awadh. Although architectural details of the building are not available, it

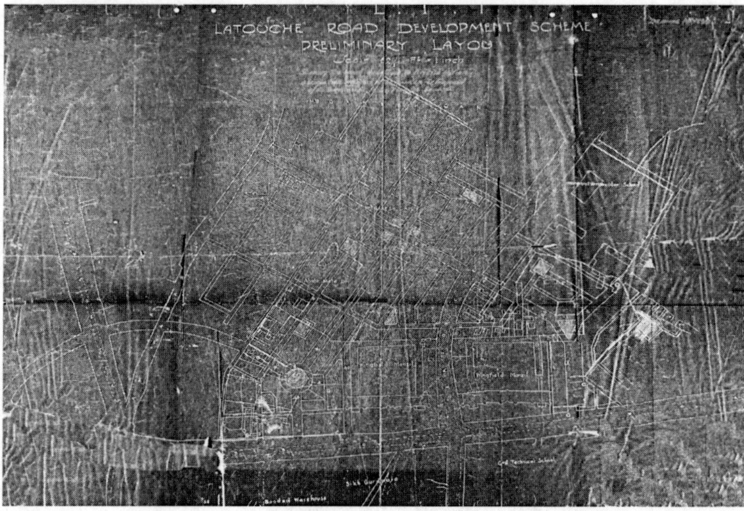

Figure 49: Blueprint of La Touche Road Development Scheme by Lucknow Improvement Trust, UP State Archives, Lucknow.

appears to have been a substantial structure situated on Forsyth Square (present day Bansmandi Chauraha). A blueprint of the La Touche Road Development Scheme of the Lucknow Improvement Trust (Fig 49) clearly shows the two wings of the building complex, bisected by the La Touche Road as it intersected Abbott Road (present day Vidhan Sabha Marg). Wingfield Manzil served as temporary quarters for *ta'aluqdars* who arrived in Lucknow but had no permanent residence in the city. The BIA also provided portions of the building complex to the colonial government from time to time, as "the Association was always prepared to obey the order of the government" but later, requested it to be vacated with the same alacrity. For example, the Elementary Industrial School, already discussed above, functioned from the western quadrangle of Wingfield Manzil, being rent-free accommodation provided by the British India Association from 1892 onwards, after "clearing the verandahs, removal of existing occupants, followed by cleaning, white-washing and addition of an additional shed, if necessary." However, the colonial government was pressurised by the BIA to vacate the premises by 1897. The Manzil premises had earlier been utilised for temporarily accommodating the Poor House (already discussed), and that was also shifted away to another location in due course of time.

Later the BIA requested the Government for additional land near the Wingfield Manzil, for the proposed extension of the building. But the proposal could not materialise. In present times, it is difficult to visualise the Manzil in the densely populated and congested commercial area today, with a flyover in the vicinity.

Chapter - VI

Educating the Natives

A single shelf of a good European library was worth the whole native literature of India and Arabia.

- Lord Thomas Babington Macaulay

Historical Background

Elected to the House of Commons of the United Kingdom in 1830 as a Member of the reformist Whig party, Thomas Macaulay held western culture in high esteem and was dismissive of Indian customs and practices, including education, which he perceived to be archaic and obsolete. As an inaugural member of the Governing Supreme Council of India in 1834, he spent the next four years of his career in India, focussing primarily on liberty of the press and of the equality of Europeans and Indians before the law. Simultaneously, based on his personal perceptions, he also tried to establish an educational system based on the western model, which he termed as a "civilising mission." thereby damaging the oriental system of education in the Indian sub-continent. On February 5, 1835, he advised the Governor General of India, Lord William Bentick to stop subsidizing advanced instruction and scholarship in Arabic and Sanskrit and to subsidize advanced instruction in English literature instead.

Another onslaught on Indian customs and practices, including education and religion was the rise of Evangelicalism - a strong religious movement which had started in Europe in the 1730s, had influenced various religious and social denominations there, which had landed in India too, in due course of time. The prospect of preaching in India was very attractive for Evangelical missionaries. Apparently for them, "the twenty million inhabitants of India, sunk deep in Hindu idolatry, seemed to cry out for conversion" and so began the campaign from 1793 onwards to open up the missionary route to India. Although Christian missionaries had been originally banned from the territories of the East India Company for fear of upsetting Indian religious sentiments, they were allowed to operate after 1843, in parallel with a rising utilitarian and evangelist fervour in Britain and within certain Company circles. Their activities often blurred the distinctions between moral improvement, social reform, education, law and order, proselytization and outright conversion. Other than the missionaries, it was no secret that many officers of the Company too were resolute Christians, and were not above professing their religious views and attitudes on natives. However, after the annexation of Awadh in 1856, the situation rapidly changed for the worse.

The various colonial-era schools and institutions of Lucknow (and elsewhere) came up in the backdrop briefly described above. Most (but not all) remained intimately linked with the Church or the colonial administration, and in the initial stages, were happy to report religious conversions as achievements; they were also eager to toe the official line in their day-to-day activities. The schools were most often referred to as "missionary" schools or "convent" schools, clearly indicating their overt and covert links with Christian missionaries, the primary aim of the "missionaries" being to preach the Gospel, to convert the weaker section of Indians into Christianity and to "serve the suffered" through Christian missions. The term "convent" unequivocally indicated the involvement of nuns or religious Christian sisters in the educational process.

The La Martiniere Schools

Claude Martin died in 1800, leaving behind a vast estate which faced litigations for nearly four decades. Finally as per his will, the first La Martiniere Schools were established in Calcutta in 1836:

Figure 50: Constantia, 1876, Unidentified Artist.

"I GIVE and bequeath the sum of two hundred thousand Sika Rupees to the town of Calcutta for to be put at interest in Government Paper or the most secure mode possible, and this principal and interest to be put under the protection of Government, or the Supreme Court, that they may devise an institution the most necessary for the public good of the town of Calcutta, or establishing a School for to educate a certain number of children of any sex to a certain age, and to have them put prentice to some profession, when at the conclusion of their school and to have them married when at age, and also wishes that every year premium of few rupees or other thing and a medal be given to the most deserving or virtuous boy and girl or both to such that have come out of the school."

Other than Martin's folly - Constantia, the Obelisk or Lat / Lath opposite the main building, standing on a shallow lake, was built around 1815, long after Claude Martin's death. Architecturally, it would serve as an inspiration for the Ochterloney Memorial, to be built later in the Maidan of Calcutta in 1828. Both shared common "hybrid" features, having a rare combination of three Eastern architectural styles: the stylobate and pedestal (base) being Egyptian, the column Doric, while the dome being typically Turkish. Both stemmed from a common design of Charles Knowles Robinson, put into practice by JP Parker, but the term, "Indo-Saracenic" architecture was not in vogue then. The La Martiniere School for Boys was established in Lucknow in 1845, in the premises of Constantia - the massive, ornate villa that he had built as his residence, but instead became his mausoleum. Also known as Luckperra or Lakhi Perra (apparently one lakh / million trees had been cut during its construction), Martin specifically mentioned in his will:

"*My house at Luckperra or Constantia House with all the ground and premises belonging to the house and all the ground around it, none is to be sold or detached from it.*" The Will went on to define his purpose, which was *"to keep the said Constantia House for school or College for learning young men the English language and Christian religion if they found themselves inclined.*"

The school was opened on October 1, 1845, with a nominal register of 97 pupils. By March 1847, 132 were enrolled; "one-fifth Christians, two-fifths Musalmans, and two-fifths Hindoos." According to Keene (1875), only 65 Christian boys entered the Residency on June 18, 1857 with the Principal, George Schilling. Of these, four were boarders and sixty one foundationers (*sic*); two of the former died during the siege, but among the latter, there were no casualties, and only two were returned as wounded. The elder boys were armed and did military duty; others worked the telegraph, and a number were usefully employed in hospital in attending the sick. Due to their contribution during the siege of the Residency, they were awarded the Indian Mutiny Medal in 1858. The School was awarded

Figure 51: La Martiniere Boys' School in Constantia, Lucknow, 1858, Robert & Harriet Tytler.

Figure 52: La Martiniere Girls School in Khurshid Manzil, Lucknow, Unidentified Photographer.

the British Army regimental-style ‘colour’ or Battle Honour in 1938 by the British Government - the only school in the world to have been honoured with such a title. After India’s Independence in 1947. the lines between the “victorious” and the “enemy” naturally became blurred and such an honour for a school became redundant in the Indian context. However, it cannot be denied that British schoolboys and their teacher had done a commendable duty towards their country at that point of time in history.

Alexius Abbot Saunders, formerly a Major General in the Bengal Army was Commissioner of Lucknow during 1858 - 1863. His wife had established the Lucknow Girls’ School in the premises of Moti Mahal, which was later shifted to the Khurshid Manzil palace and renamed as La Martiniere Girls’ High School; the palace had been built by Sa’adat Ali Khan, the sixth Nawab of Awadh as a residence of his chief consort, Khurshid Zadi. Designed by Duncan McLeod, a British army engineer, it resembled an European manor, complete with turrets and a moat. Mrs Saunders was provided with Rs 60,000/- from Claude Martin’s ‘Female Education Fund’. Initially, the children were divided into five classes, and their education described as "plain, practical and religious." Subjects taught ranged from Bible and Scripture History to Map Drawing, Grammar, Needlework, Knitting and Housekeeping. In 1888, the school was granted additional land from the Taaron Wali Kothi compound (now the State Bank of India). Khurshid Manzil was struck by lightening on March 12, 1891, but no harm to life or property was reported. By 1895, a hospital, kitchens and dormitory buildings had been added to the premises, so the school became truly spacious with the passage of time.

To quote Daroga Ubbas Ali's tongue-in-cheek comment (1874): "As a contrast to the purpose that the Khoorshaid Munzil (*sic*) was probably intended to serve, and the demoniac purpose that it did attempt to serve, it is now turned to a heavenly purpose: it is the Martiniere Girls' School; the scarped ditches now a bright green lawn for the children's play-ground, the towers make airy bedrooms for the little girls, and all the inmates seem to be supremely happy."

Catering primarily to European children, the La Martiniere schools remained outside the ambit of any Parish or Church. Later, the schools started admitting Indian children but the interference by the Church in the day-to-day administration has remained negligible through the years.

Lalbagh Girls School and Isabella Thoburn College

Isabella Thoburn, sister of Rev. James Mills Thoburn, a Methodist Episcopal missionary in Lucknow, was the first American woman Methodist missionary to sail to India in 1869, after the Women's Foreign Missionary Society (WFMS) of the Methodist Episcopal Church was founded in Boston to champion the cause of women in India. On April 18, 1870, the Christian Girls School was started by Isabella Thoburn. According to her, "No people can rise higher as a people than the point to which they educate their women." Her vision was noble and the school progressed rapidly from one-roomed premises in Nazirabad, with just six girls, to being named Christian Girls' Boarding School (a year later), being re-located to Lalbagh, in the premises of Shah Bihari Lal's regal house and surrounding grounds, under the auspices of the Women's Foreign Missionary Society (Lal had been an affluent merchant and Treasurer to Ghazi-ud-Din Haider, the first king of Awadh). With time, many other structures, including a second storey to the original kothi, verandas all around, an L-shaped extension and even a clock tower was added to the then school building. The school was upgraded to the Lucknow Women's College in 1886 (under Calcutta University) and renamed as Isabella Thoburn College after Ms. Thoburn's death in 1901; in 1910, a Hazzard Memorial building was erected for accommodating lecture rooms, study hall and dormitories. However, within five years, it collapsed in September 1915, during "a cloud burst and floods", although the original old kothi stood strong. The shifting of the college to its new premises away from Lalbagh was accompanied by much heartburn as "there was a gracious dignity of the kothi, its great high-ceilinged rooms storied with a long past. The wide verandas, the spiral stairway up which one creaked to the terrace to sleep under the summer stars, the mighty vibrations of the striking clock, the darkly mysterious underground rooms, the legend of buried treasure...." The college had been earlier offered a parcel of

Figure 53: Vintage View of IT College in Old Campus at Lalbagh, Unidentified Photographer.

Figure 54: Vintage view of IT College in New Campus at Chand Bagh, Unidentified Photographer.

land measuring 8 acres, adjacent to the upcoming Wingfield Park by the Lucknow Improvement Trust, but vacillation on the part of the college administration resulted in delays, and at one point of time the Board of Directors in America even contemplated on "Isabella Thoburn College to lose its BA section if necessary and be an intermediate college only." The management of the college finally decided to shift to the "wilderness" beyond the University, in an area known as Chand Bagh or "Moon Garden." The new buildings were constructed by an English firm, M/s Martin and Co, "under the vigorous supervision of one Mr Bridges" who was a nephew of the poet, Robert Bridges.

"Chand Bagh, Chand Bagh,
Moonlight on thy walls,
White, white lightly falls,
O Chand Bagh."

IT College had the distinction of being the first Christian College for Women in South Asia. The premises regretfully left behind in

Lalbagh continued to function as Lalbagh Girls School - the latter was subsequently re-named as Emma Thompson School in 1979.

Centennial School and Lucknow Christian College

The nucleus of this prominent educational institution of Colonial Lucknow was laid in 1862, in the form of a school in Hussainabad area, by Rev. James H Messmore, a pioneer educationist American Missionary. The Hussainabad area was prone to heavy floods during the monsoons and was very densely populated, so in 1871, Rev. James Mills Thoburn (see above) and JH Messmore purchased the Inayat Bagh, containing few run-down buildings, which was to form the nucleus of the Centennial School, so named because the funds for its small endowment were first collected in the centennial year of American Methodism. In 1878, another building was purchased near the Roshan-ud-Daula Kothi to house the school, but that too proved unsatisfactory. The school finally moved to its new premises in Golaganj, in 1883. Non-Christian students were also admitted

Figure 55: Vintage View of Reid Christian College, Unidentified Photographer.

to the school, in the hope that "the daily contact with Christian teachers may be the means of bringing many of the others to Christ, and that the institution may thus become a powerful evangelizing agency."

In 1882, when Rev. John Morrison Reid, Secretary of the Missionary Society of the Methodist Episcopal Church, New York, visited Lucknow, he had indicated that he might aid in providing Centennial School with a new building. This raised hopes of raising the status of the school to that of a college, and in 1887, at the Annual Conference of the Mission, the Board of Trustees of the School were finally authorised to raise the said school to college grade, after securing affiliation with Calcutta University. A vacant plot of land adjoining the Centennial School was purchased, for setting up the Lucknow Christian College (also known as Reid Christian College for a while) in 1888. The College was described as "an American college built on Indian soil, under the protection of the British flag, attended by Indian students, following the English system of education and supported by American money" and like IT College, was affiliated to Calcutta University. Although the College received its affiliation to run the B.A. and B.Sc. course in 1889, due to lack of students, it became functional only in 1891.

The Foundation Stone of the new College building, with its prominent clock tower was laid on August 06, 1891. Rev. BH Badley, the man who actually laboured for the new building, passed away on Nov. 20, 1891. One of the Blocks, which now houses the Botany, Zoology and the Mathematics Departments of the Degree College and some portion of the Intermediate College as well, was named after Rev. Badley as the Badley Block. Earlier known as Reid Christian College after JM Reid (see above), it was decided to later decided to rename the institution as Lucknow Christian College, which continues till today. The Christian Training College, set up in 1932 to meet the growing needs for trained teachers at Higher Secondary level was part of the Lucknow Christian College. It was the first Non Government Training College of the United Provinces, now Uttar Pradesh.

The Loreto Schools: Loreto Convent and St. Agnes Loreto

In 1872, a group of seven Loreto Sisters (Sisters of the Institute of the Blessed Virgin Mary, founded by Mary Ward in 1616; the name "Loreto" having been coined earlier in 1821 at Ireland by Frances Teresa Ball) led by Mother Joseph Hogan, had arrived in Lucknow from Darjeeling at the invitation of Rev. Paul Tosy, the Catholic Bishop at Lucknow. Hogan had been born and brought up in Ireland. She had attended school at Loreto Abbey, Rathfarnham in Dublin and had been a sister for twelve years when Mother Teresa Ball decided to send a second contingent of sisters to India and chose her to lead it. She left for Calcutta on March 21, 1844.

The contingent of sisters were warmly welcomed by the Parish Priest, Father Lewis, who led them to a "house" adjoining the St Joseph's Church, Hazratganj, that he had secured for them. It was in this property that the first Loreto School started in Lucknow on November 4, 1872. The Sisters later shifted to temporary accommodation in the Hussainganj area (the premises would later become the Royal Hotel) in April 1873.

In 1880, the Cantonment Hotel was purchased and wings were gradually added to accommodate the ever increasing number of students. After establishing the school, Mother Hogan returned to Darjeeling where she died in 1884 and was interred in the little Convent cemetery there. In 1915, the school building at Lucknow suffered heavy damages due to floods. It is said that " the Nuns were compelled to spend entire nights under umbrellas. Arches gave way and the roof of the Chapel collapsed, crushing every prie-dieu (a type of prayer desk primarily intended for devotional use) and chair under its weight but the Sisters escaped death." The northern part of the building had to be rebuilt where it is exists today as Loreto Convent Intermediate College.

Earlier, in 1904, the Loreto sisters had been requested to open a day school for girls, as a result of which the St. Agnes' School opened in rented premises on Barrow Road, to cater to the less affluent members of the Anglo-Indian community of Lucknow. The present impressive building of the school on Station Road was designed by

M/s Labanti (who is credited for having built several colonial building during that period) and blessed on November 23, 1913.

Cathedral School and St. Francis' College

In 1885, Rev. Fr. Norbert of Tossignano began teaching two boys, Isaac & Charles Claudius, on the verandah of the priest's house in the premises of the St. Joseph's Church established earlier in Hazratganj (described elsewhere). Realising the pressing need of primary education, in 1890, he established St. Francis Boarding and Day School where the present Cathedral School exists. In 1908, the land where St. Francis College now stands on Shahnajaf Road, was purchased by the Bishop of Allahabad, Rev. Petronius Gramigna. On May 6, 1915, Fr. Celestine laid the corner stones of two imposing and spacious buildings on either side of the central bungalow. One building (present day Concert Hall) was meant to house the school hall and classrooms while the other (present day Gymnasium) was to be a dormitory for boarders. In the foreground was a spacious "front field" - suitable for games and other school outdoor activities.

Figure 56 : Vintage View of erstwhile Chrysostom (Primary) Block of St Francis College, Lucknow Unidentified Photographer.

The building contract was given to M/s. P. Labanti & Co (see above) who, despite the restrictions and high cost of material due to the war years, was able to complete the building by January 1918, when St. Francis School was shifted to its present location on 8, Shahnajaf Road. At the rear of the out-houses was a large plot of vacant land; this was acquired for a sum of Rs. 6,644/- which became the "back field" of the school. In 1921, the school secured recognition as a High School and affiliated itself to the Cambridge University for the Senior Cambridge Examination. Two years later in 1925, Fr. Celestine realised his long cherished dream by providing the school with an Infirmary (Present Principal office and Staff Room) and Chapel. In 1929, another urgent need was supplied by the erection and equipment of a Science Laboratory.

On January 20, 1942, Rev. Fr. Conrad de Vito was appointed the Parish Priest of St. Joseph's Cathedral in Hazratganj. On July 8, 1950, St. Joseph's Private Day School came into existence with Rev. Fr. Edward Albertazzi, as the Founder Principal with 60 children and four class rooms. On July 16, 1952 due to a government notification, St. Joseph's Private Day School at Hazratganj was renamed as Cathedral School, which then consisted of eight to ten class rooms with 150 children on its roll.

McConaghey Free School and Christ Church College

The McConaghey Free School was started with only two students in 1878 by one H. McConaghey, which was situated on Cantonment Road, Lucknow. The school was then registered as a Society; it was only in 1927, that it came to be known as Christ Church McConaghey Memorial School. A "medium sized building standing on a land of two bighas, close to the Civil and Military Hotel, south-west of it conveniently placed near the habitations of the poor Europeans and Eurasian community. It instructed the students both in mental and physical science, having a kindergarten system attached to it, and a staff strength of seven lady teachers. It also gave to children, whose parents could not afford, clothes and boots." The Foundation Stone of Christ Church School at the present site, in the compound of Christ Church (discussed elsewhere) was laid on January 31, 1939 by

Lady Haig, wife of Sir Harry Graham Haig, then Governor of the United Provinces. For many years, this school was only upto class VIII, with about 250 students, mostly Anglo-Indians. Post independence, from 1960 onwards, the school saw rapid expansion with the addition of the Junior and Senior Wings and Science Laboratories, together with the Principal's Residence, the Auditorium and the Administrative Block. It was recognised as a college due to its affiliation with the Council of Indian School Certificate Examinations, New Delhi for the holding the ISC examination from 1975 onwards.

King George's Medical College

Raja Tassaduq Rasul Khan of Jahangirabad first mooted the idea of commemorating the visit of King George V in 1905, then Prince of Wales to Lucknow with the establishment of a Medical College. This was appreciated by Sir Harcourt Butler who wrote, "It must ever be a source of pride to you to think that the first suggestion of such a movement came from you absolutely spontaneously." On March 22, 1906, the Secretary, United Provinces of Agra and Oudh Government

Figure 57: Opening Ceremony of King George's Medical College, 1914, Unidentified Photographer.

Figure 58: Opening Ceremony of New Bridge on Gomti River by Lord Hardinge, January, 1914, which would be known by his name; Unidentified Photographer.

wrote to the Registrar, Allahabad University that, "It is the desire of subscribers to the Foundation of King George's Medical College that this College should be the best in the East and it will be aim of Government that the College shall give to its students the best education possible." The project was enthusiastically supported by the *ta'aluqdars* and *zamindars* of Agra and Oudh, who gave princely donations for its fruitful completion.

The Foundation Stone of the Medical College was laid by His Royal Highness, the Prince of Wales in 1906, during his second visit for the Coronation Durbar as King Emperor, His Majesty was pleased to give his consent and to designate the College by his name. Initially, the medical college was to have been named as Prince of Wales Medical College. After initial hiccups regarding its location, supply of water and electricity, campus layout and other concerns, the College buildings were completed and the work of the first medical session was started in October 1911, though the ceremonial opening of the College by Lt. Governor John Prescott Hewett did not occur until January 27, 1912. The architect of the College buildings was

Swinton Jacob, who ensured that the buildings were in harmony with the Nawabi structures in the vicinity; this hybrid style would later gain credence as Indo-Saracenic architecture, throughout the Indian sub-continent. The "buildings were made mainly of bricks faced with lime plaster, the colour of which resembled Mirzapur stone, which was freely used for pillars and for the lighter, more ornamental features of the exterior, marble and Mirzapur stone was extensively used in the interior. In its general design and equipment the best European models were followed and adapted to the peculiar conditions of the Indian climate and people."

The main College campus of about 14 *bighas*, occupying much of the area of the erstwhile Nawabi Macchi Bhavan fort, consisted of an Administrative Block, an Anatomical block, a combined Pathological and Physiological block and a Medico-Legal Department. As soon as the College was completed, the construction of the Hospital itself was commenced. The work for Out-patient Department was finished by April 1913 and the main-building a few months later. The number of beds provided was 232 and besides the main Hospital block, there were an Isolation Block and separated Cottage wards. The formal inauguration of King George's Hospital, together with the opening of the New Bridge (later known as Hardinge Bridge) over the river Gomti River opposite the Hospital was performed in January 10, 1914 by His Excellency the Viceroy Lord Hardinge, accompanied by Maharaja Ganga Singh of Bikaner; the new Bridge replaced the Nawabi Pucca Pul or Stone bridge, some "50 yards downstream", which was demolished. Earlier, it had even been suggested that the placement of the College hostels should be across the river, since the New "Hardinge" Bridge would provide easy connectivity between the hostels and the College campus.

On April 1, 1929, the Government transferred the Nawabi Asylum for Lepers, to the newly built Medical College. In 1921, the College along with the Hospital became a constituent College of the Lucknow University.

Colvin Taluqdars' College

The Foundation Stone of the College (initially School) was laid by

Sir Auckland Colvin, then Lt. Governor of the United Provinces and Chief Commissioner of Oudh on March 11, 1880. Aimed at providing education on the western model to the sons of British administrators and aristocratic families *viz.* the *ta'aluqdars* of Awadh, it became functional by 1889, remaining under the control of the British India Association. The institution was built opposite Badshah Bagh, in an area called Haiderabad. Both Haiderabad and Badshah Bagh had been founded by Ghazi-ud-Din Haider, the first king of Awadh during Nawabi rule. The vast premises of the College were spread over 60 acres, with an immense residence for the Principal, the Motto of the College being *Noblesse Oblige,* which, briefly translated into English meant that one was obliged to be noble at all times. The aristocracy clause for students was done away with from 1933 and the college threw open its gates for the fairer sex from the year 2020-21.

Canning College and Lucknow University

In 1864, the Canning High School at Lucknow came into existence as a nondescript school, named in honour of Charles Canning, the last British Governor General of India, and the first Viceroy of British India. The school initially started from leased premises in an old Nawabi property in Khayaliganj (Aminabad), Lucknow, being funded by few *ta'aluqdars* of Awadh, through a perpetual endowment. This endowment was fixed as a percentage of the total revenue collected by them from their respective estates or talukas. A matching grant-in-aid would be provided by the colonial government, through the Chief Commissioner of Oudh. It remained a High School during the first two years of its existence, being affiliated to the Calcutta University. Canning High School was raised to the status as a College in 1866; by 1869, it had students from several walks of life, including the sons of *ta'aluqdars, zamindars*, government officials and parents having other miscellaneous professions. The sons of the *ta'aluqdars* would later migrate to the Colvin College discussed elsewhere in this Chapter. Canning College remained affiliated to the University of Calcutta, acquiring its own ornate building (discussed elsewhere in this book) in 1879.

In 1920, through an Act of Legislature, the Canning College, the King George's Medical College and the Isabella Thoburn College were brought under the newly constituted University of Lucknow at Badshah Bagh, which was generously supported by the *ta'aluqdars* of Awadh. Within a year, a sum of Rs 30 lakhs was collected from various sources "for the fulfilment of their cherished dream." However, it seems that "the support was, however, not out of any deep commitment to education (Metcalfe, 2005), but as a prestigious act charity and because their British rulers expected it of them." This could be seen as something comparable in the construction of the Hussainabad Clock tower, half a century ago, being funded by the Hussainabad Trust under British compulsion, discussed elsewhere in this book. The Lucknow University Act No. V of 1920 received the assent of the Lieutenant Governor of Oudh on November 1, at Lucknow and by the Governor General at Calcutta on November 25, 1920. The Medical College was brought under the ambit of the University in March 1921. The Canning College with all its endowments and property was transferred to the newly constituted Lucknow University at Badshah Bagh by the Canning College Act of

Figure 59 : Classes at Canning College, 1871, Unidentified Photographer.

Vol. I. No. 1. September 1922.

CONTENTS:

12844

THE LUCKNOW UNIVERSITY JOURNAL.

Vol. I.] SEPTEMBER, 1922. [No. 1.

HIS EXCELLENCY THE CHANCELLOR'S MESSAGE.

His Excellency the Chancellor has graciously sent the following Message to the Lucknow University Journal:—

"I hope and feel sure that the Journal of the Lucknow University will preserve a high standard at all times, and do much good and useful work not only in publishing the news of the University, but also in linking together generations of students, who are separated by place and in time from one another."

Figure 60: First Issue of *The Lucknow University Journal*, 1922.

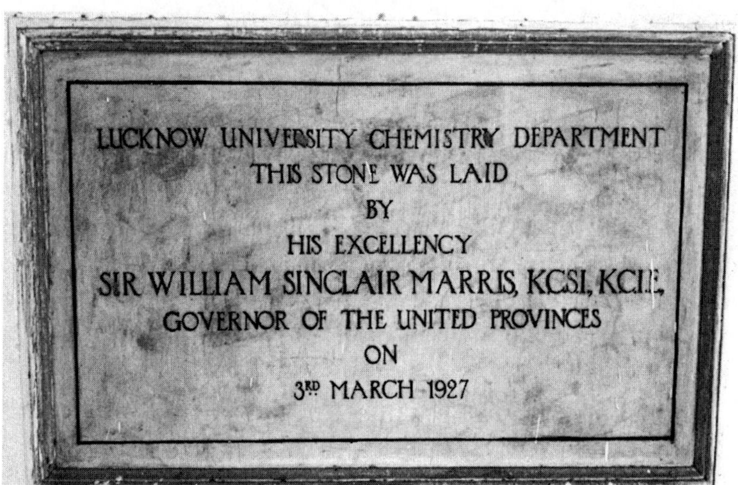

Figure 61: Foundation Stone of the Chemistry Department, Lucknow University, Author, 2023.

Figure 62: Chemistry Department, Lucknow University, 2023 by the Author, who is an Alumnus of the Department.

1922. The degree classes at Lucknow Christian College (then affiliated to the University of Calcutta) which had commenced in 1889 were also transferred to the newly constituted Lucknow University in 1922. Isabella Thoburn College became a sort of Women's Department for the University. Swinton Jacob was responsible for the now rapidly proliferating Indo-Saracenic architecture, first for the Medical College and then the University proper. The campus covered 90 acres and the buildings consisted of a main block facing the river, with a front 420 ft. in length, flanked by two double storeyed wings. However, the proposal of Walter Burley Griffin for the University Central Library could not succeed. The first issue of *The Lucknow University Journal* was published in September 1, 1922, with CJ Brown as Editor and a message of from Harcourt Butler, Lt. Governor of the United Provinces and *ex-officio* Chancellor of Lucknow University, stating that, "I hope and feel sure that the Journal of the Lucknow University will preserve a high standard at all times, and do much good and useful work not only in publishing the news of the University, but also in linking together generations of students, who are separated by place and in time from one another."

Today, the magnificent churches, schools and colleges established by the British in Lucknow, stand in mute testimony, surviving the ravages of time. With Gothic, Classic, Neo-Classic and Indo-Saracenic elements, they are architectural marvels in themselves. Whatever might have been the original intentions of the founding fathers - these educational institutions rank among the best in the country as a whole, and continue to be a source of pride for the city.

Chapter - VII

Of Divine Intervention

The trading explorer, the missionary, the concession hunter and the soldier follow each other with methodical certainty.

- Oliver Osborne,
The Other Man and Myself (1900)

In Nawabi Lucknow, although a number of Europeans, particularly Frenchmen, including Claude Martin (who, by accounts, was apparently a Freemason), remained in the service of Shuja-ud-Daula and Asaf-ud-Daula, there are no reports of Christian places of worship being set up in the city or in Faizabad, barring a short-lived Catholic St. Mary's Church and residential premises at *Padre Tola*, in the Golaganj area of Lucknow. This had been apparently established by one Father Josef Bernini, a Capuchin priest, who had obtained a grant of 20 bighas of land from Shuja-ud-Daula. Bahu Begum had been suffering from a carbuncle, which could be cured by the ministrations of the priest. The Nawab offered to a monetary reward to Father Josef, which the latter refused, and instead opted for land in Lucknow to establish a Christian locality, which came to be known as Padre Tola. Father Adeodatus Santuari established the Saint Mary's Chapel here in 1824. Since no remains of the Chapel or its neighbourhood (Padre Tola) exists today, the exact location of the same cannot be pinpointed, although it is surmised that it might have existed near the present day Bazar Jhau Lal. However, the small cemetery or burial ground of Padre Tola continues to survive till today. Known as *Kaiser Pasand Cemetery*, it had been incorporated within the Kaiserbagh palace complex by Wajid Ali Shah and named after Roshan-ud-Daula's kothi, which the King had appropriated for himself and renamed as Kaiser Pasand. Among other ruinous graves and tombs, the Padre Tola or Kaiser Pasand cemetery has the mausoleum of Sultan Mariam (Mary) Begum or Vilayati Begum, wife of Ghazi-ud-Din Haider. Mary Angela Short was the elder daughter of Dr. James Short, a Roman Catholic in the service of the EIC in Kanpur, through his Armenian wife, Mary Minas. Mary Short had converted to Islam on her marriage with the King in 1817, but reverted as a Roman Catholic as a widow in 1827, bequeathing substantial endowments for the maintenance of Christian establishments in her will. But we are digressing.

The Madiaon cantonment (discussed elsewhere), came into existence and a small Anglican chapel, called Christ Church, completed in 1842, catered to the religious needs of the soldiers and their families stationed in there. Henry S. Polehampton, Chaplain and JP Harris, Assistant Chaplain, were active in Lucknow, during 1856 – 57. Polehampton, who had been educated in Eton, stayed at the Madiaon Cantonment, reputedly in a haunted house (discussed elsewhere). His provided religious services for the Company's soldiers stationed in Lucknow, as well as for civilian British residents in the city, with attendance in the hospital and churchyard, and occasional visits to distant stations, where there was no Chaplain. He carried out notable work in caring for the sick and injured during the siege of the Residency, but his life was cut short as he fell victim to a stray shot. He died on July 20, 1857. His wife, Emily, continued to nurse the sick and the wounded within the Residency. Harris' wife, Georgina, also gained acclaim for her book, *A Lady's Diary of the Siege of Lucknow* (1858), which gave a vivid description of life within the Residency during the siege.

That the British had already embarked on the process of religious defilement of native places of worship, as can be gauged from Martin Gubbins' account in *An Account of the Mutinies in Oudh and of the Siege of the Lucknow Residency* (1858), about the Kadam Rasul as, "Directly north of the barracks, and close to the river, stood an old tomb, where was preserved a stone brought from Mecca, supposed to bear the impress of the foot of the Prophet. It was hence called the Kuddum Russool. This had been repaired, and converted into a powder-magazine, and was protected by a native sepoy guard. Some days later, the gunpowder was removed from the Kuddum Rassool tomb and placed in the Muchee Bhowan." William Forbes-Mitchell in his *Reminiscences of the Great Mutiny 1857-58* (1910), later confirmed this by stating that, "The Kuddum Russool was a strongly-built domed mosque, not so nearly large as the Shahnajaf, but it had been surrounded by a strong wall and converted into a powder magazine by the English between the annexation of Lucknow and the outbreak of the Mutiny." Thus, the intentions of the British to defile Indian and particularly Islamic places of worship had been amply clear, even before the actual outbreak of 1857. However, despite the religious cauldron that had been slowly coming to a boil before the events of 1857, the actual sepoy revolt had myriad reasons, and religion was just one immediate cause. The Uprising, however, soon degenerated into a war having significant religious overtones, with many Muslim leaders declaring the freedom movement as a *jihad* (holy war), with *fatwas* (religious proclamations) being issued on a regular basis by maulvis and ulemas (Islamic religious leaders) and the Muslim freedom fighters being termed as *ghazis* or *jihadis* and *mujahidin* by the British, who did not refer to Hindu freedom fighters contemptuously in the context of their religion, but merely as *pandies*, after Mangal Pandey. Pandey's actions at Barrackpore cantonment had set off a chain of events, culminating in the First War of Independence for Indians. The cynical terminology above, as devised by the British, tried to introduce a dichotomy in the freedom movement based on religious lines, implying that unlike the Hindus, the Muslim rebels were fighting for a religious and not political cause. The British also indulged in capturing / damaging / shelling and deliberately desecrating as many Islamic places of worship as possible. To illustrate this point, the Kadam Rasul had already been desecrated and then abandoned by the British in 1857, and the Shahnajaf had been repeatedly shelled by them during 1857 – 58. After the final capture of the city in 1858, the great Asafi Masjid and Imambara were used as arsenals by the British till 1884. The neighbouring

Alamgir Mosque (Teele Wali Masjid) was used as a medical aid center for European soldiers. Initially, the tomb of Sa'adat Ali Khan and then the mausoleum of Amjad Ali Shah or Sibtainabad Imambara (popularly known as *Maqbara* in local parlance) were appropriated for religious use by the British themselves, till the completion of the new Anglican Christ Church in 1860, which was built in the memory of British soldiers who had died in Lucknow during the Uprising. Lord (Clemency) Canning had even attended divine service in the Sibtainabad Imambara during his visit to Lucknow in October 1859.

In 1857, both the Madiaon and the Golaganj churches suffered damages; the Golaganj property was subsequently sold off.

An Anglican St Mary's Church had existed earlier since 1810, in the Residency premises. It was a handsome Gothic structure, which could accommodate a hundred and thirty people. Having imitation windows and like most buildings of its time, it was cooled by punkah coolies. The last service to be held there was in May 1857, after which it was converted into a granary. Its proximity to the outer lines made it extremely hazardous, and therefore it was abandoned shortly - the grain being moved out at night through a breach in the eastern wall of the building - the breach can still be seen and a plaque has been installed near it. The victims of the surprise rebel attack in the Madiaon cantonment were the first to be buried in St. Mary's churchyard. Burials continued here long after 1857 - but only members of the original garrison and their families were permitted to be buried here, which accounts for the comparatively recent graves in the churchyard.

The Christ Church mentioned above was consecrated by Bishop Cotton on November 26, 1860. It was constructed at a cost of about Rs 60,000/-, "of which the larger portion was contributed by the Government." It was also referred to as the Martyr's Memorial Church - because of the numerous commemorative plaques it displayed of British "heroes" and soldiers who had perished in Lucknow during 1857 - 58. Surprisingly, it also had a plaque in honour of Kavanagh, comparing his exploits "with the devotion of an ancient Roman taking his life in his hand" who had spent much of his lifetime in Lucknow (Chapter II), but had died in Gibraltar. A memorial plaque in the honour of Rev. Polehampton (see above) also existed, together with several other brass and marble tablets. Christ Church was built on typical Gothic lines of that period, being designed by General Hutchinson, having a capacity to seat 130 persons. It is said that the cross on the steeple of the church initially faced Hazratganj, but was wrenched out of place after a storm in 1933 to face the Post Office, which is continues to face even today.

Tradition has it that among the last utterances of Henry Lawrence to the besieged community at the Residency was, "Let a Christian Mission be established in Lucknow." After the British regained control of the city, "as a result of diligent search, premises for the future Mission was found in Hussainabad, which was acquired and repaired." This would form the nucleus of the Lalbagh Girls School and Isabella Thoburn College (Chapter VI), together with the Wesleyan Church. Religious and missionary activity picked up post-1858, with the quick establishment of churches and missionary schools in the city. The American Methodist Episcopal Mission was opened in Hussainabad "during the cold weather of 1858." Missionaries occupied the Asafi Kothi and the Kala Kothi and remained there till 1866. After the clearing of the ground in the neighbourhood of the Macchi Bhavan and the consequent decrease in the population, the missionaries removed their headquarters to Lalbagh and Inayat Bagh. While at Hussainabad, they refrained from purchasing any property, but after their move, they began to buy land and build institutions. Architects James Ransome, the consulting architect for the Government together with Frank Lishman are credited for having designed a number of colonial institutions in Lucknow during the period: 1869 – 1938. They were subsequently succeeded by John Begg and his team.

Figure 63: Vintage View of Anglican Christ Church, Unidentified Photographer.

Figure 64: All-Saints' Garrison Church, Lucknow Cantonment, 2020, Author.

Figure 65: St Paul's Church, Lucknow Cantonment, 1870,
Robert & Harriet Tytler.

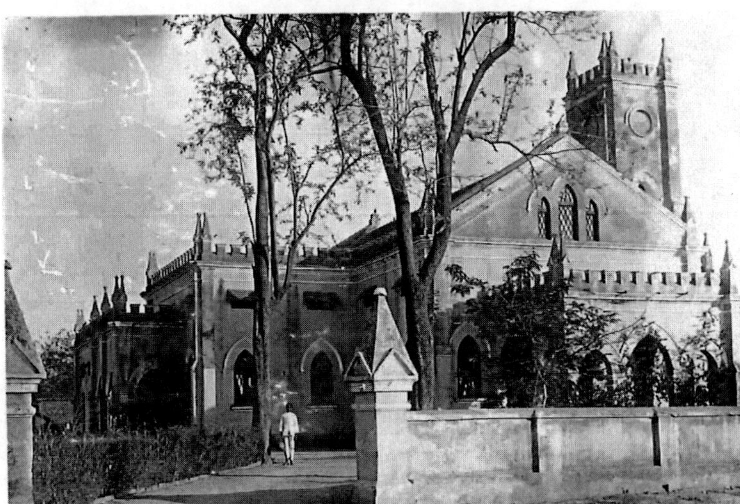

Figure 66: Vintage View of Central "Hindustani" Methodist Church,
Unidentified Photographer.

Figure 67: Vintage view of Lalbagh "English" Methodist Church, Unidentified Photographer.

The Catholic Diocese established the St. Paul's Church or Cantonment Church in the Dilkusha in as early as 1862 for European soldiers in the newly formed Cantonment, together with the St. Joseph's Church (later Cathedral) in Hazratganj, for the British civilian population. According to some writers, a Lucknow United Church had also been established in the Cantonment area during the same period (1870). It functioned from 1870 - 1877, after which, due to reasons unknown, the property was sold off after the church building had been demolished. It is said that joint services of Presbyterians and Methodists were held in that church during its short existence. At present, St Paul's Church is the oldest Catholic church of Lucknow.

In 1858, a young Irish priest and Catholic missionary, William Gleeson arrived at Lucknow. Apparently, from the money obtained from the sale of the Golaganj church described above, and also through subscriptions raised from the public, he purchased a plot of land at Hazratganj (Civil Lines), adjacent to the Kankar Wali Kothi. In 1860, he built a church and dedicated it to St. Joseph. Both St. Paul's and St Joseph's Churches were blessed on the same day by Bishop Anastasius Hartmann on May 10, 1862, although they were only partially complete. However, the original St. Joseph's saw many avatars; soon after its completion, it was observed to have weak foundations and had to be demolished. A new church came up in 1871, which was again demolished in the 1960s, to give way for the modern St. Joseph's Cathedral we see today.

The origins of Zahur Baksh Kothi and Imambara in the Lalbagh area are not clear. It appears that Zahur Baksh was built by Agha Mir, the Prime Minister of Ghazi-ud-Din Haider; it was later used by Hakim Mehdi, the successor of Agha Mir for convalescing, who later died here. Being a *nazul* property, the British sold Zahur Baksh and its compound to one Father Leopold, for a sum of Rs 33,400/- in 1859. The Church Missionary Society built a small chapel here, which came to be known as Mission Church of Lucknow. The Foundation Stone of the present Epiphany Church was laid on November 8, 1875. After the church was ready in two years, the first service was held here on December 25, 1877, to celebrate Christmas. The building has an impressive brick-red facade, built in Gothic Revivalist style, having several turrets and a five storeyed steeple or church tower, the latter having rectangular ventilators and arched windows. Its nave (prayer hall) is similar to Christ Church discussed previously.

The All Saints' Garrison Church had humble beginnings in the Cantonment area in 1860. The present church replaced the older smaller church in 1902. Its architecture was inspired by Magdalen College, Oxford, and its original design by Ransome was modified by other engineers, after the original engineer had proceeded to England. Ransome also designed St Mungo's Church discussed later. One of the unusual features of the church is that the pews have niches for supporting guns - so any surprise attack by future mutineers could be thwarted (!). The church has two memorial plaques, in honour of the soldiers of the 3rd Company, 8th Battalion Royal Artillery and the soldiers of the Perthshire Regiment, who had perished during 1857 - 58. The Church compound also bears a marble plaque, indicating the site of the alter of the original church, the first one to be built in the Dilkusha cantonment area in 1860, which was later demolished.

Figure 68: Vintage View of the Second St Joseph's Church, Hazratganj, Unidentified Photographer.

Methodism arrived in India in 1856, and the Methodist Church in India (MCI) is an "autonomous affiliated" Church in relation to the United Methodist Church, a Protestant Christian denomination of India. The Old Methodist Church in Ganeshganj started its services in 1891, but the first official congregation was formally held in 1870. The compound where the Church is situated was initially rented from the Raja of Balrampur; later the plot was purchased from the Raja. The Ten Commandments are inscribed on the main eastern entrance of the Church which is an unique feature.

The Central "Hindustani" Methodist Church of the Methodist Episcopal Mission came up in 1869 on the Cantonment Road and it was intended for the native Christian population. The Central

Methodist Church has an imposing building carrying projecting portico, a square tower having Indo-European design parapets and circular ventilators having the small and solid towers over the corners. The spacious prayer hall had tri-arched windows with the central one being the biggest in size, being able to accommodate 2000 worshippers at a time. It was the first Methodist Christian Church of Lucknow today.

The construction of Lalbagh "English" Methodist Church started in 1875 and it was completed in 1877, although the congregation had begun worshipping here in 1870 when, on the invitation of James Thoburn, brother of Isabella Thoburn (discussed elsewhere), the famous world famous preacher and missionary, William Taylor delivered his first sermon here on November 25, 1870. Taylor "began his work by preaching to the English speaking people in the evenings, and to the Hindustani people, through an interpreter, in the mornings. The impression produced was immediate, deep, and abiding" and the Church came to be known as the English Methodist Church because its services were held in English, as compared to the earlier Methodist Church, where services were conducted in Hindi. The parsonage came up in the Church compound in 1894; the Duncan White Institute for Sunday School was added in 1910. The first Indian Pastor of this church was William Jeffroy, who worked here in 1942 - 1944. After him, again a succession of expatriate Pastors continued till 1972.

The preaching of John Wesley, primarily against slavery and the hymns of his brother, Charles, had led to a spiritual awakening in England. The Lucknow and Benares district of Wesleyan Methodist Church came into being in 1879. In January 1880, six Methodist ministers met at Lucknow and formed the first synod of the Lucknow-Benares district. This district began with three circuits (Lucknow, Faizabad and Benaras) - the membership of which consisted mainly of British soldiers and civil servants. A Methodist church was reported to have been built in Sa'adatganj area of old Lucknow in the late 1880s. The parsonage was located within the church compound. Later, this parsonage was illegally occupied and the matter ultimately reached the courts, where, after prolonged litigation, the occupant was evicted from the premises. By this time, the area had become

Figure 69: St Mungo's Church, Lucknow Cantonment, 2019, Author.

Figure 70: Epiphany "Zahur Baksh" Church, 2022, Author.

Figure 71: St Thomas Church, Lucknow Cantonment, 2021, Author.

heavily encroached upon by illegal occupants, as a result of which the Executive Board of the church decided to sell the land to the local inhabitants of the area, after demolishing the church and the parsonage. Thus, ended the sad story of the Sa'adatganj Methodist Church.

St Thomas Church, situated on present day Nehru Road, Lucknow Cantonment was built in 1908. Popularly known as Dilkusha Church, the Church building was comparatively smaller in size, if compared to the other churches of Lucknow Cantonment (accommodating at best 250 people), although the Church compound is vast, with an equally spacious parsonage. It was also known as the British Methodist Church, but in 1970, it was amalgamated with the CNI. The church was used for a film shoot for the Hindi film, *Junoon* in 1978 (based on the 1857 revolt), in which the steeple was seen to be taller than what is observed today - the reason being that the tower was later damaged by lightning and was never restored to its original height.

St. Mungo's Church of Scotland was consecrated on November 31, 1909 at Lucknow Cantonment, by the Rev. GT Chree (Presidency

Senior Chaplain of Bengal) - St. Mungo being the patron saint of the city of Glasgow, Scotland. In Wales and England, this saint is known by his birth and baptismal name "Kentigern." A number of churches dedicated to St. Mungo exist in the UK, as well as in Canada and New Zealand. It is no secret that Scottish Highlanders had a prominent presence in Lucknow, from 1857 till Independence. The Highland regiments, in kilts, plaid uniforms and playing bagpipes (often called *petticoated devils*) represented a romantic visual of British exploits in India.

After 1947, the devout had all but vanished; as per reports, on August 14, 1952, the Indian Government had requested the Secretary, Church of Scotland Chaplaincy Board, to assume control of this Church. Receiving no response, the Ministry of Defence was instructed to take over the Church on October 3, 1955. Being de-consecrated in 1976, it is now no longer a place of worship, but a casual warehouse for army supplies. A view of the majestic, Gothic ruins give an indication of how this church might have been in its better days. It is too strongly built to collapse and vanish on its own, and it's too prominent to be bull-dozed and levelled to the ground. And so it stands, ignored, its spire towering and dwarfing neighbouring structures, waiting for its slow, imminent and eventual end.

The Foundation Stone of St Peter's Church was laid by Bishop George Herbert on March 21, 1914, the same day he also laid the Foundation Stone of Charbagh Railway Station. Both had a common thread as the Railways were involved - the Church being built for the benefit of railway men and their families in the area. Hence it is also known as Railway Church and its Pastor was addressed as Railway Chaplain for quite some time. The Church was consecrated on April 8, 1915, the architect being Frank Lishman again. Initially it was an Anglican church under the Anglican Diocese of Allahabad which came under the Episcopal area of Diocese of Lucknow in 1970 when Church of North India was formed. Two inscriptions bearing the Ten Commandments are affixed at the entrance of the Church in 1989, perhaps drawing inspiration from the Old Methodist Church in Ganeshganj discussed earlier. St Peter's is moderately spacious, with a capacity to seat around 500 persons. Its compound also houses the parsonage within its premises.

We get some official details of the missionaries' presence and their activities by 1916 in Colonial Lucknow, from the District Gazetteers of the United Provinces of Agra & Oudh of the same year:

"The Church Missionary Society has a large establishment in Lucknow. There are three clergymen, one of whom is an Indian. One of the Europeans is in-charge of a number of Indian preachers and also supervises a free library situated near the Chauk (*sic*) which is frequented daily by a number of young men. Another has charge of the Mission High School. It was opened originally in 1859 as a Middle School but some 20 years ago was moved to a site close to the Kaiserbagh. The present fine building is largely the work of the Rev. A.I. Birkett (see Annexure I), for many years Manager of the school and now houses some 400 boys. In 1913, a large hostel for both Christian and non-Christian boys together with a residence for the manager of the school and provided with spacious playing grounds was built in Cantonment Road, not far from the school. There is also an Anglo-Vernacular middle school near the city station worked by the Mission and a mixed school is held in the church compound. The headquarters are known as Zahur Baksh, a pre-mutiny building, said to have been built by one of the royal family of Oudh and in this church (*sic*) of the Epiphany at Lucknow, a handsome Gothic structure of red brick with a fine spire. The congregation consists chiefly of Eurasians and Indian Christians. Working in connection with the Church Missionary Society is a branch of the Zenana Bible and Medical Mission, which also has a station in Nigohan. The staff consists of six European missionaries and teachers. The principal institution of this mission is the Lady Kinnaird Memorial Hospital in Shah Mina. This hospital was considerably enlarged in 1897 and has some 40 beds for in-patients. The dispensary is open daily and is attended by a large number of out-patients.

The remaining missions deserving of mention in Lucknow comprise the Wesleyan Methodist Mission to which a high school situated in the cantonments is attached. There is a church for Indian communicants on Banks Road and a church in the cantonments, which is used for both English and Indian services. The high school is recognised for the school leaving certificate examination and has a hostel attached to it. There are three girls' schools in Lucknow and a female dispensary in Amethi. The number of native communicants is about 200.

The mission owns the Memorial Soldier's Home in cantonments on Napier Road. There is also a Roman Catholic Mission, which as two churches: one in the cantonments and one in the Civil Lines. There are also three schools attached to this mission, the Loreto Convent with 115 pupils, St Agnes School with 120 pupils, and St Francis School with 110 pupils."

1932 saw the Wesleyan Church coming up in Lalbagh, Lucknow. Also known as Lal Girjaghar due to its prominent red colour, it is situated in a large compound and has a cruciform layout. In 1970, during the reunification and amalgamation of several churches under the umbrella of the CNI, this Church also came under the administrative control of the CNI, although apparently, the Church property and assets continue to belong to the British Association Trust and not the CNI.

The Holy Redeemer Church, Mawaiya was established in 1934, primarily for railway employees and their families residing in the Charbagh and Alambagh area. The St Joseph's Church at Hazratganj being too far off for Catholic families to attend service, the movement for building a church in this area started in 1922, and it was in 1932, that Fr. John Chrysostom could get the plot sanctioned from the Railway authorities, on which the Church, with its prominent spire could be built. Fr. Chrysostom would later become the Principal of St. Francis High School (1935 - 36; 1941 - 42), which was attached to the St Joseph's Church discussed earlier.

Other notable Colonial era churches in Lucknow include the Calvary Evangelical Church (1910), Daliganj Methodist Church (1925), Assembly of God Church (1925), Seventh Day Adventist Church (1938) and Dua Ka Ghar / House of Prayer (1940).

A brief note on the Methodist (later Lucknow) Publishing House would not be out of place at this juncture. Feeling the need for printed material for distribution (including hymns, Catechism lessons and gospel materials), the Methodist Episcopal Mission at Bareilly approached the Newal Kishore Press at Lucknow for purchase of their small printer. However, the cost being prohibitive (Rs 1062/-), the matter was dropped. In 1860, a small hand press was purchased from Roorkee for Rs 500/-, said to "have been made from cannon used in the mutiny and cast by trained native labourers under European supervision." The first production from this fledgling Mission Press "in the language of these millions was a tract on the *Witness of the Holy Spirit*, written by Brother Parsons." In 1862, the first edition of *Masihi Git Ki Kitab*, containing 50 hymns was issued. By 1866, due to logistic reasons, it was decided to move the Press to Lucknow, where it was installed in Hussainabad, in a room about 16 ft. x 20 ft. in size, and six nos. staff. Due to the Gomti floods in

Figure 72: Lucknow Publishing House in Hazratganj, Unidentified Photographer.

1870, which inflicted considerable damage to the Mission properties, the Press was removed to a safer place in the Inayat Bagh property (discussed elsewhere), where it was installed in the godown of one of the bungalows at this site.

In 1873, "a large, substantial and well situated building on the main business street of Lucknow" was identified (an obvious reference to Hazratganj) which "afforded an abundance of room for the present and ground sufficient for any extension." In the following year, the Press, despite the handicap of relocation and moving, managed to churn out 36 new books, with an aggregate total of 3,265,36 pages, which was no mean achievement. Known originally by the name of Mission Press, in 1874, it adopted the name of "The American Methodist Mission Press". In 1905, "a desirable piece of property lying west of the Civil and Military Hotel was available" which was acquired. The Publishing House would thus be relocated to its final destination on this site on Cantonment Road, Lucknow in due course of time. On January 25, 1932, it was decided to change the name of the press to "The Lucknow Publishing House" with a sub-title "Of The Methodist Episcopal Church." By this time, the output of the press was enormous, publishing Weeklies (e.g. *Indian Witness, Kaukab-i-Hind, Lucco Life*), Monthlies (e.g. *United Church Review, Indian Temperance News*), Quarterlies (e.g. *Christian Education, Collegian, Chand Bagh Chronicle*), Half Yearly (*Burma Mission Herald*), Religious Pamphlets, Tracts in Hindi and Urdu and text books containing hymns, gospel stories and similar materials. It also published a Dictionary and *Hilton's Guide To Lucknow.*

By 1961, similar presses at Calcutta, Bombay and Madras had been closed down due to various reasons, but the Lucknow Publishing House continued to flourish, with modern offset equipment and trained, dedicated staff.

Chapter - VIII

From a Jack to a King

European Reminiscences

"*The subjects of his Majesty of Oude are by no means desirous of participating in the blessings of British rule. They are a richer, sleeker, and merrier race than the natives in the territories of the Company*"

- Fanny Parkes, *Wanderings of A Pilgrim* (1850)

The British formally ruled Lucknow from 1856 to 1947, although they had been indirectly controlling the territory of Awadh from 1764 onwards, after their victory against Shuja-ud-Daula in the Battle of Buxar. The appointment of British "Residents" or "Political Agents" in successive Nawabi courts, the persistent demands to expel French officials from Faizabad and then Lucknow, the constant interference of the Residents in day-to-day administration, the stream of administrative instructions under the guise of "reforms" from EIC Governor Generals stationed at Calcutta, the relentless demands for money and concessions from successive Nawabs / "Kings" and the signing of fresh Treaties each time a native ruler took over, may not have been "colonial rule" but a parallel system of governance of the "Company Bahadur" had already commenced, after Shuja-ud-Daula had been reinstated, the latter under severe constraints. Later, the severance of all ties whatsoever from the Mughal court at Delhi during the times of Ghazi-ud-Din Haider was another indication of British hegemony; Ghazi-ud-Din Haider was anointed as "King" by the Marquis of Hastings (Lord Moira) "with a strange looking crown designed for the occasion, rather like the crown of Charlemagne as worn by the kings on a pack of playing cards (Mount, 2015). History would be witness that the "Kings" of Awadh from circa 1818 onwards were mere titular heads, with little influence on matters of state, while the real administrative power was centred around the British Resident, who maintained a parallel court from the Residency. To quote Captain Godfrey C. Mundy (1833), who accompanied Lord Combermere, Commander-in-Chief as aide-de-camp during the latter's tour across India: "Oude was (until, for value received, acknowledged as an independent kingdom by the all-powerful Company) a province of the Mogul (*sic*) or Delhi empire; and the Nawaub (*sic*) Vizier of Lucknow was, as the title literally signifies, the deputy or the vicegerent of the Emperor. Ostensibly his Nabobship (*sic*) has been promoted from the rank of servant to that of Lord; virtually, he has only changed masters; for, like all other native potentates who have admitted British residents at their courts, he is so strictly supervised, that he can scarcely add an extra wife or two to his establishment, much less enact any important state measure, without the interference of his super-attentive allies." Of course, we cannot ignore the idiosyncrasies and irregularities prevailing in the Nawabi court also, which periodically included the King, his begums and courtiers, giving an opportunity to the Resident to set things right and create the impression that all was not right in Awadh. This situation reinforced the idea that the British should either play a more active part in the administration of the "kingdom" or annex it altogether and assume direct control. The actions of Sleeman, Outram and Dalhousie in this regard have been documented by various authors and need not be reiterated here. The actual "annexation" has also been likewise described in detail by historians and it would served no purpose to repeat the same here, but to set the record straight, the following points may be emphasised for the information of the reader:

- The territory or "kingdom" of Awadh had long served as a buffer state between the British in the east and growing Maratha influence in north India. The Governor General at Calcutta now wanted direct control over Awadh's riches and military might, instead of dealing through a succession of Residents and recalcitrant Nawabs (later "Kings").

- Military successes of the British in other parts of the Indian sub-continent had made them over-confident and foolhardy.
- Policies such as Doctrine of Lapse (e.g. Jhansi) or direct military offensive (e.g. Mysore / Seringapatam) were not applicable on Awadh, since by all practical purposes, the rulers of Awadh were British supporters and there had never been any conflict between Calcutta and Lucknow after Shuja-ud-Daula's defeat at the Buxar (despite the constant undercurrent of tension between successive Nawabi rulers and British Residents).
- The British tried to coax and cajole and even threaten Wajid Ali to abdicate, on the grounds of "extensive misrule", "cruel oppression which prevailed throughout His Majesty's dominions", the "deplorable condition of Oude (Awadh)" as a whole and "ill-health" of the king himself. The latter was offered a substantial pension, the Dilkusha palace to settle down with his retinue and enjoy the remainder of his life with his wives and titles, devoid of any authority or responsibility.
- As evident from the despatches between Calcutta and Lucknow, the East India Company in Calcutta with its Court of Directors at London, had already started using the terms "British Government" and "Government of India" interchangeably with itself, although neither the Crown nor British Parliament were directly involved in the Company's machinations in the Indian sub-continent. Extracts of instructions January 23, 1856 to Outram (the officiating Resident at Lucknow) from Calcutta are quite revealing:

    1. "The Governor General in Council having thereupon resolved to proceed at once to the establishment of the new policy which he had proposed, and to carry into effect the instructions of the Honourable Court for the assumption of the Government of Oude...."

2. "You will point out to the Minister (Ali Naqi Khan, Prime Minister of Awadh) that the resolution of the British Government to assume forthwith the administration of Oude, in one form or the other, has been finally taken, and is inflexible..."

3. "The Resident will inform the King .... the Governor General has instructed him to state, that the resolution of the Government of India is irrevocably taken... "

- Against such insurmountable odds, Wajid Ali proved to be surprisingly adamant about retaining his titles / position and all attempts by the British to take control of Awadh started floundering. As per plan, the British next issued an ultimatum that either the King should sign on the Draft Treaty which was basically an Instrument of Accession within three days, or the Governor General would anyhow, assume control of Oude (Awadh), but in that case, the British would not provide guarantees, as regards the king's titles, payment of stipend or personal security.
- Without signing any document or "Treaty", Wajid Ali simply walked out of his palace, urging his citizens to keep calm and not to revert to arms or violence. He planned to meet the Governor General at Calcutta and eventually reach London to petition Queen Victoria.
- The British quickly stepped into the political and administrative vacuum created by Wajid Ali's departure from Lucknow and tried their best to introduce their own model of governance, which would later prove to be a failure.
- Wajid Ali Shah was never *exiled* to Calcutta. He was an unwelcome guest, not a prisoner or a king in exile and his presence remained an object of curiosity, his medieval life style an anachronism - which baffled both the British as well as the local populace of Calcutta.

With increasing British influence in Awadh, first there was a trickle of curious visitors and settlers from Europe, which turned into a deluge, with passing time. The general impression among the visiting Europeans was that there would be easy pickings in the Nawabi court, and ample opportunities existed to earn wealth, which one could take back home to England. Today, a crude analogy can be drawn with this thought process with the California Gold Rush of America and Klondike Gold Rush of Canada, almost a century later. Initially, on arrival at Indian shores, Europeans were appalled at the state of the natives, in terms of the latter's social mores, religious beliefs / practices and personal languid lifestyles. In fact, all aspects of native life invited derision. The latter were basically black heathens and idolaters, who needed to be proselytized and put to work either as "coolies" or at best, as petty clerks, for their white masters, in this god-forsaken land, which was seemingly cursed with a terrible climate and infested with vermin and disease. And yet, a fabulous wealth seemed to be hidden from the eyes - the splendid lifestyles of the native princes who ruled from their lofty palaces was proof of this.

After the formal annexation of Awadh in 1856, the British could now justifiably regard themselves as masters of the Indian sub-continent, and conduct themselves accordingly. Low paid Company officials, often with unimpressive family, financial and educational backgrounds, could now stay in commodious palaces, strut about on vast palace grounds wearing sola topis or canter around on horseback, lording over the local populace – such was the miserable fate of the original inhabitants of the city, in that dark phase of Lucknow's history. Many travellers, officials (and their wives) as well as settlers - the neo Nabobs or White Sahibs penned their memoirs, describing the Lucknow of those times. These prove to be important sources of historical detail about colonial Lucknow, albeit with a distinct racist bias. In this Chapter, we shall selectively peruse few of these memoirs and writings, some of which are factually correct and quite informative, while others are apt to be totally erroneous and occasionally hilarious.

Descriptions of Lucknow's palaces and places of worship are many, and we need not repeat them here. But Captain Leopold Von Orlich (1845) actually discovered a torture chamber in the king's

Figure 73: Lord Charles Canning, 1857-58, Unidentified Photographer.

Figure 74: Major General Robert Napier with ADC, 1857, Unidentified Photographer.

Figure 75: Lt. Col. Saunders Alexius Abbot, 1858, Unidentified Photographer.

Figure 76: Judge Edward Gustavus Fraser, 1858, Unidentified Photographer.

Figure 77: Dr EW Bonavia, 1885, Unidentified Photographer.

Figure 78: Sir Auckland Colvin, 1875, Unidentified Photographer.

Figure 79: Sir Harcourt Butler, 1920, Unidentified Photographer.

Figure 80: Sir William Sinclair Marris, 1930, Unidentified Photographer.

Figure 81: Lord and Lady Curzon at Governor's House, Lucknow, 1920, L De Gruyther.

Figure 82: Visit of Edward, Prince of Wales to Lucknow, 1921, Unidentified Photographer.

palace complex, referred to as the Furrahbaksh, "Among the lower apartments, we accidentally discovered a room hung with black cloth, on which skeletons were painted, and where all sorts of instruments of torture were kept. We were informed that Hyder (Nasir-ud-Din Haider) used here (*sic*) to confine those women who withstood his orders, and had actually suffered two of them to perish in this horrible chamber." Orlich, however, was appreciative of the "fair women of Lucknow; they were all bare-headed, and their beautiful black hair fell down in braids, or was interwoven with jewels; most of them wore large nose-rings, which hung over the corners of the mouth, and their long ear-rings touched their shoulders. Very few of them could be called pretty, but they have piercing eyes, which look the more brilliant because their eyelids are blackened with antimony. A coloured scarf was thrown lightly and gracefully across the neck and shoulders, and displayed rather than concealed the fine contour of the upper part of their persons. They did not fail to make many remarks upon us, and sought to draw our attention, by laughing, joking and tittering."

Fanny Parkes or Parks née Frances Susanna Archer (1794–1875) was an iterant traveller-writer, known for her extensive journals about colonial India, where she lived for 24 years. A detailed and rather flattering account of Badshah Bagh (present day Lucknow University campus) had been given by her as below:

"We crossed the river to a new house and garden, built by the present king called Padshah Bagh; of which I must give a description, it being the most luxurious palace I have seen in India. A large space has been enclosed as a garden within a high wall; it contains three houses and two gateways; the first house is a most delightful one, all you can wish for in such a climate as this; beautiful rooms, with six fountains playing in them, and everything in fairyland style; then such a hummām! Or steam baths, containing rooms heated to different temperatures, the heat of each increasing until you arrive at the steam bath itself. The apartments are made of white variegated marble, and the roofs arched; the rooms are so delightful, we felt every inclination to remain in the hummām, the temperature was so luxurious.

Crossing from this palace to the center of the garden, we entered another elegant building, supported on white marble pillars, beautifully finished, and adorned and furnished with crimson and gold. On the left of the garden is a third palace, sacred to the ladies of the zenāna; this house if built of marble, and covered with flower-work of pounded tālk (talc), which has exactly the same appearance of silver, giving an eastern style to the place. There are two handsome gateways, a steam engine to supply the fountains, and a superb tiger in a cage. Every luxury of life may be contained within the walls of this garden; it is at present scarcely finished, but displays great taste and beauty."

William Howard Russel (1859, 1860) was an Irish reporter with The Times, London, considered to have been one of the first modern war correspondents. His description of Lucknow was, "a fairy tale city, more vast and brilliant than Paris; a vision of palaces, domes azure and golden, cupolas, colonnades, long facades of fair perspective in pillar and column, terraced roofs - all rising up amid a calm still ocean of the brightest verdure... spires of gold glitter in the sun. Turrets and gilded spheres shine like constellations." Russel was one of the first Europeans to have personally observed the marauding British and Sikh soldiers who had laid waste Kaiserbagh during 1858. Among the mayhem and plunder, Russel noted, "Imagine courts as large as the Temple Gardens, surrounded by ranges of palaces, or at least of buildings well stuccoed and gilded, with fresco-paintings here and there on the blind-windows, and with green jalousies and Venetian blinds closing the apertures which pierce the walls in double rows. In the body of the court are statues, lines of lamp-posts, fountains, orange groves, aqueducts, and kiosks with burnished domes of metal."

Passing through Badshah Bagh with the relief force, Russel had observed that, "in the days of its full magnificence, it must have been glorious. Such forests of orange trees, such trickling fountains, shady walks, beds of flowers, grand alleys, dark retreats and summer-houses, all surrounded by a high and massive wall, and forming, as it were, the approaches to a snug little palace of pleasure." He described how he had mounted the flat roof of one of the towers, which provided a pleasant view of the "enemy's works." Russell observed that "in one of the rooms was a portrait of the late King of Oude, which he was permitted to cut out of the frame and carry it off with him - a small bit of loot of very little value."

Russell described his first view of Vilayati Bagh as, "a walled garden filled with cypresses, summer-houses, plaster statues with kiosks and pleasant walks "mid orange trees. Beneath it flows the Goomti, about 500 yards from us, coming down with many a curve from the city of Lucknow. It must have been a very pretty spot - opening on the river by a flight of steps, with alcoves, covered walks, orange trees, kiosks, abundant statuary in plaster, a platform for dancing, an orchestra, the ornamented roofs covered with gilded bosses and spires - tall cypresses and tamarinds bordered the orange plantations, and a wilderness of flowers sprang up in their neglected beds. Everything was fast going to decay; the irrigation canals were choked up, the foundations were dry, the statues falling to pieces, the lattices in the kiosks broken."

Russel returned to Lucknow in January 1859. One of his despatches, dated February 14, 1859 stated, "What is to be done with the Kaiserbagh? A mere shell is all that now remains of rows of palaces. The wind whistles as it lists through unglazed windows and shattered Venetians - through doorless corridors and battered walls. The gardens still remain, but the fountains have ceased to play; the statues - marble and plaster - are all gone. The grand mausoleum of Saadat Ali, the last wise and good Nawab who reigned over Oude, is closed, and the ruin of cannon shot and shell is aggravated by the unresisted effects of rain and wind. A few of the buildings are used as quarters, but by far the greater portion of the palaces of the Kaiserbagh is untenanted."

Frederick Wyman (1866) undertook a journey by train "from Calcutta to the Snowy Range" on a holiday tour and recorded his memoirs, which make for an extremely interesting read, particularly so because he chose to travel by the newly introduced railways and not by dak gharry (Annexure X) or the river route. After several hilarious if derogatory observations on the Indian railways, as compared to the one in England ("It is almost a matter of impossibility to understand the name of the station as shouted by the attendant porter" or "The stations are at night miserably lighted; unless you are very careful, you will come into collision, on alighting to stretch your limbs, with one of the many stray packages and huge bundles of native wraps and cloths, invariably left by the Up-country travelling aborigines exactly where they should not be; while their unfortunate owners rush about in wild excitement and confusion, followed helplessly by their women and children, in search of the 3rd or 4th class ticket-office, before which a seething, unsavoury crowd of straggling passengers are fighting for place, the baboo or clerk behind the partition dispensing tickets by the light of a dirty chiragh, with irritating slowness, utterly regardless of the Babel going on around him."), he eventually reached Colonial Lucknow and recorded his impressions. Wyman "had prepared himself for a modernised impression of Lucknow" (as compared to earlier descriptions "when it was ruled by a King of Oude") and certainly found his impressions more than agreeably realised. "The extreme cleanliness of the Station, its broad and splendidly kept roads, green and neatly fenced maidans, and the many shady and beautiful trees around, with a general aspect of thorough control, supervision, and regularity - all these leave a most gratified impression on the mind; an impression certainly not eradicated in favour of any other Eastern city I have seen." Wyman was appreciative of Nawabi architecture and the "very respectful demeanour of all classes of the natives, having till then understood that since the Mutiny, they had become more upstart and insolent; and certainly having seen no evidence till then to the contrary." Major Chamberlain, "the then worthy and energetic magistrate, explained that such insolence had been common enough after the Mutiny, but that the evil had been remedied by promptly punishing all cases brought to notice." In other words, within a span of half a decade, the native Indians had been browbeaten into submission under colonial rule, and the "vast reforms which have taken place since the Mutiny already indicated that it will not be many years before Lucknow can truly boast of being a model city of the East."

About the newly built cantonment, Wyman stated that, "The south-eastern part of the city is skirted by the military cantonments, a series of well-built barracks in echelon, stretching from Dilkoosha (*sic*) to Alumbagh (*sic*). These are capable of accommodating two line regiments, a cavalry regiment, besides several batteries of artillery; and the most elevated and open space around Lucknow appears to have been chosen for their site. The cantonments also contain a commodious if not a very handsome church, and a soldiers' institute, which is used as a theatre, lecture-room, &c." Hazratganj was a "wholesome-looking market-place, and several large Mahomedan (*sic*) buildings with imposing gateways" while the "Goomtee (*sic*) offered a very pleasing view, extremely picturesque, much resembling in size the Thames at Richmond."

Edward Gustavus Fraser held several posts during his career under the colonial government, in addition to his personal contribution to the activities of the Anglo-Indian Christian Mission, American Presbyterian Mission and the Baptist Mission Society. His daughter, Isabel was born in Agra. After 1857, he was posted as Civil Judge at Lucknow. According to Cupples (1923), "At first, they lived in one of the palaces belonging to the late King of Oude, named the Chutter Munzil (*sic*), from being surmounted with a large copper of bronze umbrella thickly gilt, and hence so resplendent as to be popularly believed a dome of pure gold. The rooms were large and grandly decorated, uncomfortably so. There they remained for about a year, then removed to a house on the other side of the river Goomtee (*sic*), called the Kabutar Walla Kotee (*sic*) or Pigeon-House, having been formerly the King's pigeon-house. Here pigeons, bought for thousands of rupees, were kept. Rascals from all parts of the country came, pretending they had pigeons of rare breeds and great value, so that often as much as a thousand rupees were paid for a pair. The pigeons had been cleverly painted, their feathers twisted about in all directions to make them appear rare, while all the time they were actually of the most common kinds. The King amused himself flying them; at other times Persian cats were let loose among them, while the King and his nobles wagered with each other as to whose cat would kill the greatest number.

Lucknow is one of the finest stations in Upper India, abounding with palaces, mosques, tombs and towers of most gorgeous description. As the capital of the most fertile and populous province of the British Empire, it will always be a place of interest, and the startling events of the Mutiny make it more especially attractive. The occurrences of that time were such as to make Lucknow a solemn household word in the homes of Europeans for generations to come; and under wazirs and kings of Oude in previous years, it had undergone remarkable vicissitudes and incidents of its own, which make it equally interesting to inquiring travellers. Indeed, in no part of the world can millions of intelligent people dwell for several centuries without a history rich in stories, and buildings more or less connected with them."

Isabel learnt about the siege from her father's friends, many of whom had personally witnessed the mutiny themselves. Soon, she could identify the room in the Residency where Henry Lawrence had died, "The Alum Bagh (*sic*), a fortified garden where Havelock died and the Secunder Bagh (*sic*) where a terrible massacre had taken place." At Lucknow, her father's position was influential, and from the way in which he conducted the duties of office, Mr Fraser not only enjoyed the society but the friendship of some of the highest officials of Oude. Many of the old retainers of the late King called upon him, and from their conversation, Isabel learned much of the inner life of the King and of his Ministers, and of the causes that led to the annexation of the state. "Raja Man Singh, the 'wily Rajpoot (*sic*) chief' would add with a laugh, "Without doubt, I deserved to be hanged, but by the kindness, or perhaps stupidity of the British Government, I have been rewarded with an estate!"

Isabel Fraser was married to Dr Colin Valentine of Jaipur; "The ceremony took place in the Bibiapur palace, that had been built by Ausuf-u-dowla (*sic*) for a country residence in his sporting excursions. It is a two-storied building, thoroughly in the English style, General Martin being its reputed architect. The site is well chosen, upon a considerably elevated spot at a bend of the river Goomty (*sic*). To this retreat the Prince-Regent was in a habit of making excursions in a small steam boat, constructed in 1819 by an English engineer, the first steam-vessel known in India."

According the Fanny Parkes (see above), Beebeepore (*sic*) had earlier been the residence of George Cherry, who had been Resident at Lucknow in 1793 – 1796, during the reign of Asaf-ud-Daula. Cherry was later murdered in Benaras in 1799 by Wazir Ali, Asaf-ud-Daula's successor.

Edith E. Cuthell, was the wife of Lt. Col. Thomas George Cuthell of the 38th Foot and later the 13th Hussars. She spent a number of years in India before settling in Surrey, and many of her works feature India as a setting. Her experiences when her husband Thomas (whom she constantly referred to as Captain Sahib) was posted in Lucknow were summarised in a substantial compilation called *My Garden in the City of Gardens* (1905). Edith was no racist, but we cannot blame her for being appalled at the venomous, and sometimes ferocious wildlife in and around her cantonment residence; the leper in her garden, the cholera patients, the troublesome servants and maidservants. She loved gardening and her book is more about her

Figure 83: Vintage View of Hardinge Bridge, Unidentified Photographer.

Figure 84: Unidentified Tomb Converted to a Colonial Bungalow, unidentified Photographer.

efforts on raising local, exotic varieties of flowers, vegetables and fruits in the compound of her bungalow, without any trace of bias or rancour. Sometimes, her historical statements are jumbled up. For example, she writes, "Two evenings ago we went for a drive by the Botanical Gardens. These lie in an immense stretch of ornamental grass, carefully watered and forested, behind the Civil Lines. After the Third Relief, the native city, which was some twenty miles in circumference, was much demolished and reduced, and the environs laid out in drives with trees. In the midst of the gardens rises a square marble summer-house with flights of steps. It was brought from the great palace, "Caesar's Garden (= Kaiserbagh)," is called a baradari, and is a fine specimen of Moghul architecture, the tessellated floor is excellent for dancing. Round the baradari was some good ribbon-gardening, with tiny gravel paths." It is obvious that Edith was confusing between Wingfield Park, where the Nagine Wali Baradari had been translocated from Kaiserbagh and not the Botanical Gardens, formerly Sikandar Bagh. She further continues, "On our way home, we looked in at the Garden of Alexandra (= Sikandar Bagh). Once a palace of Wajid Ali Shah, built for a favourite Mahal, it is now a ruin, enclosed in a high wall, which was carefully loopholed and strongly held by the rebels in November 1857. The inside, gloomy enough in appearance and in memories - for in the courtyard some two thousand mutineers were cut to pieces - this November afternoon was a glory of beautiful gardening, as are all the Lakhnao (*sic*) ruins."

Edith's quaint references to Nawabi heritage places in western context are rather delightful: "We took boat at the English Garden (= Vilayati Bagh) below Heart's Delight (= Dilkusha). Here, in the early nineteenth century, Nasiruddin Haider, second King of Oudh, laid out a garden and planted it with European trees, hence its name (it was actually Ghazi-ud-Din Haider, who laid the Vilayati Bagh). Though by no means to be approved of as a man and monarch, he had a nice taste in gardening, and the situation is pleasant, steps leading down to the river and a high wall all around, to seclude his ladies from outside gaze. The river at Laknao is crossed by five bridges, which carry on as it were in chronological order the development of the city from an obscure hamlet to a capital. The railway bridge which we passed under first, in all its naked utilitarian ugliness, is of course the most modern production. The old builders please the eyes better. Round the first bend we came upon the park, imposing obelisk, dome and towers of the Martiniere, facing us among trees, and giving an odd, partly rococo, partly eastern, and partly mediaeval touch to the landscape. Poor old General Claude! What a poor substitute he must have found the Gumti for his native rushing Rhône!

Now we turned city wards, and under the Pile Bridge (= Nishatganj Bridge), busy with traffic, the heavy bullock hackris lumbering over our heads. On our left lay a line of palaces and public buildings, each in woody gardens, many half in ruins, all the scenes of past splendours of Oudh sovereignty, all the scenes of battle and murder and sudden death, and of British heroism. Then under Bruce's Bridge (= Monkey Bridge), built in 1866, and here a fine view down the long straight reach, spanned by the iron bridge (= Rennie's Bridge) ordered from England by Ghaziu-din Haider (*sic*) in 1816 (actually it was ordered by Sa'adat Ali Khan), to Asufu-daula's (*sic*) picturesque, high-pitched stone bridge of 1780, with its thirteen gothic arches (actually it was a masonry bridge paved with stone). At a little distance from Bruce's Bridge, on the opposite side of the river, lies the King's Garden (= Badshah Bagh), only a thousand yards from the Residency, from where the Mutineers planted a battery. I turned away, regretting that I had not known India in those more splendid days, and we pulled across the stream to the steps of the beautiful Parasol Palace (= Chattar Manzil); and so to tea and gossip in its vaulted and traceried halls, once the abode of Nasiru-din's (sic) beauties, and now given over to the club."

Edith refers to the Bada Imambara as the "Mahommedan Cathedral of Lakhnao" the Alambagh as a "lordly pleasure-house' (it was not so), the Macchi Bhavan as "Fish Market Fort" but her description of Mohammad Bagh as "Prophet's Garden" is quite enlightening and gives a fair idea of how the colonial-era Mahomed Bagh Club evolved from being a Nawabi garden of Asaf-ud-Daula's times: "I drove round recently to have a look at the ferneries in the Prophet's Garden. Here was one of those royal garden houses, on the outskirts of the city, and was used as an outpost by Sir Colin Campbell in the Second Relief. It has been razed, the site gardened, and bisected with a broad Mall, shaded with mangos, a soft sand ride on either side. In the middle stand the Cantonment Club, theatre, cricket ground, and bandstand, among flower beds and pergolas of jaffri work, which shelter palms and ferns. It is marvellous in this climate what a little shade and water can effect." Her account of old Lucknow, possibly Chowk and a traditional Muslim home, cannot be faulted with: "The streets are too narrow to allow of a carriage passing, so we proceeded afoot down the narrow lanes of mud and plaster, thatched, windowless houses, each opening into an interior courtyard. We stopped before an arched gateway bearing the Oudh royal crest painted in the stucco. In the outer, or men's, courtyard lounged a number of tatterdemalion servants in scarlet livery. A coarse curtain of sacking, hung across the opposite archway, prevented the bold male gaze from penetrating into the further court allotted to the women." She also provides an interesting snippet of information from her visit to Kaiserbagh: "There in front of the main buildings was a canal with marble sides and a very handsome carved marble bridge over it. The imposing and beautiful throne which is now in the king's garden at Windsor Castle stood near it." So had Wajid Ali's throne remained at Kaiserbagh for so many decades, before being "smuggled" off to Windsor Castle? This statement needs to be verified.

Bithia Mary Croker (1848 - 1920) was an Irish novelist, her work describing life and society in Colonial India. About her experience of Lucknow (1906), she wrote, "We arrived in Lucknow in November, when the cold weather is delightful to me. The bustle and life of a great Indian station, the novelty of my surroundings, the early morning rides, picnics down the river and dances at the "Chutter Munzil" (*sic*), made me look upon Lucknow as a paradise on earth; and in this light I still regarded it, until a great change came over the temperature, and the month of April introduced me to red-hot winds, sleepless nights and the intolerable "brain fever" bird. With a large cool bungalow, plenty of punkahs, khus khus tatties, ice and a thermantidote, surely we could manage to brave May and June - at any rate, the attempt was made. Gradually the hills drained Lucknow week by week; family after family packed up, warned us of our folly in remaining on the plains, offered to look for houses for us and left by the night mail. By the middle of May, the place was figuratively empty. Nothing can be more dreary than a large station in the hot weather - unless it is an equally forsaken hill station in the depths of winter, when the mountains are covered with snow, the mall no longer resounds with gay voices and the tramp of Jampanies, but is visited by bears and panthers, and the houses are closed, and, as it were, put to bed in straw! As for Lucknow in the summer, it was a melancholy spot; the public gardens were deserted, the chairs at the Chutter Munzil (*sic*) stood empty, the very bands had gone to the hills! The shops were shut, the baked white roads, no longer thronged with carriages and bamboo carts, gave ample room to the humble ekka, or a dhobie's meagre donkey, shuffling along in the dust.

Of course, we were not the only people remaining in the place, grumbling at the heat and dust and life in general; but there can be no sociability with the thermometer above 100° in the shade. Through

Figure 85: Visiting the Residency Ruins during Colonial Rule was a popular pastime - I, Unknown Photographer.

Figure 86: Visiting the Residency Ruins during Colonial Rule was a popular pastime - II, Unknown Photographer.

Figure 87: Ruins of Alambagh during Colonial Rule, 1860, Shepherd & Robertson.

the long, long Indian day we sat and gasped, in darkened rooms, and consumed quantities of Nimbo (*sic*) pegs, i.e. limes and soda water, and listened to the fierce hot wind roaring along the road and driving the roasted leaves before it; and in the evening, when the sun had set, we went for a melancholy drive through Wingfield Park or round Martiniere College, and met our friends at the library, and compared sensations and thermometers. The season was exceptionally bad (but people say that every year)."

At long last, when the children grew listless and sick in Lucknow's summer heat, Mary finally decided to go up to Naini Tal, but by then, every hotel and home was already full. With great difficulty, the family managed to find a house called Briarwood, but it was quite far away from the main town. That it was haunted and hence unoccupied, is the subject of another story, which is beyond the scope of the present book.

Speirs (2013) has given several interesting references of Europeans visiting or staying in Lucknow during colonial rule. Among them, was James Acheson, in charge of the "great Central Telegraph Office", who described Lucknow as a "big, famous and decaying city" where "even the tonga drivers spoke the Urdu of the text books." Marian Hume, sister of Andrew Hume, an ICS officer described the luxurious official residence of the Principal of KGMC, Dr (Col.) Stott. One Thomas Brownsden, who was posted in Lucknow as Assistant Commissioner, was provided with "excellent bachelor accommodation in the club", actually the Chattar Manzil United Services Club, which Thomas mistakenly refers to as the "local Gymkhana Club." Almost all visitors to Lucknow during those times refer to the Chattar Manzil (by varying names, including "Chutta Manzil") which seemed to have awed them. They were also suitably impressed by life in the bungalows which had come up in the city and the cantonment areas with accompanying servants or "lackeys". Of course, not all were lucky. Hilda Seebohm and her friend Lucy, during their "world tour" were accommodated in the Moti Mahal palace compound in tents, not within the palace proper, despite their connections in the colonial government.

Following the departure of the British from India in 1947, it became the self-assumed duty of the Eurasians, often referred to as "Anglo-Indians," to endeavour to uphold the legacy of the British Empire within India, including places such as Lucknow, particularly with regard to language, lifestyle and religion. However, their rapidly declining numbers, exacerbated by ongoing emigration to more favourable destinations like Britain and Australia, would herald the decline of the *Burra Sahib* and *Chokra Boy* culture within a few decades after India achieved independence from colonial rule. Meanwhile, the Anglophiles, who often identified more closely with British customs and life-styles than the British themselves, would find themselves trapped in a peculiar temporal limbo, existing in a state of disconnect from the evolving society around them.

ANNEXURES

Annexure - I

Pictographic Memories of Colonial Lucknow

Hotels

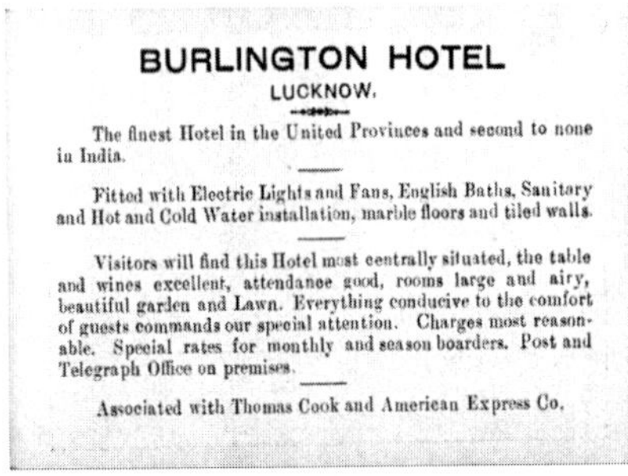

Letters, Postcards and Advertisements

Dr PC Sarka

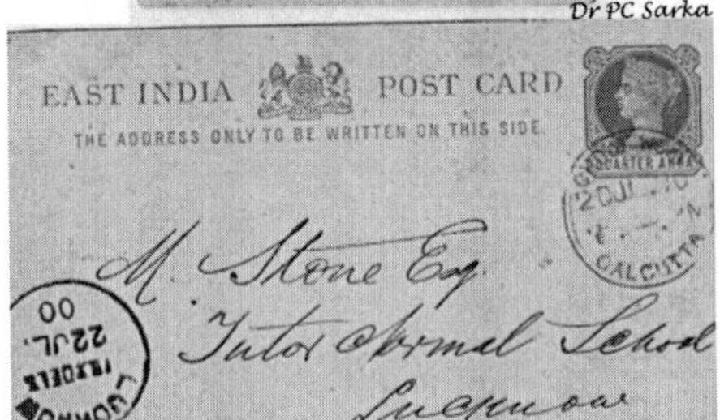

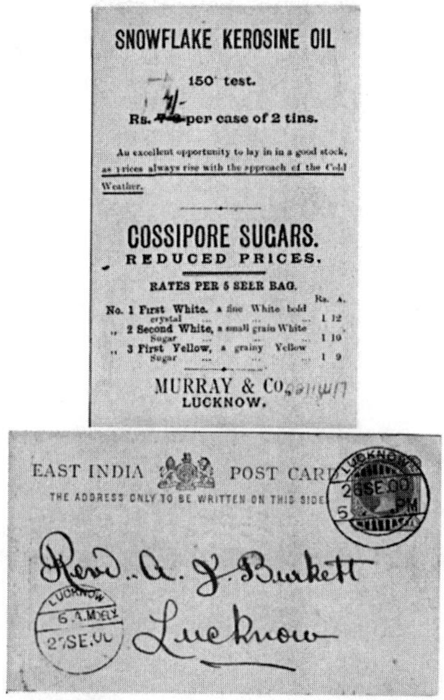
SNOWFLAKE KEROSINE OIL
150° test.
Rs. 4/- per case of 2 tins.
An excellent opportunity to lay in a good stock, as prices always rise with the approach of the Cold Weather.
COSSIPORE SUGARS.
REDUCED PRICES.
RATES PER 5 SEER BAG.
Rs. A.
No. 1 First White, a fine White bold crystal ... 1 12
„ 2 Second White, a small grain White Sugar ... 1 10
„ 3 First Yellow, a grainy Yellow Sugar ... 1 9
MURRAY & Co., Limited
LUCKNOW.
EAST INDIA POST CARD
THE ADDRESS ONLY TO BE WRITTEN ON THIS SIDE
Revd. A. J. Burkett
Lucknow

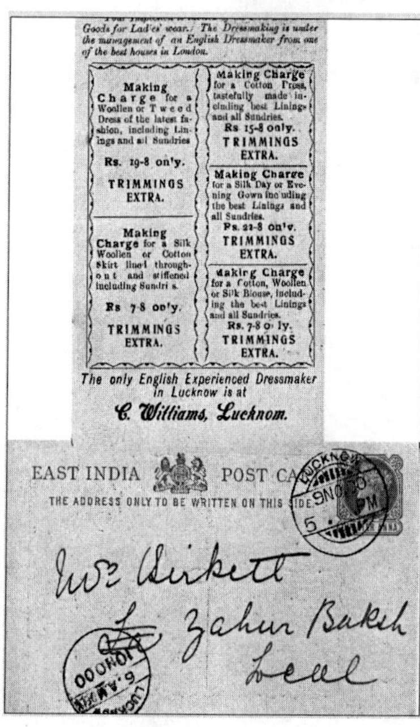
Goods for Ladies' wear. The Dressmaking is under the management of an English Dressmaker from one of the best houses in London.
Making Charge for a Woollen or Tweed Dress of the latest fashion, including Linings and all Sundries
Rs. 19-8 only.
TRIMMINGS EXTRA.
Making Charge for a Silk Woollen or Cotton Skirt lined throughout and stiffened including Sundries.
Rs 7-8 only.
TRIMMINGS EXTRA.
Making Charge for a Cotton Dress, tastefully made including best Linings and all Sundries.
Rs 15-8 only.
TRIMMINGS EXTRA.
Making Charge for a Silk Day or Evening Gown including the best Linings and all Sundries.
Rs. 22-8 only.
TRIMMINGS EXTRA.
Making Charge for a Cotton, Woollen or Silk Blouse, including the best Linings and all Sundries.
Rs. 7-8 only.
TRIMMINGS EXTRA.
The only English Experienced Dressmaker in Lucknow is at
C. Williams, Lucknow.
EAST INDIA POST CARD
THE ADDRESS ONLY TO BE WRITTEN ON THIS SIDE.
Mrs Birkett
Zahur Bakhsh
Well

III HUSSARS
Regimental Theatre.
Beresford & Dagmar's
SPECIALITY COY.
FRIDAY, AUGUST 17th
THE NIGHT OF THE SEASON
GENERAL
STAFF NIGHT
Under the Distinguished Patronage of
Major-General R. M. Jennings, C. B.
SPECIAL ATTRACTIONS
NEW SONGS!
NEW DANCES!
NEW SKETCH!
Plan can be seen at Murray & Co.
Book early to avoid confusion.
S. L. BERESFORD,
Manager.
EAST INDIA POST CARD
THE ADDRESS ONLY TO BE WRITTEN ON THIS SIDE
European Residents
Lucknow

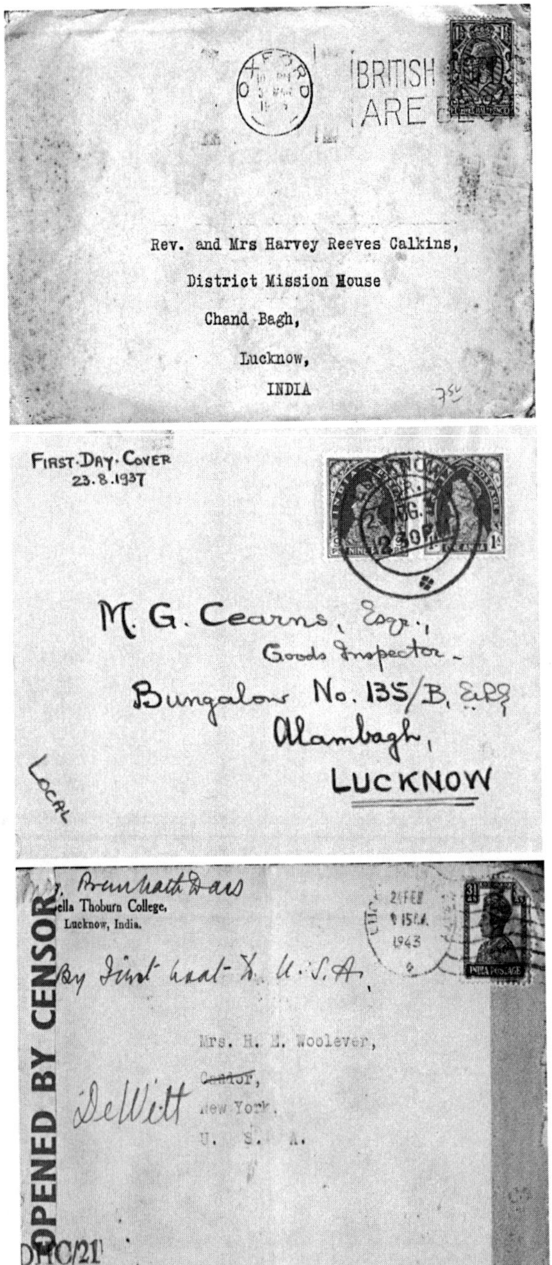
OXFORD
BRITISH
ARE
Rev. and Mrs Harvey Reeves Calkins,
District Mission House
Chand Bagh,
Lucknow,
INDIA
FIRST-DAY-COVER
23.8.1937
M. G. Cearns, Esqr.,
Goods Inspector.
Bungalow No. 135/B,
Alambagh,
LUCKNOW
LOCAL
Isabella Thoburn College,
Lucknow, India.
OPENED BY CENSOR
By First boat to U.S.A.
1943
INDIA POSTAGE
Mrs. H. E. Woolever,
New York,
U. S. A.
DeWitt
DHC/21

INDIA POST CARD

THE ADDRESS ONLY TO BE WRITTEN ON THIS SIDE

India Service Post Card.

(The address only to be written on this side; the address includes the signature and official designation of the senders.)

Regr. No. 893—1,931—24-10-02.

T. 144.

OUDH AND ROHILKHAND RAILWAY.

NOTICE OF ARRIVAL.

Station ______ 190

The undermentioned consignment addressed to you from ______ arrived here this day. Be good enough to send for same as soon as possible, as it will remain here entirely at your risk, and demurrage will accrue after midnight of the ______. When sending, please forward the original receipt and endorse thereon the name of the person to whom it is to be delivered.

Your Obedient Servant,

Station Master.

Nature of Consignment.	Address.	To Pay. Rs.	As.	P.
1 Trunk 238—		68	4	

Here enter date

Goods and Parcels will not be delivered unless the receipt granted for the same at sending station is given up. Should the receipt have been lost, an Indemnity Note, on a paper bearing an impressed stamp will be required...

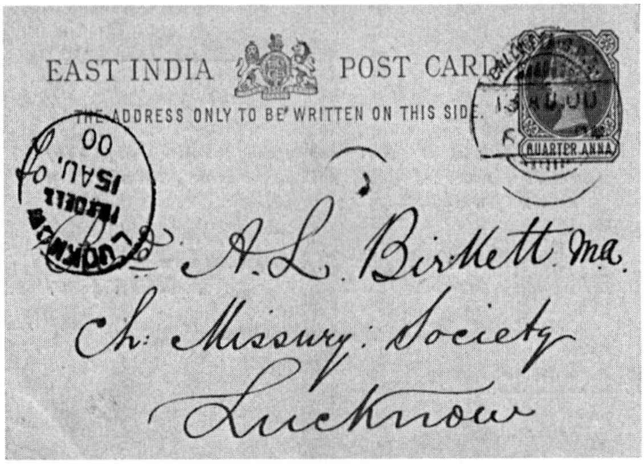

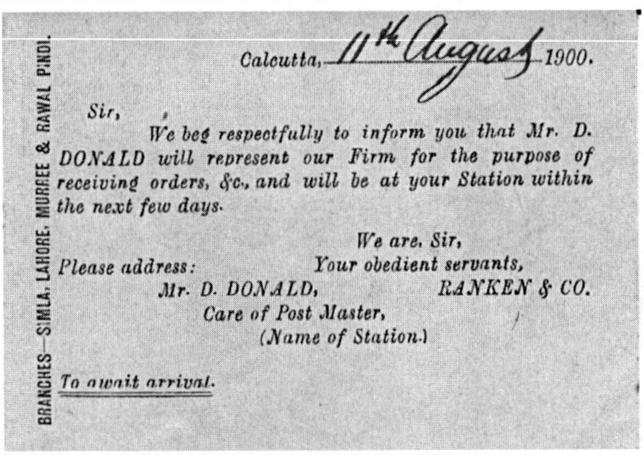

BRANCHES—SIMLA, LAHORE, MURREE & RAWAL PINDI.

Calcutta, 11th August 1900.

Sir,

We beg respectfully to inform you that Mr. D. DONALD will represent our Firm for the purpose of receiving orders, &c., and will be at your Station within the next few days.

We are, Sir,
Your obedient servants,
RANKEN & CO.

Please address:
Mr. D. DONALD,
Care of Post Master,
(Name of Station.)

To await arrival.

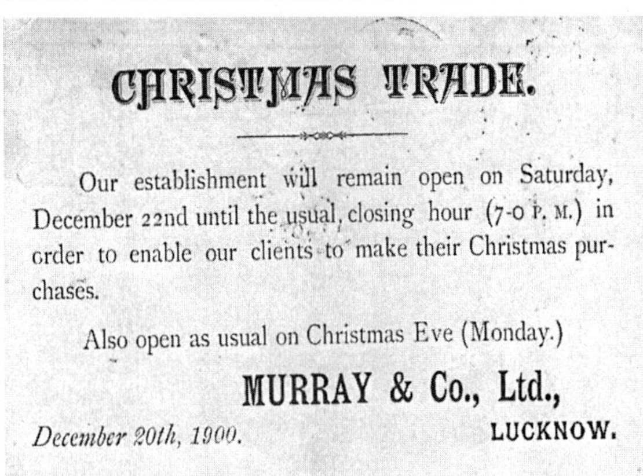

CHRISTMAS TRADE.

Our establishment will remain open on Saturday, December 22nd until the usual closing hour (7-0 P. M.) in order to enable our clients to make their Christmas purchases.

Also open as usual on Christmas Eve (Monday.)

MURRAY & Co., Ltd.,
LUCKNOW.

December 20th, 1900.

BY AIR MAIL
PAR AVION
CARD
LUCKNOW
DELY.
27 DEC. 35
DILKUSHA
DELY.
27 DEC. 35
5 – P.M.
LUCKNOW
Miss B. Heard,
Sandes Soldiers,
Lucknow,
United Provinces,
India

ON ACTIVE SERVICE
NO 175
UNIT CENSOR
B 217
Lieut
Mrs. R.N. Bourke.
Nathans Building
10. Lalbagh
Lucknow.
U.P.

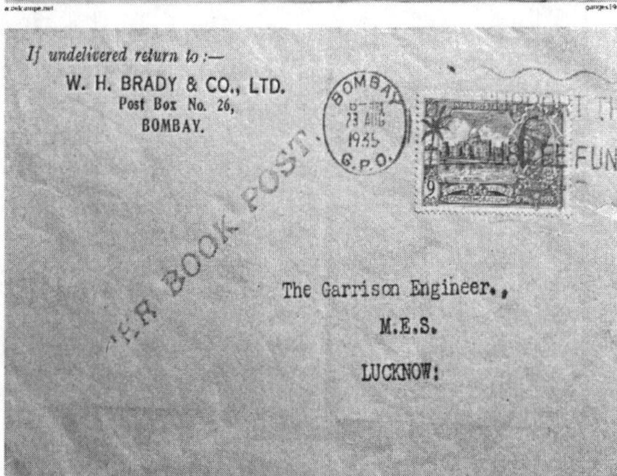
If undelivered return to :—
W. H. BRADY & CO., LTD.
Post Box No. 26,
BOMBAY.
BOMBAY
23 AUG
1935
G.P.O.
BOOK POST
The Garrison Engineer.,
M.E.S.
LUCKNOW:

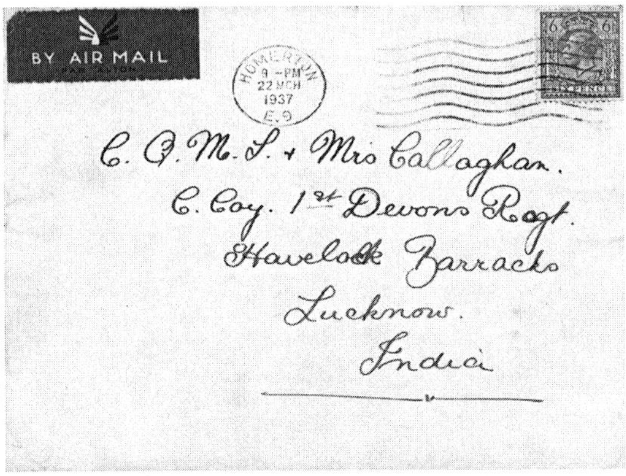

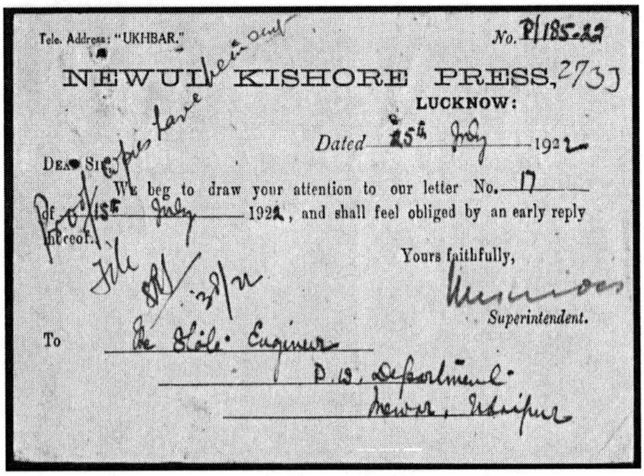
Tele. Address: "UKHBAR." No. P/185-22

NEWUL KISHORE PRESS, 2733

LUCKNOW:

Dated 25th July 1922

Dear Sir,

We beg to draw your attention to our letter No. 17 of 15th July 1922, and shall feel obliged by an early reply thereof.

Yours faithfully,

Superintendent.

To The State Engineer

P.W. Department

Mewar, Udaipur

Christmas and New Year Cards.

A very large and Choice Assortment of the latest and most Up-to-date Cards has just been received. We would advise an early selection, as the latest date for posting home, will be by the Mail leaving Lucknow on December 6th. We shall be glad to send carefully selected parcels to our Out-Station Customers to choose from.

PEAKE, ALLEN & CO.,
LUCKNOW.

Annexure - II

Colonial Lucknow Streets and Areas

Colonial Name	Present Status
Abbot Road	Vidhan Sabha Marg, Guru Govind Singh Marg, Gurudwara Road (in parts)
Alexander's Garden	Sikandar Bagh
Allum Nugger	Alamnagar
Ameenabad	Aminabad
Ameenabad Road	Nazirabad Road
Bagh Jagar Sahib	Vivekanand Puri
Bandariya Bagh Road	Vikramaditya Marg
Banks Road	BN (Bishweshwar Nath) Road
Barrow Road	Kunwar Jagdish Marg
Belaitee Bagh; Vilaiti Bagh; Willaitee Bagh	Vilayati Bagh
Blunt Square	Extant
Bruce's Bridge	Monkey Bridge (demolished; replaced by Hanuman Setu)
Bruce Ganj	Nishatganj
Buland Bagh Road	Nabiullah Road
Butler Ganj	Butler Palace Colony
Butler Road	Extant
Caesar's Garden	Kaiserbagh
Campbell Road	Extant
Canning Road	Hazrat Mahal Marg
Canning Street	Subhash Marg
Capper Road	Extant
Cassels Road	Extant
Chamberlain Road	Moti Mahal Road
Chandganj Khurd	Chota Chandganj
Chandganj Road	University Road
Chauk	Chowk
China Bazar Road	Osama Talha Road
Circular Road	Dr RK Tandon Road
Clay Square	Extant
Clive Road	Extant
Clyde Road	Rana Pratap Marg

Crommelin Road	Khun Khunji Road
Dil Khoosah	Dilkusha
Dilkushà Road	Kalidas Marg
Dollygunge	Daliganj
Forsyth Road	Dayanidhan Park Road
Frampton Square	Bansmandi Chauraha
Golah Gunge	Gola Ganj
Goral Purwa	Shakti Nagar
Grant Road	Bahadur Shah Marg
Gwynne Road	Extant
Hardinge Bridge	Pucca Pul / Lal Pul (Extant)
Havelock Road	Sarojini Naidu Marg
Havelock Road (Cantonment)	Usman Marg
Hewett Road	Shivaji Marg
Hope Road	Extant
Iron (Rennie's) Bridge	Demolished after 1960s floods; replaced by Daliganj Bridge
Jopling Road	Lajpat Rai Marg
Junglee Gunge	Jangali Ganj
Khealee Gunge	Khayali Ganj
King George's Medical College & Hospital	King George's Medical University
La Touche Road	Gautam Budh Marg
Lacknow Horticulture Gardens	National Botanic Gardens
Lady Dufferin Hospital	Veerangana Avanti Bai Mahila Chikitsalaya
Lalbagh Road	Newal Kishore Halwasiya Road
Lawrence Road	Newal Kishore Road
Lawrence Road (Cantonment)	Cariappa Road
Lawrence Terrace	Extant
Mahomed Bagh; Prophet's Garden	Extant (as Club)
Mall Avenue	Extant
Mall Road	Extant
Mayo Road	Subhash Marg (Cantonment)
McConaghey Free School	Christ Church College

Montgomery Road	Tagore Marg
Mowyah	Mawaiyya
Murriaon	Madiaon, Aliganj
Napier Road	Prabhu Dayal Marg
Napier Street	Hardoi Road
Narhai / Narhie	Narhi
Narhai Road	Ram Tirath Marg
Naval Road	Atal Road
Nayagaw	Naya Gaon
Neil Road	Rani Laxmibai Marg
Neil Road (Cantonment)	Lal Bahadur Shastri Marg
Oliver Road	Sapru Marg
Outram Road	Ashok Marg
Park Road	Ambedkar Marg
Peel Road	Rani Lakshmibai Marg
Pile Bridge	Replaced by Nishatganj Bridge after 1891 floods
Queensway / Civil Lines / the Mall / Huzrutgunge	Hazratganj
Quinton Road	Extant
Routledge Road	Valmiki Marg
Ruby Garden	Lalbagh
Saunder's Road	Madan Mohan Malviya Marg
Station Road	Motilal Nehru Marg
Strand Road	Mahatma Gandhi Marg
Sudder Bazaar	Sadar Bazar
Tal Kathura	Talkatora
Urjan Ganj	Arjun Ganj
Victoria Memorial Park	Begum Hazrat Mahal Park
Victoria Street	Tulsidas Marg
Wingfield Park	Wajid Ali Shah Zoological Gardens
Yahiaganj	Yahyaganj; Yahiyaganj

Annexure - III

The Canning College Act, 1922

[29th April, 1922]

Adopted and modified by the Adaptation of Laws Order, 1950 An Act to merge the Canning College in the University of Lucknow and to transfer all the property and liabilities of the Canning College to the University of Lucknow. Whereas by the Lucknow University Act, 1920, the University of Lucknow was constituted and founded at Lucknow with power to confer decrees and other distinctions and whereas the Canning College situate at Lucknow, hereinafter referred to as "the Canning College" has under section 46 of the said Act ceased to be a College affiliated to the University of Allahabad, and whereas the Governing Body of the Canning College are desirous and it is expedient that the Canning College should be merged in the University of Lucknow and maintained as a College, and that all its property and liabilities should be transferred to and vested in the University of Lucknow, hereinafter referred to as "the University", and whereas the previous sanction of the Governor General has been obtained under sub-section 80-A of the Government of India Act; It is hereby enacted as follows : 1. For Statement of Objects and Reasons, see Gazette, 1922, Part VIII, p. 82. Sec Gazette 1922, Part VII, p. 107.

1. **Short title**:

   This Act may by called The Canning College Act, 1922.

2. **Transfer of the College to the University:**

   From the commencement of this Act the Canning College shall be and become by virtue of this Act a College maintained by the University, and all property movable and immovable of every description and all endowments, rights and privileges of the Canning College which immediately before that date belonged to or were vested in that College shall, by virtue of this Act without any conveyance or other instrument be transferred to and vested in the University, and shall be applied to the objects and purposes of the Canning College as a College maintained by the University.

3. **Transfer of debts and liabilities:**

   From the commencement of this Act, all debts and liabilities of the Canning College shall by virtue of this Act be transferred and attached to the University, and shall thereafter be discharged and, satisfied by the University.

4. **Saving for agreements, deeds, actions, etc.** All agreements, articles, contracts, deeds and other instruments and all actions

and all proceedings and causes of action or proceedings which immediately before the commencement of this Act were existing or pending in favour of or against the Canning College shall continue and may be carried into effect enforced or prosecuted by or in favour of or against the University to the same extent and in like manner as if the University instead of the Canning College had been party to or interested in the same respectively.

5. **Adjustment of property and liabilities, etc.:**

(1) The University shall by agreement with the Governing Body of the Canning College as constituted immediately before the commencement of this Act adjust and settle and questions arising with respect to any endowments, powers, privileges authorities, debts, liabilities, obligations or expenses in which the parties to the agreements are interested and also with respect to any other College matters. (2) An agreement under this section may provide for the transfer, retention, division, apportionment or commutation of any endowments, property, debts, liabilities or obligations and for payment being made by either party to the other in respect of any such transfer, retention, division or apportionment or commutation or in respect of the salary or remuneration of any officer of person and generally may make as between the parties to the agreement any provisions necessary or proper for carrying into effect the purposes of this Act. (3) In default of agreement on any such question as aforesaid or so far as such agreement does not extend, the question shall be referred to a Board to Arbitration consisting of: (1) the Minister of Education, (2) one representative of the University, (3) one representative of the British Indian Association of Oudh, on the application of either party and their award may provide for any matter for which any agreement might have provided. Every such reference shall be deemed to be a submission to arbitration within the meaning of the Indian Arbitration Act, 1899, 1 and all the provisions of that Act, with the exception of section 2 thereof, shall apply accordingly: Provided that nothing in this section shall be deemed to affect the provisions of section 6 of the Canning College and British Indian Association Contribution Act, 1920. 1. See now the Arbitration Act, 1940 (Act No. X of 1940).

6. **Saving for existing staff:**

All Professors and other members of and persons attached to or associated with the teaching staff of the Canning College and all salaried or paid officers and servants of the Canning College shall hold as nearly as practicable the same offices and places in the

College as they held in the said College immediately before the commencement of this Act upon the same terms and conditions unless and until the University shall subject to the provisions of section 4, otherwise decided.

7. **Constitution of the Board of Management:**

Any power or right of the Government of 1[Uttar Pradesh] or any power or right of the British Indian Association of Oudh as such to be represented on the Governing Body of the Canning College shall from the commencement of this Act be transferred to and may be exercised by the University: Provided that upon any Board of Management of the Canning College appointed by the University under section 25 of the Lucknow University Act, 1920, not less than one-half of the members shall be persons who are members of the court of the University and are also members of the British Indian Association of Oudh. 1. Substituted by the AO 1950 for "the United Provinces".

8. **Contribution under U.P. Act IV of 1920:**

Nothing in this Act shall be deemed to affect the liability of persons named in section 3 of the Canning College and British Indian Association Contribution Act, 1920, to contribute in accordance with the provisions of that Act for the maintenance and support of the Canning College as a College maintained by the University.

Annexure - IV

Some Commercial Establishments in Colonial "Huzrutgunge"

Name	Commercial Service Provided
Dr Louis J Bischoff	Dental Surgeon (American)
M/s AC Nichols & Co.	Mechanical engg. firm
M/s Aktor & Company	Hairdressing salon
M/s AN James & Co.	Pharmacy
M/s Anderson Bros.	Tailors and outfitters
M/s Auto Stores	Dealer in motor cars
M/s Baejee Deote & Co.	Auctioneer
M/s Blackwood, Bryson & Co.	Typewriter dealer
M/s BN Mohan & Co.	Auditor
M/s Britannia Bookstall	Bookseller
M/s British Pharmacy	Chemists & Druggists
M/s British Radio House	Radio suppliers
M/s C Williams	Draper
M/s Carlton & Co.	Boot maker
M/s Charles Nephew & Co.	Exhibitors
M/s Charlton Crawshaw & Sons	Electrical contractor
M/s Chicago Telephone & Radio Co. (Motwane Bros.)	Radio and sound system suppliers
M/s Cooper & Co.	Aerated water manufacturer
M/s C Mull & Co.	Photographer
M/s Dare & Co.	Auctioneer
M/s DD Capur & Sons	Insurance services
M/s Devi Radiograms	Radio and sound system suppliers
M/s Electric Trading Co.	Electrical goods
M/s ER DeAbreu	Confectioners
M/s ES Beg & Co.	Leather goods
M/s Fitu	Ladies' corsets and apparel
M/s French Motor Car Co.	Dealer in motor cars
M/s GD Punn & Co.	Sterilised and aerated water supplier
M/s GW Lawrie & Co.	Photographer
M/s Harold Brothers	Hardware merchant
M/s Hathaway & Co.	Draper
M/s Hevzog & Co.	Cakes and confectioneries
M/s R. Hormusjee & Co.	Coach Builders, General merchants
M/s Ice Machine Supply Co.	Ice merchant
M/s J Pownes & Son	Boot maker

M/s Jewellers Ltd.	Jeweller
M/s JR Croke	Sterilised and aerated water supplier
M/s JR Fanthome & Co.	Auctioneer
M/s L Landau & Co.	Watch maker / repairer
M/s Lawrence & Mayo Ltd.	Opticians
M/s London House	Clothiers and drapers
M/s Lucknow Engineering & Electric Works	Electrical contractor
M/s M. Rubenstein & Co.	Cosmetics and costumes
M/s Mangal Prasad & Sons	Hosiery works
M/s Minoo & Dinshaw	Watch dealer, silverware,
M/s Moore & Co.	Dress maker
M/s Murray & Co.	General merchant
M/s Muthra Dutt & Co.	Trophies, souvenirs and memorabilia
M/s Nortons	Ladies tailor
M/s NL Roy & Co.	Watch maker / repairer
M/s Oriental Motor Car Co.	Dealer in motor cars
M/s Oudh Cocogem & Provision Store	Chemists & Druggists; provisions; wine and liquor
M/s Oudh Motor Works	Dealer in motor cars
M/s Peake, Allen & Co.	Chemists & Druggists, stationery items
M/s Perry & Co.	Watch maker / repairer/ jeweller
M/s Ramble & Co.	Engineering contractor
M/s Remington Rand Inc.	Typewriter dealer
M/s Rufener & Co.	Jewellers
M/s Saldana & Sons	Dealer in musical instruments
M/s Salon-De-Musiq	Dealer of musical instruments, gramophones
M/s SH Clarke & Co.	Provisions, including wines
M/s Sharman & Co.	Electrical contractor
M/s Sohrabjee	Wine merchant
M/s Standard Electric Company	Electrical contractor
M/s Standard Radio Corporation	Radio suppliers
M/s Standard Typewriting Co.	Typewriter dealer
M/s Taraporewala	Sewing Machines
M/s Upper India Electrical & Mill stores	Electrical contractor
M/s Upper India News Agency	News agent
M/s W Achenwall	Chemists & Druggists
M/s Whiteaway, Laidlaw & Co.	Departmental Store
M/s Wood & Metal Works	Furniture makers
Madame Kate Allen	Dress maker
M/s Viccajee's	Automobile showroom

Annexure - V

Establishment of Lucknow Zoo

Copy of the Memorandum and Rules and Regulations of the Association of the Prince of Wales Zoological Garden, Lucknow registered on the 17th August 1926

REGISTRAR OF JOINT STOCK COMPANIES

SEAL

U.P., AGRA AND OUDH

1. The name of the Society is "The Association of the Prince of Wales Zoological Gardens, Lucknow."
2. The objects for which the Association is established are as follows:
   (1) To maintain a Zoological Garden in Lucknow.
   (2) To provide recreation, instruction and amusement to all classes of the community subject to any limitation and restriction that the Association may impose.
   (3) To provide facilities for observation of habits of animals.
   (4) To breed, acclimatize and domesticate animals.
   (5) To promote the Science of Zoology.
   (6) To do all things that are incidental or conducive to for the attainment of objects mentioned above.

List of Members of the Governing Body to whom by the Rules of the Association the management is entrusted:

1. Commissioner, Lucknow Division, Lucknow.
2. Raja Muhammad Ejaz Rasul Khan C.I.E., President, Jahangirabad, District Barabanki.
3. Chaudhari Mujtaba Husain, Bar-at-Law, Hony. Secretary, Lucknow
4. Khan Bahadur Shaikh Makbul Hussain, C.I.E, Magistrate and Collector, Jaunpur.
5. Rai Bahadur Kunwar Ram Bahadur Sah, Singahi, District Kheri.
6. Hon'ble 2nd Lieut. Nawab Muhammad Ahmed Said Khan C.I.E., M.B.E., Chattari, District Bulandshahr.
7. Raja Suraj Buksh Singh, O.B.E., Kasmanda, District Sitapur.
8. W.E. Betting Esqr., Lucknow.
9. Chairman, Improvement Trust, Lucknow.
10. Chairman, Municipal Board, Lucknow.
11. Babu Bishan Narain Bhargava, Lucknow.

12. Superintendent, Horticultural Gardens, Lucknow.
13. Dr K.N. Bahl, M.Sc., D. Phil., Professor, Lucknow University, Lucknow.
14. Curator, Lucknow Museum, Lucknow.
15. Raja Indrajit Pratab Bahadur Sahi, Tamkohi, District Gorakhpur.
16. Nawab Ghulam Hussain, Golaganj, Lucknow.

We the undersigned wish to form ourselves into a Society to be registered under the Societies Registration Act (Act XXI of 1860) in pursuance of the above Memorandum of Association.

1. Sd/- W.S. Cassels, Commissioner 4.8.26
2. " Trilok Nath Bhargava, Chairman, Municipal Board.
3. " Bishan Narain Bhargava.
4. " Nawab Ghulam Hussain, Golaganj, Lucknow.
5. " W.E. Betting.
6. " Prayag Dayal, Curator, Provincial Museum.
7. Sd/- Mujtaba Husain.

Witness to the above signatures:

Sd/- Ishtiaq Ali

2, Mall Road, Lucknow.

Introduction

His Excellency Sir Harcourt Butler, G.C.I.E., K.C.S.I., the then Governor of the United Provinces convened a meeting at Government House, Lucknow on the 20th November, 1921 of the provinces of Agra and Oudh to consider the proposal for commemorating the visit of his Royal Highness the Prince of Wales to these Provinces. Since the need for a Zoo for the Province had been long felt, his Excellency's suggestion to establish a Zoological Garden in Lucknow as memorial of the Royal visit was unanimously and most enthusiastically accepted. Subscription amounting to Rs 7,30,357/- were promised at the meeting and Col. J.C. Faunthorpe, C.I.E., O.B.E., Commissioner, Lucknow Division and Shaikh Makbul Husain, C.I.E., Registrar of Cooperative Societies were appointed by his Excellency as President and Secretary of the Movement Committee of Management was formed consisting of donors and others.

The original site selected for the location of the large portion of the Zoo was the low lying land on the east of Wingfield Park, but it had to be discarded as unsuitable for the purpose, after the experience of the flood of 1923 and only small portion of it has been retained for water fowl and aquatic exhibits. The Zoo has therefore been located in the Wingfield Park area, the whole of which will be converted into the Zoological Garden subject to the condition that the Baradari and the ornament garden and park found it are maintained as at present. It is intended that the admission to the Park will for the present be free. Since the ground is the property of Government, it has been placed at the disposal of the Prince of Wales Zoological Garden Committee for the purpose of extension and development of the Zoo.

The chief features of the Scheme of Management of the institution of memorial of his Royal Highness, the Prince of Wales are:

1. To provide recreation, instruction and amusement for all classes of the community.
2. To facilitate scientific observations of the habits of animals.
3. To encourage the acclimatisation, domesticate and breeding of animals.
4. To improve the science on Zoology by adopting suitable means.

The Gardens Committee have already fulfilled some of the obligations by collecting a large variety of animals both by means of purchase and as presents from generous donors. They have erected paddocks for deer and antelopes, aviaries for birds and houses for carnivora, where the exhibits are on view. The designs of the structures and buildings of the Zoo are unique in many ways and the crowds which are attracted to the place bear ample evidence of the interest shown in it by the public. The success of the establishment of the Zoo as an attractive place for the recreation, instruction and amusement for all classes of the community is no longer in doubt. It is an established fact and no further justification is necessary for its existence. It does provide the greatest pleasure to the greatest number.

RULES

Constitution of the Prince of Wales Zoological Garden Association

MEMBERS

A. Extraordinary members

PATRON

President of the Association

One or more Vice Presidents

DONORS

1. Life Governors:

Life Governors are donors of Rs 19,000/- and upwards and also either persons who by their special interest and influence have assisted in the development and success of the Zoo.

2. Life Members:

   Life members are donors of Rs 5000/- and upward. They shall have their names inscribed on a tablet to be put up at a conspicuous place in the Zoo.

3. Honorary Members:

   Honorary members are donors of Rs 1,000/- and upwards. They shall have their names entered on a list which will be placed inside the Zoo at a frequented place.

4. Ordinary Members:

   Ordinary members are donors of Rs 250/- and upwards and others who may be their special fitness be selected as member and who otherwise would not become member of their own accord.

   The number of members of the Association will be unlimited.

REGISTRAR OF JOINT STOCK COMPANIES

SEAL

U.P., AGRA & OUDH

This Committee is the chief administrative body for the management of the Zoo. It consists of a Chairman and an Honorary Secretary both appointed by Local Government and twelve members, six of whom elected by the Association, the Chairman of the Improvement Trust, Lucknow, the Chairman of the Lucknow Municipal Board and one member to be elected by the Executive Council of the Lucknow University. The remaining three to be co-opted by the Committee of Management by reason of their usefulness for the Committee of Management.

The Prince of Wales Zoological Gardens has been instituted. It is maintained at the cost of the members of the Association aided by the Government.

1. This Association shall meet once a year on a date to be fixed by order of the President or oftener if the President desires.
2. The Honorary Secretary of the Association will ordinarily be the Chairman of the Committee of Management unless the President may appoint some other person.
3. At its annual meeting the Association will (a) Consider the annual report of the Committee of Management, (b) Pass the Budget and the annual account submitted by the Committee of Management and (c) Frame proposals for the development and extension of the Gardens and the efficiency of its management.
4. Any member of the Association shall be entitled to receive at the

meeting any information which he may require respective the management and the affairs of the Garden.

5. The information shall so far as possible be furnished provided a requisition in writing is made by the member or sent to the Secretary of the Association before the date and time of the meeting specifying clearly the information required.
6. Notice of the date, time and place of the meeting will be issued to the members by the Secretary at least thirty days before the date of the meeting.
7. Eleven members shall form a quorum. No quorum will be required for an adjourned meeting.
8. The minutes of the meeting shall be recorded by the Secretary in a special book and will be signed by the President.

COMMITTEE OF MANAGEMENT

1. The members of this Committee shall be elected for a period of three years and will be eligible for re-election.
2. The time of the sitting members will expire at the end of the current year. Fresh election of the members of this committee will be made before the end of the current year for the period beginning from the year 1929.
3. This committee will ordinarily hold its meetings quarterly
4. The date of the meeting will be fixed by order of the Chairman and the Honorary Secretary shall cause the notice of the date, time and place of the meeting issued to the members
5. Five members including the Chairman and Honorary Secretary shall for a quorum. For an adjourned meeting quorum will not be required.
6. At its meeting the Committee will dispose all business concerned with the duties devolving on this executive body.

The Garden will be managed by the Committee of Management through its Chairman and Honorary Secretary with a paid establishment.

The ordinary duties of the Committee are:

1. The custody and disposal of the funds of the Zoo.
2. To determine the cost and number of paid establishment.
3. To fix the standard of food of animals and its cost.
4. To make the alignment of roads, paths, and sites and to prepare the structures for the reception of animals.

5. To make rules and byelaws for the preservation of order for the custody and disbursement of funds and for other matters connected with the administration of the Zoo.
6. To accept contributions and to collect subscriptions and donations.
7. To purchase, exchange and dispose of the stock.
8. To control and supervise the income and expenditure of the funds.
9. To prepare the annual budget of the income and expenditure of the Gardens.
10. To lease or acquire land for the purpose of the Zoo.
11. To do all other acts compatible with the internal economy and improvement and extension of the Gardens.

The Chairman of the Committee of Management will exercise all or any of the powers which the Committee may delegate to him.

The Chairman shall have emergency powers which he may exercise subject to the approval of the Committee.

The Honorary Secretary shall be the Chief Executive Officer-in-Charge of the Gardens under the control of the Chairman.

The paid establishment of the Garden will be under the orders of the Honorary Secretary.

The Superintendent of the Zoo will exercise control over the paid staff of the Gardens and will be primarily responsible for every detail of Management of the Gardens.

The appointment, dismissal and punishment of the employees of the Zoo will be made by the Chairman and the Secretary in the following manner:

The Chairman will deal with cases of employees of the Gardens drawing salary of above rupees fifty while the Honorary Secretary will exercise the same power in case of servants of the Gardens on a salary below rupees fifty.

The Honorary Secretary shall be in-charge of the Garden's Offices and shall carry on all correspondence except when Government is to be addressed. The Chairman will correspond with the Government.

The Committee of Management shall frame Regulations from time to time for the preservation of orders in the Zoo and for the protection of animals and Gardens.

We, the undersigned certify that it is a correct copy of the original rules of the Association.

1. Sd/- W.S. Cassels, President, 4.8.26
2. " Bishen Narain Bhargava
3. " Mujtaba Husain, Assistant Secretary.

Annexure - VI

Establishment of Lucknow Museum

(Extract from Minutes of The Management Committee from August 1883 to 31st March 1888, The North-Western Provinces and Oudh Provincial Museum, Lucknow)

The want of a public Museum having been much felt in Oudh, a province which had in other respects taken the lead in the civilisation of North-West India, Colonel Abbott, then Commissioner of Lucknow Division (June 1862), solicited the aid of Government in establishing a Museum at Lucknow, proposing to locate the institution in the Lal Baradari building under the superintendence of an efficient Curator on Rs 500 a month, with a subordinate establishment, the cost of which was estimated at Rs 200 a month.

The proposal was not sanctioned by the Government of India on financial grounds.

In March of the following year, 1863, Colonel Abbott again made a strong representation on the subject to the Chief Commissioner.

The Chief Commissioner, while acknowledging the benefits that would be derived by establishing a Central Museum at Lucknow and placing it under the superintendence of Dr Bonavia, whose scientific attainments duly qualified him for the charge, did not sanction the use of the Lal Baradari building for a Museum, but added that he would make over the large Baradari*, which was formerly used as a jail, provided that arrangements were made to remove the Police Hospital, which then occupied the latter building to some other place.

The large Baradari was inspected by the Commissioner and Dr Bonavia and was found unsuitable for a Museum. Accordingly, it was suggested that the institution could not be better located than in the Tara Kothi, which was used as an observatory during the Native Government.

The use of the Tara Kothi for the Museum was sanctioned by the Chief Commissioner (13th June, 1863).

In July 1863, the Commissioner suggested the constitution of an organised body for the conduct of the affairs of the Museum, and a committee composed of the following gentlemen was formed with the approval of the Chief Commissioner:

- E.G. Fraser, Esq.
- W. Handford, Esq.

* Possibly the Sikche Wali Baradari was being referred here

- Dr Skelton
- Charles Currie, Esq.
- Colonel Barrow, C.B.
- Nawáb Mohsan-ud-daula
- Babu Dakhina Ranjan Mukerji Bahádur
- Mahárája Mán Sinha Bahádur, Kaīm-i-Jung
- Dr. Bonavia, M.D.

There appears a break in the correspondence at this stage of the proceedings; but it is clear that a Museum was opened in the Chatr Manzil building and the management of the institution was entrusted to Dr. Bonavia.*

By some mistake the Tara Kothi was leased to the Bank of Bengal, and it was in December, 1863, that the Commissioner again took up the question of a suitable building for the Museum and insisted on its being located in the Lál Baradari.

In December, 1864, Dr Bonavia submitted a report on the condition of the Museum as it then stood, from which it appears that the institution was maintained by a municipal grant of Rs 100 per mensem, and that it had created much interest among the native population of the province.

Colonel Barrow forwarded Dr Bonavia's report to Government, recommending that the monthly allowance be raised to Rs 200.

As the three years' lease on which the Bank of Bengal held the Tara Kothi had half expired about the end of March, 1863, and the authorities of the Bank were anxious to know if a fresh lease would be granted them after expiry of that period.

The Commissioner proposed to inform them that the building was required for other public purpose, i.e. for the Museum as was arranged before. The Commissioner's proposal was approved by the Chief Commissioner, and the Secretary, Bank of Bengal, was informed accordingly.

In March, 1867, Sir John (then Mr.) Strachey, Chief Commissioner of Oudh, intimated his desire to convert the Lál Baradari (which was then used as the Municipal Engineer's Workshops) into a Museum and requested the Commissioner of Lucknow to draw up a design and an estimate for carrying out the scheme, adding that the cost of the work shall fall on the Local Funds, and not on the Municipal Board of Lucknow.

---

* Emanuel W. Bonavia, born in July , 1829 was an authority on natural history, economic botany, and pioneered horticultural research in Lucknow. He was the first Superintendent of the Lucknow Provincial Museum and the founder of the Lucknow Horticultural Gardens.

The Municipal Engineer of Lucknow was requested, through the Deputy Commissioner, to prepare an estimate for the above project.

From a printed memorandum by the Chief Commissioner, dated 25th March, 1867, it appears that Dr. Bonavia, on his services as Assistant Civil Surgeon of Lucknow having been dispensed with by the Government, was appointed in 1867, Superintendent of the then newly created Department of Science in Oudh, which included among its functions the supervision of the Museum, the Observatory and the Agri-Horticultural Gardens of Lucknow, on a total monthly salary of Rs 900, of which Rs 300 was to be paid by the Municipality of Lucknow for his services as Health Officer of the station.

An estimate of Rs 190,035 for adapting the Lál Baradari into a Museum was sanctioned by the Chief Commissioner, and the institution was subsequently removed to that building.

At the instance of Colonel Barrow, Commissioner of Lucknow, a sub-committee composed of the following gentlemen was formed to discuss matters relating to the improvement of the Museum:

- Inspector General Innes, C.B. President
- Major Chamberlain
- Captain Lang, R.E
- Dr E Bonavia

As the funds of the institution were very limited, the sub-committee unanimously agreed to ask the Local Government to place at their disposal such sums as they considered necessary for the collection and preservation of exhibits and suggested that the district officers in Oudh be requested to send contributions to the Museum from their respective districts.

The attention of the Deputy Commissioners was directed to the necessity of lending support to the Museum, and they were requested to send specimens of coins which might be received in the Government treasuries, their bullion value being in all cases paid by Government.

After this (April 1868) there was no correspondence to show to what extent funds were allotted by Government for expenditure on the Museum, or when the latter was removed from the Lál Baradari.

In September, 1877, or a few months after the amalgamation, Dr Bonavia expressed a wish to resign his appointment, and the Local Government asked the Commissioner's opinion as to the best way of conducting the duties performed by that officer.

The Commissioner forwarded the Local Government's letter to Dr Bonavia, who suggested that some officer of the Educational Department should be placed in charge of the Museum, and named Mr Pirie as one qualified for the appointment.

Mr Pirie was recommended to Government for the Curatorship.

The Local Government remarked that although Mr Pirie was duly qualified for the Curatorship, his connection with the Canning College was, in their opinion, likely to prevent his exercising a close supervision over the subordinate establishment, and they therefore recommended Mr. Thorpe, late Superintendent of the Oudh Secretariat, for the proposed appointment.

The appointment was accordingly offered to Mr. Thorpe, who accepted it.

On Dr Bonavia's recommendation, one clerk on Rs 25 per month was allowed to the Museum.

Mr Thorpe submitted his resignation on the 30th August, 1878, and recommended Mr Joyce for his place.

Mr Thorpe's resignation was accepted, and Mr. Joyce was appointed to the charge of the Museum (September, 1878).

In January, 1883, Mr Benett, then Director in the Department of Agriculture and Commerce of these provinces, in consultation with Colonel Forbes, Commissioner of Lucknow, drew up a scheme for the better management of the Lucknow Museum, which was then in a declining state. The project was based on a detailed reported by Colonel Pitcher on the condition of the institution, from which the following facts came to light:

1. The income of the institution amounted to a little over Rs 2,500.
2. It was located in an incommodious building in the vicinity of the Lál Baradari, in which there was not sufficient room for the exhibits in the different sections.
3. It included nearly all the departments which it now represents.
4. A lump sum of Rs 1,000 was provided in the budget of the Agriculture Department for expenditure on the Museum.

In April 184, His Honor the Lieutenant-Governor and Chief Commissioner, in a visit to Lucknow, met the Members of the Museum Committee, and on the 18th of the same month the Secretary to Government conveyed His Honor's approval of the Committee's proposal to locate the Museum in the Lál Baradari, with the remark that the work of selecting and rejecting specimens from the old collection be undertaken without delay.

From a letter dated 7th July, 1884, from the Secretary, Managing Committee, to the address of the Commissioner, it appears that the work of removing the Museum to the Lál Baradari was completed by the end of June, 1884.

Annexure - VII

The Oudh Taluqdars' Relief Act, 1870

Act No. 24 of 1870

[7th *September,* 1870.]

Passed by the Governor General of India in Council.

(*Received the assent of the Governor General on the* 7th *September* 1870.)

An Act to relieve from encumbrances the estates of Taluqdárs in Oudh.

PREAMBLE.— WHEREAS many of the taluqdárs of Oudh are in debt, and their immoveable property is subject to mortgages, charges and liens; and whereas it is expedient to provide for their relief in manner hereinafter appearing; It is hereby enacted as follows:—

I— PRELIMINARY.

1. Short title.— This Act may be called "The Oudh Taluqdárs' Relief Act. "

2. Interpretation-clause.— In this Act—

'Chief Commissioner' means the Chief Commissioner of Oudh:

'taluqdár' means a person whose name is entered in the first of the lists mentioned in the Oudh Estates' Act, 1869, section eight:

'heir' means the person for the time being entitled under the same Act as heir to a taluqdár.

II—VESTING ORDER.

3. Power to vest management of taluqdár's property in an officer appointed by Chief Commissioner.—Whenever, within twelve months after the passing of this Act, any taluqdár,

or (when such taluqdár is an infant, or of unsound mind, or an idiot) his guardian, committee, or other legal curator,

or the person who would be heir to such taluqdár if he died intestate,

or (when such person is an infant, or of unsound mind, or an idiot) his guardian, committee, or other legal curator,

applies in writing to the Chief Commissioner, stating that the taluqdár is subject to, or that his immoveable property is charged with, debts of liabilities other than debts due, or liabilities incurred, to Government, and requesting that the provisions of this Act be applied to his case,

the Chief Commissioner may, with the previous consent of the Governor General of India in Council by order published in the local official Gazette, appoint an officer (hereinafter called the Manager), and vest in him the management of the immoveable property of or to which the taluqdár is then possessed or entitled in his own right, or which he is entitled to redeem, or which may be acquired by or devolve on the taluqdár or his heir during the continuance of such management.

4. Effect of order.— On such publication, the following consequences shall ensue:—

Bar of suits against taluqdár.— *first*, all proceedings in respect to such debts of liabilities which may then be pending in any Civil Court in British India, shall be barred; and all processes, executions and attachments for or in respect of such debts and liabilities shall become null and void;

Taluqdár freed from arrest.— *secondly*, so long as such management continues, the taluqdár and his heir shall not be liable to arrest for or in respect of the debts and liabilities to which the taluqdár was immediately before the said publication subject, or with which his immoveable property or any part thereof was then charged, other than debts due, or liabilities incurred, to Government;

and his moveable property from attachment for prior debts.— nor shall their moveable property be liable to attachment or sale, under process of any Civil Court in British India, for or in respect of such debts and liabilities other than as aforesaid; and

Cessation of his power to alienate.— *thirdly*, so long as such management continues,

(*a*) the taluqdár and his heir shall be incompetent to mortgage, charge, lease or alienate their immoveable property or any part thereof, or to grant valid receipts for the rents and profits arising or accruing therefrom,

Immoveable property freed from attachment.— and (*b*) such property shall be exempt from attachment or sale under such process as aforesaid, except for or in respect of debts due, or liabilities incurred, to Government.

III—DUTIES OF MANAGER.

5. Manager to receive rents and profits,—The Manager shall, during his management of the said property, receive and recover all rents and profits due in respect thereof; and shall, upon receiving such rents and profits, give receipts for the same.

From the sums so received, he shall pay—

and pay therefrom the Government demand,—*first*, the Government revenue, and all debts or liabilities for the time being due or incurred to Government in respect of the said property:

an annual sum for maintenance of the taluqdár and his heir,—*secondly*, such annual sum as appears to the Chief Commissioner requisite for the maintenance of the taluqdár, his heir and their families:

costs of repairs and improvements,— *thirdly*, the costs of such repairs and improvements of the property as appear necessary to the Manager and are approved by the Chief Commissioner:

costs of management, and the debts and liabilities.— and the residue shall be applied in discharge of the costs of the management, and in settlement of such debts and liabilities of the taluqdár and his heir and their immoveable property, as may be established under the provisions hereinafter contained.

IV.—SETTLEMENT OF DEBTS.

6. Notice to claimants against taluqdár.— On the publication of the order vesting in him the management of the said property, the Manager shall publish in the local official Gazette a notice in English and Urdú, calling upon all persons having claims against the taluqdár or his immoveable property to notify the same in writing to such Manager within three months from the date of the publication.

Copies of notice to be exhibited.—He shall also cause copies of such notice to be exhibited at the Tahsildárs' Kachahrís in the District or Districts in which the said property lies and at such other places as the Manager thinks fit.

7. Claim to contain full particulars.—Every such claimant shall, along with his claim, present full particulars thereof.

Documents to be given up.—Every document on which the claimant founds his claim, or on which he relies in support thereof, shall be delivered to the Manager along with the claim.

Entries in books.—If the document be an entry in any book, the claimant shall produce the book to the Manager, together with a copy of the entry on which he relies. The Manager shall mark the book for the purpose of identification, and, after examining and comparing the copy with the original, shall return the book to the claimant.

Exclusion of documents not produced.— If any document in the possession or under the control of the claimant is not delivered or produced by him to the Manager along with the claim, the Manager may refuse to receive such document in evidence on the claimant's behalf at the investigation of the case.

8. Debt or liability not duty notified, to be barred.—Every debt or liability (other than debts due, or liabilities incurred, to Government) to which the taluqdár is subject, or with which his immoveable property or any part thereof is charged, and which is not duty notified to the Manager within the time and in hereinbefore mentioned, shall be barred:

Provision for admission of claim within further period of nine months.—Provided that, when proof is made to the Manager that the claimant was unable to comply with the provisions of sections six and seven, the Manager may admit such claim within the further period of nine months from the expiration of the said period of three months.

9. Determination of debts and liabilities.—The Manager shall, in accordance with the rules to be made under this Act, determine the amount of the debts and liabilities due to the several creditors of the taluqdár and persons holding mortgages, charges or liens on the said property or any part thereof.

10. Appeal.—An appeal against any refusal, admission or determination under sections seven, eight or nine shall lie, if preferred within six weeks from the date of such determination, to the Commissioner of Division to whom the Manager is subordinate, and the decision of such Commissioner, or of the Manager if no such appeal has been so preferred, shall be final.

11. Scheme for settlement of debts and liabilities.—When the total amount of such debts and liabilities has been finally determined, the Manager shall prepare and submit to the Chief Commissioner a schedule of such debts and liabilities, and a scheme for the settlement thereof; and such scheme, when approved by the Chief Commissioner, shall be carried into effect.

Power to return scheme for revision.—Until such approval is given, the Chief Commissioner may, as often as he thinks fit, send back such scheme to the Manager for revision, and direct him to make such further enquiry as may be requisite for the proper preparation of the scheme.

12. Restoration of taluqdár to his property.—When all such debts and liabilities have been discharged,

or if, within six months after the publication of the order mentioned in section three, the Chief Commissioner thinks that the provisions of this Act should not continue to apply to the case of the taluqdár or his heir,

the taluqdár or his heir shall be restored to the possession and enjoyment of his immoveable property, or of such part thereof as has not been sold by the Manager under the power contained in section nineteen, but subject to the leases and mortgages (if any) granted and made by the Manager under the powers hereinafter contained.

Revival of barred proceedings and debts.—Where the taluqdár or his heir is so restored under the circumstances mentioned in the second clause of this section, the proceedings, processes, executions and attachments mentioned in section three (so far as they relate to debts and liabilities not settled by the Manager), and the debts and liabilities barred by section eight, shall be revived, and any mortgagee dispossessed under section seventeen shall be reinstated unless his claim under the mortgage has been satisfied;

and in calculating the periods of limitation applicable to such revived proceedings and to suits to recover and enforce such revived debts and liabilities, the time intervening between such restoration and the publication of the order mentioned in section three shall be excluded.

V.—POWERS OF MANAGER.

13. Power to call for further particulars.—The Manager may, from time to time, call for further and more detailed particulars of any claim preferred before, him under this Act, and may at his discretion refuse to proceed with the investigation of the claim until such particulars are supplied.

14. Power to summon witnesses and compel production of documents.— For the purposes of this Act, the Manager may summon and enforce the attendance of witnesses and compel them to give evidence, and compel the production of documents by the same means, and, as far as possible, in the same manner, as is provided in the case of a Civil Court by the Code of Civil Procedure.

15. Power to administer oaths.— The Manager may administer an oath in such form as he thinks fit to any person examined before him touching the matters to be enquired into under this Act.

16. Investigation to be deemed a judicial proceeding.— Every investigation conducted by the Manager with reference to any claim preferred before him under this Act, or to any matter connected with any such claim, shall be taken to be a judicial proceeding within the meaning of the Indian Penal Code.

Statements of persons examined, to be evidence.—And every statement made by any person examined by or before the Manager with reference to such investigation, whether upon oath or otherwise, shall be taken to be evidence within the meaning of the same Code (45 of 1860).

17. Manager to have powers of a taluqdar.—The Manager shall have, for the purpose of realising and recovering the rents and profits of the said immovable property, the same powers as the taluqdár would have had for such purpose if this Act had not been passed.

Power to remove mortgagee in possession.—And if such property, or any part thereof, be in the possession of any mortgagee, the Manager may apply to the Court of the Deputy Commissioner within whose jurisdiction the property is situate, and such Court shall cause the same to be delivered to the Manager as if a decree therefor had been made in his favour; but without prejudice to the mortgagee preferring his claim under the provisions hereinbefore contained.

18. Power to lease.—Subject to the rules made under section twenty, the Manager shall have power to demise all or any part of the said property, for any term of years not exceeding twenty years absolute, to take effect in possession, in consideration of any fine or fines, or without fine, and reserving such rents and under such conditions as may be agreed upon.

19. Power to raise money by mortgage or sale.—The Manager, with the previous assent of the Chief Commissioner, shall have power to raise any money which may be required for the settlement of the debts and liabilities (other than as aforesaid) to which the taluqdár is subject, or with which his immoveable property or any part thereof is charged,

by demising by way of mortgage the whole or any part of such property for a term not exceeding twenty years from the said publication,

or by selling, with the previous consent of the taluqdár and of the person (being of full age) who would be his heir if he died intestate, by public auction or by private contract, and upon such terms as the Manager thinks fit, such portion of the same property as may appear expedient.

And no mortgagee advancing money upon any mortgage made under this section, shall be bound to see that such money is wanted or that no more than is wanted is raised.

Manager's receipts.—And the receipt of the Manager for any monies paid to him upon any mortgage or sale made under this section, or for any rents or profits received by him under section five, shall discharge the person paying the same therefrom and from being concerned to see to the application thereof.

The power to mortgage conferred by this section shall not be exercisable until six months have elapsed from the publication of the order mentioned in section three.

VI—MISCELLANEOUS.

20. Power to make rules.—The Chief Commissioner may, from time to time, make rules consistent with this Act in all matters connected with its enforcement.

Such rules, when approved by the Governor General of India in Council, and published in the local official Gazette, shall have the force of law.

21. Power to appoint new Managers.—Whenever the Chief Commissioner thinks fit, he may appoint any officer to be a Manager in the stead of any Manager appointed under this Act; and thereupon the management then vested under this Act in the former Manager shall become vested in the new Manager.

Every such new Manager shall have the same powers as if he had been originally appointed.

22. Managers to be public servants.— Every Manager appointed under this Act shall be deemed a public servant within the meaning of the Indian Penal Code (45 of 1860).

23. Bar of suits.— No suit or other proceeding shall be maintained against any person in respect of anything done by him *bonâ fide* pursuant to this Act.

24. Petitions, &c., under Act exempt from Court fees.—No petition, application, memorandum of appeal or other proceeding under this Act, shall be chargeable under the Court Fees Act, 1870 (7 of 1870).

25. Saving of jurisdiction of Courts in Oudh in respect of certain suits.— Nothing in this Act precludes the Courts of the Province of Oudh, having jurisdiction in suits relating to the succession to or rights of persons claiming maintenance from any immoveable property brought under the operation of this Act, from entertaining and disposing of such suits; but to all such suits the Manager of such property shall be made a party.

Annexure - VIII

Colonial Administration and The Administrators of Oudh / NW Provinces / United Provinces

Post 1857, the reconstituted province of Awadh under colonial rule or Colonial Oudh / Oude had four administrative Divisions: (1) Lucknow - comprising the districts of Lucknow, Unnao and Barabanki, (2) Sitapur - comprising the districts of Sitapur, Hardoi and Lakhimpur Kheri, (3) Raebareli - comprising the districts of Raebareli, Sultanpur and Pratapgarh and (4) Faizabad - comprising the districts of Faizabad, Gonda and Bahraich.

The Chief Commissioner was in charge of the entire administration of the province; he reported to the Governor General at Calcutta. He was assisted in his day-to-day duties by the Civil Secretary, Military Secretary, Judicial Commissioner and Financial Commissioner.

The Chief Commissioner was the Executive Authority of the Province. He had authority and control in all administrative departments, including the police and military departments. He was also authorised to carry out all communication with the ex-King and his family members. He had a sanctioning power of Rs 10,000/- for any single expenditure involving public works, or grant payment under any head.

The Financial Commissioner was in charge of revenue administration of the province. He also had to carry out measures which would inspire people and inculcate faith in the British government in revenue matters, which included collection, settlement, surveys, excise and even pensions. He was the final authority in all suits related to land revenue.

The Judicial Commissioner was in charge of the judicial administration of the province, both civil and criminal; he also controlled the functioning of the jails. Strangely, he was also to look into the establishment and management of ferries for public transport. Although holding independent charge in the Province, it was expected of him to obtain permission from the Chief Commissioner, before issuing any circular or order.

Each Division in the Province had one Commissioner, assisted by three Deputy Commissioners. Therefore, Awadh had a total of four Commissioners and twelve Deputy Commissioners. In their multifarious duties, they would be assisted by Assistant, Extra Assistant Commissioners and Tehsildars in the lowest rungs of the colonial administration.

Chief Commissioners of Oudh (1856–1877)

Name	From	To	Remarks
James Outram	February 1856	May 1856	–
Colville Coverley Jackson	May 1856	March 1857	Officiating
Henry Montgomery Lawrence	March 1857	July 1857	Killed at Lucknow, July 1857
John Sherbrooke Banks	July 1857	September 1857	Killed at Lucknow, July 1857
James Outram	September 1857	April 1858	–
Robert Montgomery	April 1858	February 1859	–
Charles John Wingfield	February 1859	April 1860	–
Lousada Barrow	April 1860	April 1861	Officiating
George Udny Yule	April 1861	August 1865	Officiating
Robert Henry Davies	August 1865	March 1866	Officiating
John Strachey	March 1866	May 1868	–
Robert Henry Davies	May 1868	January 1871	Officiating, Confirmed March, 1868
Lousada Barrow	January 1871	April 1871	–
George EW Couper	April 1871	March 1875	Officiating, Confirmed, December, 1873
John Forbes David Inglis	March 1875	February 1877	Officiating

Lieutenant-Governors of the North-Western Provinces and Chief Commissioners of Oudh (1877–1902)

In 1877, the Office of Lieutenant Governor was merged with that of the post of Chief Commissioner of Oudh

Name	From	To	Remarks
George EW Couper	February 1877	April 1882	–
Alfred Comyn Lyall	April 1882	November 1887	–
Auckland Colvin	November 1887	November 1892	–
Charles HT Crosthwaite	November 1882	January 1895	–
Alan Cadell	January 1895	November 1895	Officiating
Anthony Patrick MacDonnell	November 1895	November 1901	–
James John D. La Touche	November 1901	March 1902	–

Lieutenant-Governors of the United Provinces of Agra and Oudh (1902–1921)

In 1902, the province was re-named the United Provinces of Agra and Oudh and the former Commissionership was abolished.

Name	From	To	Remarks
James John Digges La Touche	March 1902	January 1907	–
John Prescott Hewett	January 1907	September 1912	–
Leslie Alexander Porter	April 1910 April 1911	October 1910 December 1911	Officiating in Hewett's absence
James Scorgie Meston	September 1912	February 1917	–
Duncan Colvin Baillie	September 1913	November 1913	Officiating in Meston's absence
John Mitchell Holmes	February 1917	February 1917	Officiating
Spencer Harcourt Butler	February 1918	January 1921	–

Governors of the United Provinces of Agra and Oudh (1921–1937)

The Office of the Lt. Governor was upgraded in 1921

Name	From	To	Remarks
Spencer Harcourt Butler	January 1921	December 1922	–
Ludovic Charles Porter	December 1922	December 1922	Officiated for 3 days only
William Sinclair Marris	December 1922	January 1927	–
Samuel Perry O'Donnell	August 1926	December 1926	Officiating in Marris' absence
Alexander Philips Muddiman	June 1927	June 1928	–
William Malcolm Hailey	August 1928	December 1934	–
George Bancroft Lambert	October 1930	April 1931	Officiating in Hailey's absence
Mohammad Ahmad Said Khan	April 1933	November 1933	Officiating in Hailey's absence
Harry Graham Haig	December 1934	April 1937	–

Governors of the United Provinces under British India (1937 - 1947)

The United Provinces came into existence from April 1, 1937

Name	From	To	Remarks
Harry Graham Haig	April 1937	December 1939	–
Mohammad Ahmad Said Khan	April 1937	November 1937	Officiating in Haig's absence
Maurice Garnier Hallett	December 1939	December 1945	–
Francis Verner Wylie	December 1945	August 14, 1947	Succeeded by Sarojini Naidu on August 15, 1947

Annexure - IX

Colonial Railways: Oudh & Rohilkund (BG) and Rohilkund & Kumaon (MG)

The Oudh and Rohilkund / Rohilkhand Railway (O&RR) was formed in 1872 by taking over the interests of the "Indian Branch Railway" / "Awadh Rohilkhand Railway." It had its headquarters at Lucknow. The Company connected Lucknow and Hardoi, Lucknow and Barabanki and Moradabad to Chandausi. It laid tracks from Benaras to Lucknow in 1874, with an extension to Faizabad known as the Fyzabad Loop.

The 4 miles long Broad Gauge (BG) line from Burhwal to Bahramghat and 17 miles long Burwhal to Bara Banki Metre Gauge (MG) line were opened on April 1, 1872, as part of the Bahramghat branch of the Oudh and Rohilkhand Railways. Upon conversion to mixed gauge, the Metre Gauge track formed part of the Cawnpore-Burhwal Railway, which was managed as part of the Oudh and Rohilkhand Railways. The Oudh and Rohilkhand Railway was merged with the East Indian Railways on July 1, 1925 but this section of the Cawnpore to Burhwal Railway was operated by the Bengal and North Western Railway and was transferred to the Oudh and Tirhut Railway on January 1, 1943. The 2 miles long metre gauge line from Benares Cantonment to Benares City was opened in 1899 as the Benares City branch of the Oudh and Rohilkhand Railway.

The first Broad Gauge (BG) station at Lucknow, served the Oudh and Rohilkhand Railway from its opening in 1867. In 1888, the Government of India took over the Oudh and Rohilkhand Railways making it a Government-run enterprise. In 1925, it was merged with East Indian Railway Company. Lucknow Junction Station was situated right next to Lucknow Charbagh Station and was the original station serving the Rohilkund and Kumaon Railway (R&KR) Metre Gauge (MG). On April 14, 1952, the Northern Railway zone was created by merging Jodhpur Railway, Bikaner Railway, Eastern Punjab Railway and three Divisions of the East Indian Railway. The present day office of the Divisional Regional Manager of Lucknow Division, Northern Railway occupies the modified colonial building which was once the Headquarters of the O & RR in Hazratganj, Lucknow.

The Rohilkund and Kumaon Railway (R&KR) was a metre gauge (MG) railway in India covering a total network of 592 miles (953 km). The Company was founded in 1883 (registered on October 6, 1882), by Scottish railway engineer Alexander Izat, who was also the Company Director until 1904. Izatnagar (present day Izzatnagar) in Bareilly is named in honour of Izat, who specialised in Bridge Engineering and came to Izatnagar in 1896. The Rohilkund and Kumaon Railway was transferred to the Government of India and merged into the Oudh and Tirhut Railway on January 1, 1943. Post Independence in 1952, the Oudh and Tirhut Railway became part of North Eastern Railway, a Zone of Indian Railway.

Annexure - X

Lingua Franca

With the passage of time, in addition to developing a home-grown hybrid architectural style, Awadh in general and Lucknow in particular also adopted the usage of several terms / words, derived from different languages, especially Arabic, *Farsi* (Persian), Hindustani and old English. An indicative, if not exhaustive list of this pidgin *lingua franca* is provided below for general readers as well as for researchers. The colonial inflexions, commonly used during colonial rule are particularly interesting.

Adawlat; Adawlut	*Adālat*; Court of Justice
Aarzii	Interim; provisional
Acbar	*Akbar* (Mughal Emperor)
Achkan	Knee length coat with circular collar, buttoned at the top
Affghan; Affghanistan	Afghan; Afghanistan
Ainawala Kothi	*Aine Wali Kothi* (demolished; present day *Hindi Sansthan*)
Ajmir	Ajmer, Rajasthan
Ajodhya; Ajoodiah	Ayodhya (town)
Ala	Superior / senior
Alexander's Garden	Sikandar Bagh
Allee	Ali (name)
Allyghur	Aligarh (town)
Almairah; Almirah	Wardrobe
Almasi (brick)	Larger than the usual *lakhauri* bricks popular as a building material in the Indian sub-continent, till early 20th century
Almorah	Almora (town)
Alumbagh	Alambagh (palace complex in Lucknow)
Amraoti	Amravati
Andaz	Style; mannerism
Andaz karna	To guess
Anglo-Indian	Eurasian; person of mixed parentage - one European and the other Indian or "native"
Arazi	Area
Ardali	Orderly, peon; lowly employee physically delivering files and papers
Áriyat	Loan
Arzi; Arzii	Petition; application
Asil; Aseel	Breed of ferocious fighter cock, rooster
Asmani	Sky blue

Astabal	Stable for horses
Atqiyaa	Pious, virtuous person
Aumeen	*Amin*; trustee
Avval	*Awwal*; outstanding; in first position
Ayah	Maidservant; matron
Azadari; Āzādāri	Mourning rituals, particularly connected with observance of Muharram
Azimgarh	Azamgarh (town)
Baadnaa	To stake a wager; to bet
Baandi	Maidservant
Baboo, Babu	Clerk
Badami	Almond shaped; colored
Badarnavisi	Audit
Badnaseeb	Unfortunate
Badshah Salamat	May God Preserve the King (salutation)
Bagheecha	(Fruit) garden
Bagla; bagula	Heron (bird)
Bahadoor	*Bahadur*; brave (honorary title)
Bahrii safar	Journey across the seas
Baksheesh; Backsheesh	Tip, pourboire
Bakshi	Paymaster
Bamba	Tap (water)
Bangash; Bangash Pathan	Tribe of ethnic Pashtuns from Afghanistan
Banyan; Bunnian; Bunneah	*Bania;* native Hindu trader / merchant
Bāqirkhāni	Crisp flat bread made of milk, sugar, flour and butter / clarified butter
Baradari; Baradwari; Baraduree	A building or pavilion with twelve entrances (or more), generally used for religious discourses
Barabunkee	Barabanki (town)
Baraitch / Baraich	Bahraich (town / district)
Barawafat	12th day of Islamic month *Rabi-ul-Awal*, signifying the death of the Prophet; *Milad-ul-Nabi*
Barek	Barracks (military)
Barkat	Blessing
Barrackpoor; Barrackpore	A military establishment on the outskirts of Calcutta, built by the British in 1772
Basti	Small settlement
Batta	*Bhatta*; allowance
Baug	*Bagh*; garden
Bawarchi	Royal chef / chef / cook
Bayan karna	To relate; relate

Bayli-garad	Baillie Guard gate (of Lucknow Residency)
Bazuband	Armlet
Bedaag	Literally "spotless." Breed of homing pigeon
Begum; Begam	Lady with title
Belaspore	Bilaspur (town)
Beldar	Labourer engaged in digging / excavating works
Beloochi	Thoroughbred horse (from Afghanistan)
Berra	Bearer; steward, as in a restaurant or club
Bhagaruttee	Bhagirathi river
Bharti karna	To enlist
Bhisti	*Bhishti*, goatskin water carrier
Bhoota	*Bhutta;* corn
Bhudist	Buddhist
Bhung	*Bhang*; hemp
Bhurtpore	Bharatpur (town)
Bigha	The *bigha* or *beegah* (Persian: بیگھا, Hindi: बीघा), roughly equal to 17500 sq. ft, is unit to measure land area, traditionally used in northern & eastern parts of India
Biradari	Clan
Biryani	Rice and meat dish, with the rice being infused by the flavors of the meat
Bismillah	An invocation used by Muslims at the beginning of an auspicious task
Biswa	Twentieth share (of land / property)
Bitur	Bithoor (town)
Boolund;	*Buland; bulandi*; elevated; of eminence
Bowlee	*Baoli*; step well
Box-walla	Travelling merchant; peddler with merchandise arranged in a metal box
Brumma	Lord Brahma, the Creator in the Hindu pantheon of Gods
Buckram; Bokeram	Stiffener in clothing e.g. collars; also book covers and hats
Buckree Ede	*Bakra-Eid*; Muslim festival *of Eid-ul-Zuha*
Budmash	Ruffian
Bugeros; Budgerows	Old-style boats, at least 60 feet in length, with a single mast and square sail
Bullea	Ballia (town in eastern Uttar Pradesh)
Bund	Embankment
Buniyaad	Foundation
Burkandaaz	Armed guard
Burra Sahib	The "big boss", typically British, in colonial India
Burrumpooter	Brahmaputra river

Bylee	Native carriage
Byrynji	Made of brass
Cabooli	Thoroughbred horse (from Afghanistan)
Cabul	Kabul (city)
Caesar's Garden	*Kaiserbagh*
Caly Yug; Calyoogum	*Kalyug*; fourth and present stage of civilisation according to Hindu belief
Candela	*Chandela* (Rajput tribe)
Canoongo	*Kanungo*; a Revenue Officer
Cashmere	Kashmir (state)
Cawnpore	Kanpur (city)
Chabutra	Tower-like structure with octagonal or pentagonal shaped open enclosure, found typically in Rajasthani architecture, later adopted by Mughals
Chajja	An overhanging eave or roof covering, found typically in Rajasthani architecture, later adopted by Mughals
Chaka Kothi; Chukkar Kothi	Chakkar Wali Kothi; Nasir-ud-Din Haider's race stand (no longer extant)
Chakla; Chakladar / Nazim	Administrative division under a province; person heading the *chakla*
Chandernagore	Chandannagar (town) in Hooghly district, West Bengal; formerly French settlement
Chapkan; Chupkan	A tight fitting long coat
Chappa-chappa	Every nook and corner
Chappar	Thatched
Char-diwari; Chahaar-diwari	Boundary; walled enclosure
Chattri	Elevated, dome-shaped pavilion used as an element in Indo-Islamic architecture
Chauk; Choke	*Chowk*; old market of Lucknow, Delhi; cross-roads
Chaupar	Traditional cross and circle board game; cruciform
Chaupoutre	*Chabutra*; platform
Cheraug	*Chirag*; small Indian lamp
Chick	Curtain made of thread and strips of bamboo
Chikni Dali	Betel nuts boiled in milk
Chilamchii; Chillumchee	Wash stand, basin; wide bowl
Chinam	*Chunam*; lime based plaster; may contain crushed sea shells
Chirag, Charag	Oil lamp
Chit	A brief letter or note
Chittel	*Chital;* spotted deer
Chobdar; Chubdar	Attendant bearing a staff

Chokedar; Chokidar; Chowkidar	*Chaukidar*; guard; watchman
Chokra (boy)	Deprecatory term for servant boy
Chongli	Conical packing made of metal / fabric / paper, for presenting individual servings of *pān*
Chota Hazry	Early morning breakfast
Choultry; Tschultri; Choltri	Rest house / inn for travellers
Chownee, Chaoni	*Chavni*; garrison, military outpost
Chowpeyra Istubul	*Chaupar Astabal*; Nawabi cruciform stable
Chucker; Chukker	Wheel; circle
Chudder	*Chadar*; (bed) sheet
Chukerbutty	*Chakravarty*; title of Bengali Brahmins
Chupatty	*Chapati*; Indian flat bread, unleavened
Chupkun	*Chapkan*; cassock worn by males in north India
Chuprass; Chuprassy; Chupprassie	A metal badge worn by a peon; lowly employee physically delivering files and papers
Chuttree	Kshatriya (Rajput)
Chuttur Munzil	Chattar Manzil (palace) in Lucknow
Circar	*Sarkar*; government
Civilian	Employee of ECI without military rank
Colney Hatch	A lunatic asylum, term being inspired by a similar asylum near London
Company Gardens; Company Baugh	Colonial-style gardens created by the British, often after modifying existing Mughal-style or Nawabi-style gardens
Compleat	Complete
Connouge; Kanog; Kanouj	Kannauj (town)
Consumah; Khansamah	Steward
Coolie	Porter; labourer
Cootub, The	Qutub Minar, Delhi
Country born	Europeans born in India
Culpee	Kalpi (town)
Cummerbund	Waist-cloth
Cutcherry	*Katchery*; courthouse
Cutwal; Katwal	*Kotwal*; police chief
Daad-raasi	Justice; one who seeks justice
Dāk	Mail (postal)
Dāk Gharry	Horse-drawn carriage or "coach", carrying mail; often allowing upto four passengers to travel inside and one passenger with the driver, on payment basis.
Dali	Basket
Darbar	Court

Daroga; Darogah	Superintendent (of police); officer-in-charge
Daroga-e-Bawarchikhana	In-charge of kitchen
Dastan	Saga
Dastarkhwan	Tablecloth, which is spread on the ground, floor, or table and is used as a sanitized surface for serving food
Dastpanah	Kitchen tongs
Deccan	*Dakshin*, southern part of the Indian sub-continent
Dekkanee	Belonging to the southern states
Demooltee	Dhanaulti (hill station)
Deobund	Deoband, town in Saharanpur district, famous for its Islamic seminary called *Darul Uloom*
Deodhi; Dyodhi	Mansion with a porch
Dewan; Diwan	Revenue collector, subordinate to a *Zamindar* or European Collector
Dewanee Khas	Hall of Audience (in a palace)
Dewanny	*Diwani;* Right to collect revenue and handle the administration of a region
Dewdwallar	*Doodhwala*; milkman
Dhal	Shield
Dhoon; Deyrah Dhoon; Doon	Dehra Dun (town)
Dhooniya	One who fluffs up cotton, prior to filling it in a mattress
Dilkhusa; Dilkoosha; Dil-Koosha; Dil Koosha	Dilkusha: Manor and grounds in Lucknow
Dilli; Dehli	Delhi (city)
Din; Deen; Diin	Faith; religion
Dooli	*Doli*; a covered palanquin; litter
Doorgah Poojah	*Durga Puja;* festival prominent in Bengal and other eastern states of India
Dootee	*Dhoti;* waistcloth
Dorundah	Doranda (in Ranchi district)
Dowr	*Daur*; period; time
Duph (grass)	*Cynodon dactylon* or *Doob* grass, also known as Bermuda grass
Durbangah	Darbhanga (town)
Durriabad	Daryabad (town)
Durzee	*Darzi;* tailor
Eidgah	Open grounds reserved for Eid prayers
Ekka	Horse drawn carriage for single rider
Elahabad	Allahabad (city)
Fakir; Fakeer	Holy man; travelling mendicant
Fana	Cease to exist / disappear

Farman	*Firman*; an oriental sovereign's edict.; a grant or permit; imperial decree
Farzand	Son; male child / offspring
Fasahat	Eloquence
Fasih; Fasiih	Elegant (of language); eloquent word or phrase
Fasl; Fasli	Harvest (of a year)
Faujdar; Sadr Faujdari	A term of pre-Mughal origins. Under the Mughals, the office combined the functions of a military commander along with judicial and land revenue functions
Firinghi; Firingee	*Firang*; An European
Firni	Sweet dish of rice, milk, sugar and garnished with chopped dried fruits, a kind of rice pudding
Fish Market Fort	Macchi Bhavan
Friseur	Hairdresser; barber
Furhut Bux; Furrad Buksh; Furra Bux	*Farhat Baksh*; palace of Nawab Sa'adat Ali Khan, former "country house" of Claude Martin
Furlough	Extended leave period availed by officials of EIC
Furruckabad	Farrukhabad (town)
Futteh	*Fateh*, victory
Futtehpur	Fatehpur (town)
Futtyghur; Futtehgur	Fatehgarh (town)
Fyzabad	Faizabad (town)
Gaazi; Ghazi	Conqueror
Gali Koocha	Lanes and by-lanes
Ganges	Ganga (river)
Garden of God / God's Acre	Alambagh
Garhi; Gurhee	Small mud fort; may also pertain to fortified religious structure
Gate ka Darwaza	Wicket gate
Gentoo	Heathen
Gharana	School; ideology (of dance / drama / music)
Gharri; Gharree	Carriage, often drawn by animals, like bullock or horse
Ghaut	*Ghat*; river bank
Ghazal; Guzzel; Gazele	Short poem in Urdu, consisting of couplets, often set to music, describing unrequited love (both spiritual as well as worldly) or the charms of intoxication
Ghera bandi	Enclosure
Ghulam Gardish	Corridor / passageway with cubicles, providing temporary shelter (for travellers / pilgrims)
Gilauri	Betel leave folded in conical shape, with a filling of areca nuts, dried fruits, lime, spices etc
Girabaaz	Famed breed of homing pigeon capable of non-stop flying for 10 - 12 hours

Gogra	Ghagra (river)
Gola	Cannon ball
Gola Kabootar	Feral wood pigeon, grey in colour, without any pedigree
Golah Ganj	Gola Ganj locality in Lucknow
Gomastah; Gomasta	Indian agent of the British East India Company, to sign bonds, to fix prices of agricultural produce
Gondah	Gonda
Goomty; Goomtee; Gumti	Gomti (river)
Goorka; Gourkah	*Gurkha*; martial tribe of Nepal
Gora Sahib	Literally "white man"
Gorackpore	Gorakhpur
Gulaab-paash	Rosewater sprinkler
Gumma	Brick
Gungootrie	Gangotri glacier
Gunje; Gunge	*Ganj*; market (typically grain market); can also denote locality
Gurrah	*Ghara*; earthen pot for storing water
Gurreeb	*Garib*; poor
Guzar	Passing through
Guzarat	Gujarat (state)
Gwallah	*Gwala;* cattle herdsman
Haberdasher	A shopkeeper selling small items used in sewing, such as buttons, zips and thread
Habshi	Negro; person of African origin; Abyssinian
Hackery; Hackerie; Hackri	A two wheeled cart, pulled by humans or bullocks
Hai Rabba	Oh God (exclamation)
Hajipore	Hajipur (town)
Hakim	Physician using traditional remedies in India and Islamic countries
Hammam	Turkish bath
Hunnooman Gurrie	Hanuman Garhi
Har-carrier	*Harkara*; messenger or courier
Hasrat	Wistfulness, sense of deprivation
Hata	Enclosure; courtyard
Hauz	Water tank
Hawas	Desire; greed
Hayrat	Wonder
Hazareebagh	Hazaribagh (town)
Hazrat	Title prefixed to the name of a prophet, or saint or devout person
Hern Khana	*Hiran Khana;* enclosure for housing deer

Hijr	Separation (from beloved)
Hindoo	*Hindu*
Hindoo Koosh	*Hindu Kush* mountain range
Hindostan	Hindustan (sub-continent)
Hindostanee; Hindostani	*Hindustani*; pertaining to the sub-continent of Hindustan or India; Hindi language
Hissa-e-rasadii	Wealth tax
Hooka; Huqqa; Houkah	*Hookah*; hubble-bubble; water pipe
Hookam	*Hukum*; an order or command
Hoolee	*Holi*
Hujum	Crowd
Hukkām	Official
Hukumran	Ruler
Hundi	Treasury bill
Hurdui	Hardoi (town)
Hurdwar	Haridwar (town)
Hurreepoor	Haripur (town)
Hussun	Hasan (as in name)
Hyder	*Haider* (name)
Hysar; Hisar	Battlement; fortified enclosure
Ijaradar	Revenue contractor
Ijarband	Cord of pyjama
Ijtihad	Reasoning / rationalising law on basis of Islamic tenets
Ilm-o-fazl	Learning
Imambara; Emamburra; Imambargah; Ashurkhana	A congregation hall for Shi'a religious discourses, especially those associated with Muharram.
Imamdasta	Mortar pestle
Insha	Letter
Ittiqaa	Piety; abstaining from evil
Jagir; Jageer; Jagirdar	A grant of the public revenues of a district; a person with power to collect the revenue
Jah-o-Jalal	Splendour (as of a royal court)
Jaidad	Landed property
Jajman; Jajmani	Familial patron; patronage
Jalousie	A blind or shutter made of a row of angled slats
Jalwa afroz	Literally "to spread radiance." Can denote "ascending the throne"
Jamghat; Jamghata	Literally "gathering." Kite flying festival observed after Diwali festival
Janab-é-Áliya; Janab-é-Ália	Her Majesty
Jān-é-Álam	Spirit of the World (title)
Janpan	A sort of sedan chair, carried by four bearers

Jarnail	General
Jawab; Jawabi	Facsimile (gateway), to maintain architectural symmetry. The responder during *soz-khwani* is also known as a *jawabi*
Jea Mhow	Jiamau (locality in Lucknow)
Jeena	Staircase
Jelalabad; Jalallabad	Jalalabad (fort) on eastern outskirts of Lucknow
Jemadar	Servant / solder with rank
Jhansie	Jhansi (town)
Jheend	Jind (town)
Jhil	Lake
Jirga	Circle, ring, group
Jounpur	Jaunpur (town)
Jowaulla Mookhee	*Jwalamukhi;* volcano
Jubbulpore	Jabalpur (town)
Jugdespore	Jagdishpur (town)
Juggernaut	Jagannath; denoting something massive (originating from Jagannath temple of Odisha)
Justaju	Search with effort
Kaafir	Idolater; infidel; beloved
Kababchi	One who prepare *kebabs* and barbecued items
Kabootar Baazi	Pigeon racing (sport)
Kabootar Khana	Pigeon house
Kahaar	Palanquin bearer
Kahn	Khan (title)
Kakoree	Kakori (town)
Kal Sira	Literally "black headed." Breed of homing pigeon
Kala Panee; Kala Pani	'Black Water' or seas
Kamalat	Place of excellence
Kana	*Kanha;* Lord Krishna
Kan-Kaiyya	Kite
Karabala; Kerbala; Karbula	*Karbala;* Holy city of Iraq and centre of Shi'a Muslim pilgrimage; burial place of Mohammed's grandson Husain; place where *Ta'zīyas* are interred
Karnama	Feat; exploit
Kartus	Cartridge
Kasba; Qasba; Qasbat	Township; settlement
Ke zariye se	By means of
Kebab	Meat patty, fried or grilled
Kernaul	Karnal (town)
Khala	Aunt
Khalifa	Muslim civil and religious ruler; Leader

Khamba	Pillar
Khanaut	Wall of tent
Khandsár-Bhandsár Bazár	Wholesale market where trade was done on the basis of samples, e.g. a sample of sugar (*khánd*) in an earthen vessel (*bhánd*)
Khanpur	Kanpur (city)
Khanqah	Lodge or rest house where travellers discuss spiritual matters, get saints' blessings and hear *Sufi* music
Khansamah	Steward
Khapanaa	Consume
Khapna	Dried up
Khas Mahal	Senior-most Begum or Queen
Khāsdān	Container or try for presenting *pān* and / or token gifts
Khasta haal	Impoverished
Khatma	The end; conclusion
Khelassy	*Khalasi*; dockyard worker, sailor, or lascar; native skilled in a profession
Kheree	Kheri (town)
Khidmat	Service
Khilaut; Kelaut; Killut	*Khilat*; ceremonial robe of honour
Khimadtgar; Khudai Khidmadtgar	Servant; Servant of God
Khud	Precipice
Khurd; Khurd Mahal	Smaller; junior Queen / Begum
Khusuusiyat	Distinctive feature; attribute
Khwajasara	Transgender; often holding high position in the Nawabi court, particularly in the women's quarters of *zenana*
Khwansama	Butler or Captain, responsible for the serving of food on the *Dastarkhwan* as per accepted norms or directions
Khyrabad	Khairabad (town)
Killar	*Qila;* fortress
Kist; Kisht	Instalment
Kitaab Khana	Library
Kittesan	Parasol
Kookeree	*Khukri*; a type of machete used by *Gurkhas* of Nepal
Kos	Unit of distance; approximately 3.2 km
Kotha	Brothel
Kothie; Kothee	*Kothi*; mansion. Large, imposing building
Kotwall, Kotwali	*Kotwal*, police or military officer responsible for law and order of a fort in medieval times; a police chief in modern times; police station

Kuddum Rusool; Kuddum Russool	*Kadam (Qadam) Rasul;* an elevated building housing impression of the Prophet's foot
Kunkur Kothi	Kankar Kothi or Kankar Wali Kothi; sold off and demolished during colonial rule
Kuppentulla	Kapoorthala, Kapurthala; princely state of British India, which remained loyal to the British during 1857
Kuskus	*Khuskhus*; poppy seeds
Kussowlie; Kussowlee	Kasauli (hill station)
Lachhmi	Laxmi
Lad Sahib; Lat Sahib	Lordship; Governor General
Lakhauri; Lakhori (bricks)	Flat, thin red coloured burnt clay bricks, popular as a building material in the Indian sub-continent, till early 20th century. Size varied from 100 x 150 x 20 mm to 100 x 150 x 50 mm
Laknow; Lakhnau; Lakhnaw; Lakhnow; Lucnow; Lacnow; Nakhlau	Lucknow (city)
Lâl Sharab	Claret; wine
Lathi	Baton
Land of Regrets	The Indian sub-continent
Landaur	Landour, a small hill station near Mussoorie, Uttarakhand
Lascar	*Lashkar*; Corps; Battery (of army), typically of artillery
Lawh	Tablet (for inscription - not medicine)
Layla and Majnun	Laila and Majnu; love story originating from Northern Arabia
Liaquat	Ability
Loab	Oil floating on top of curry dish
Logue	*Log*; people; multitude
Loll	*Lāl*; red colour. Also used for names *e.g. Jhao Loll* for *Jhau Lal* or *Loll Baugh* for *Lal Bagh*
Loodianah	Ludhiana (city)
Lustres	Glass prisms and spherical pendants in chandeliers
Lutchman	Laxman
Lutf uthana	To enjoy
Lyhaza; Lehaza	Therefore
Machan	Platform erected in a tree, originally for hunting large animals from a vantage position (presently used for watching animals in wildlife reserves)
Madad-e-Ma'ash	Revenue free land often given to learned persons
Madrasa; Madrassa	Islamic centre of learning
Mafi, Maafi (land)	Exempt. Land from where no revenue was paid either to the landlord or to the government by the tenant
Mahajan	Trader

Mahez	Simply; only
Mahi	Fish
Mahman nawazi	Hospitality
Mahomet	*Mohammad*
Mahrattas	Marathas
Mahvar; mahavari	Monthly allowance
Mahviyat	Engrossed; fascinated
Maidan	Green, open space
Majlis	Congregation
Maktab	Old fashioned method of educations in Islamic countries, focussing mainly on memorising the holy *Koran*
Malli	*Mali*; gardener
Manja	String of kite coated with powdered glass (opposite of *saddi*, or plain string)
Mānqulāt	Orthodox science
Mansab	Office, post
Mansabdar	A civil or military officer holding rank (*mansab*) in the Mughal administration
Manzuri	Approval
Maqbara	Tomb, revered as a shrine
Māqulāt	Rational science
Marhaba	Bravo; hail
Markaz	Centre (of learning)
Marsiya; Marsiya-khwani	Elegy; reading of elegies (related to Muharram)
Masalchi	One who prepared spices according to the cook's menu (*Bawarchi*) and instructions
Masnad; Musnad; Masnad nashin	Royal seat; ruler sitting on *masnad* / royal seat
Matam	Mourning
Mauza	Village / hamlet
Mazar	Grave of a Muslim religious leader or saint
Mazuli	Removal; dismissal (in disgrace)
Mehfil	Cultural gathering
Mehfil; Mahfil	Assembly; congregation
Mesyu	Monsieur (French)
Metranee	*Methrani*; sweepress; a sweeper's wife
Mihrab	Arch; prayer niche in mosque
Millinery	Profession of making or selling women's hats
Milkiyat	Private land ownership of *Zamindars*, often cultivated by contract or bonded labourers
Mir Atishi	Commander of artillery
Mir Bakshi	Head of military
Mir Manzil	Camp superintendent

Mir Munshi	Head clerk
Mithoolee	Mitauli. A *tehsil* in present day Uttar Pradesh
Mohavrat	Idiomatic expressions
Momin	True believer of Islam; staunch Muslim
Momiya	Coating with wax (waxing)
Moofty; Muftee	*Mufti*; A legal expert who is empowered to give rulings on Islamic religious matters; Eastern style of dressing
Mooltan	Multan (city)
Mooluck	*Mulk;* kingdom; one's country
Moolvee	*Maulvi*; Islamic scholar; a learned and religious man; interpreter of Islamic law
Moonshee	*Munshi*; clerk
Moonsif	*Munsif;* judge/ arbitrator in lower court
Moora	Small stool
Mooradabad	Moradabad (town)
Moorshedabad	Murshidabad (town)
Moslem; Mussulman	Muslim
Motee	*Moti;* pearl
Motimahul	Moti Mahal (palace)
Mouzah	*Mauza;* Village / hamlet
Muchee Bhowun; Muchi Bawan	Macchi Bhavan; old pre-Nawabi fort of Lucknow
Muddat	For a long time; period
Mugger	Crocodile
Mughlai	Pertaining to the Mughals, who ruled the Indian sub-continent for three centuries
Mujahid	Crusader; warrior fighting for his faith
Mujra	Dance performance by female dancers, to the accompaniment of vocal and instrumental music
Mujtahid	Individual who is qualified to exercise *ijtihad* in the evaluation of Islamic law
Mukarrar	Encore, as in a recital of poetry
Mukhtasar	Short; in brief
Mulazammin	Servants; employees
Munsarowar	Mansarovar glacier
Munzil	*Manzil;* generally denotes a large building, although the term has other connotations e.g. destination, floor
Musgid	*Masjid;* mosque
Muqarrar	Settle, confirm
Muraqqa	Album of miniature paintings in book form
Murriow	Madaion cantonment
Musahib	Courtier; friend and advisor

Mushaira	Congregation of poets during which Urdu poetry is recited, typically taking the form of a contest
Musjed	*Masjid;* mosque
Mussooree	Mussoorie (town)
Must	*Musth;* seasonal condition in bull elephants characterised aggressive behaviour and rise in reproductive hormones
Mustaydi	Alertness
Mut'ah	Ancient Islamic practice uniting man and woman as husband and wife for a limited time, on mutual agreement
Mutawasit	Paymaster
Muttra	Mathura (town)
Mynporee	Mainpuri (town)
Naanbai	One who prepares flat breads such as *roti, kulcha, sheermal* etc.
Naaz-aafriin	Coquettish lover
Naaziriin	Viewers; spectators
Nabob	*Nawab*; provincial Governor, often *de facto* ruler
Nafa	Profit
Nafs	Body; flesh
Nagpore	Nagpur (city)
Naib; Nayb-e-Khas	Second in command; a deputy
Najib	High born; superior; outstanding
Naka bandi	Check post;
Naqdi; jama	Revenue deposit
Naqqar; Naqqarkhana	Short, flat drum; pavilion where drums are beaten at intervals, or to announce royalty
Nasl	Race
Nath	Nose ring
Nath utarna	Ceremonial sexual intercourse with a virgin prostitute
Nawab Gunge	Nawabganj
Nawab Wazir	Person holding dual charge of *Nawab* or provincial governor e.g. in Awadh, and also *Wizarat* or Prime Ministership of the Mughal court at Delhi
Nazabaz	Lancer
Nazim	First officer of a province; minister of the department of criminal justice
Nazir	Court official
Nazm	Urdu poetry, that is normally written in rhymed verse and also in modern prose-style
Nazul; Nazool	Confiscated (estate)
Nilgherries	Nilgiri hills in South India
Nigrani	Keeping watch

Nikah	Matrimonial ceremony under Islam
Nimish; Makhan Malai	Light dessert based on set cream, flavoured with saffron and rose water
Nipal	Nepal (Himalayan country)
Nishapuri	Belonging to Nishapur, Persia
Nizam; Nizamat	A hereditary ruler; territory, office, or authority of the *Nizam.*
Notch girl; nautch girl	Derived from the Hindi word, *Naach*, meaning dance
Nourjehan	*Nur Jahan* (Mughal Empress)
Nullah; Nulluh	Small stream; drain
Nusseeb	*Naseeb;* fate
Nuwabgunge	Nawabganj (administrative sub-division in Bareilly)
Nuzzer	*Nazar*; ceremonial gift presented in court to royalty / nobility
Nynee Tal	*Naini Tal*; hill station town in present day Uttarakhand
Ooddeen	ud-Din (as in name)
Oonao; Onao	Unnao (district)
Oordoo	Urdu (language)
Oudh; Oude	Awadh (state)
Padre	A Christian priest
Padshah	*Badshah*; king
Palkee; Palankeen	*Palki*, palanquin
Paltan	Battalion; platoon
Pān	A preparation of betel leaves, with condiments such as areca nuts, herbs, lime and dried fruits
Panah lena	To take refuge
Panah-gazin	A refugee
Panapna	To prosper; survive
Pāndān	Box for storing *pān* (see above)
Pandy	Derogatory term used by the British for Indian freedom fighters, with reference to Mangal Pandey
Parantha; Paratha	Shallow fried, layered flat bread
Parasol Palace	Chattar Manzil palace, Lucknow
Pargana	A revenue unit, consisting of several *mouzas* (smallest unit for collecting revenue)
Pari Khana	Abode of fairies
Parterre	Garden with symmetrical flower beds
Patan; Pathan	Afghan tribesman
Patang Bazi	Kite flying
Patialah	Patiala (town)
Patta	Land deed issued by the government to an individual
Patwari	Village accountant
Paundan	*Pāndān* (see above)

Payravi	Follow through
Pehra	Patrol
Pehra dena	To keep watch
Pench ladana	Combat (as in kite flying)
Peon	Footman; foot solder; pawn; lowly employee physically delivering files and papers in an office
Pergola	Outdoor garden with a pillared passageway and / or shaded sitting area, often supporting creepers or climbing plants
Pergunnah	*Pargana*; administrative sub-division of a district
Pertabgurh; Pertabghar	Pratapgarh (town)
Peshcush	*Pesh-kash*; an offering; proposal
Phaeton	Four wheeled carriage, drawn by a pair of horses
Phirni	Flavored rice pudding
Phool Sira	Literally "spotted head" (as if with tiny flowers). Breed of homing pigeon
Pindarry	*Pindari;* plunderer; highway robber
Pinjara	Cage
Pir; Peer	A Muslim saint; holy man
Pirich	Saucer
Pishpash	Meat-based rice stew
Plassey	Palashi - Site of a decisive war between British East India Company and Nawab of Bengal, fought in 1757. Name derived from the local tree called *Palas* (*Butea monosperma*), bearing red flowers commonly called "Flame of The Forest"
Pleader	An advocate in a court of law
Poojari	*Pujari*; Hindu priest
Poppadam	*Papad*; seasoned dry flatbread
Prophet's Garden	Mohammad Bagh
Pucca and Cutcha	*Pakka* and *Katcha*; literally signifying cooked and raw, although meanings could be different, depending on context
Puharree	*Pahari;* inhabitants of hilly regions
Punchayat	*Panchayat;* a village council
Punjaub	Punjab (state)
Punkah; Punkha; Punkah coolie	*Pankha*; fan; a lowly employee who manually operated the fan
Punsaree	*Pansari*; Indian native seller of indigenous medicines
Purdah; Purdahnashin	Literally curtain; religious and social practice of female seclusion prevalent among Muslim and Hindu communities; a woman who practices *purdah*
Purza	Component; part (of mechanical contraption)
Pyke	Night watchman in a village; runner / messenger

Qaahir	Dominant; oppressive
Qahar; Khuda ka qahar	Wrath (of God)
Qaraar denaa	To fix, determine, adjudge
Qasiida	Eulogy
Qatl-e-aam	General massacre
Qaul-o-qarar	Agreement
Qayda; Beqayda	Regular; irregular
Qazi	Magistrate or judge of a *Sharia* court
Qibla	Direction towards *Kaa'ba*
Qil'a-band	Imprisoned (in a fort)
Qil'adaar	Commander of fort
Qil'a-e-Fort Vylyam	Fort William (Calcutta)
Qissa; Qissa goii	Story; recitation of story
Qizilbash	Turkic warriors who settled in Afghanistan in large numbers
Qubuliyat	Acceptance; receipt
Rahgir	Traveller
Rajah	Raja; King
Rajapoot	Rajput
Rakabdaar	The waiter or steward, presenting food, as per the *Khwansama's* instructions. May also be involved in preparation of sweets / desserts
Ramghur	Ramghar cantonment town
Rampoor	Rampur (town)
Ranee	*Rani*; queen
Raptee	Rapti (river)
Raseed	Receipt
Ratub; Ratib	Food for dogs
Raunaq	Lustre; elegance; cheerfulness
Rauza; Rouza	Tomb of Muslim saint, (with garden) serving as a shrine
Reign of Terror	The period of the Indian Mutiny or First War of Independence (1857 - 58)
Reis; Rais	Moneyed class; wealthy
Risaldar	Commander of the mounted troop
Rishvat-sitaanii	To get bribe
Riyasat	State
Rob; Raub	Awe, fear
Rora	Pebble; obstruction
Roy Bareilly	Rai Bareilly (town)
Rumali; Roomali Roti	Very thin flat bread, almost like an handkerchief
Rumna; Ramna	Park; hunting ground

Russoulpore	Rasoolpur (town)
Ryasala	Cavalry
Ryot; Ryut	Peasant; tenant farmer
Saalan	Curry; gravy dish
Sada mezaji	Simplicity (of character)
Saharumpore	Saharanpur (town)
Sahib	A man of authority, typically European
Sajjada Nashin	Descendant of a *Sufi* saint or *Pir*; descendant of disciple of such holy man
Sālan	Curried (meat) preparation
Santipore	Shantipur city (in present day Nadia district of West Bengal) famous for silk saris
Sardari	Command
Sarkar	Division of a *Subah* or province
Sarzamin	Land; territory
Sataanii	Praise
Saudagar	Merchant
Saz-o-saman	Supplies
Secunder; Secundur; Sekundra Bagh	*Sikandar* (as in Sikandar Bagh); for Alexander (the Great)
Seda Bearer	*Sardar*; head or leader of palanquin bearers
Seetapoor; Seetapore	Sitapur
Seikh	Sheikh; typically an Arab chieftain
Sepoy	*Sipahi*; native soldier
Caravan serai	*Serai; Serai Khana*; shelter for travellers
Shab-é-Baraat	Fifteenth night of the month of *Shaban* (Islamic calendar) when Muslims pray and make offerings in the name of deceased relatives
Shah Nujif; Shan Nujjuff; Shan Nugguf	Shah Najaf; tomb of Ghazi-ud-Din Haider in Lucknow
Shahanshahi	Imperial
Shahi Tukda	Sweet dish, made of fried pieces of bread soaked in flavoured sweet milk
Sham-e-Awadh	Colourful evenings of Awadh (Lucknow), often compared with *Subah-e-Banaras* (dawn in Varanasi) and *Shab-e-Malwa* (nights of Malwa)
Shamshir	Sword
Shekarry	*Shikari;* huntsman
Shemianah	*Shamiana;* ceremonial tent, shelter or awning, commonly used for outdoor events
Shervani	A long cloak like garment for males, favoured by Lucknow aristocracy
Shikarnama	Account of a hunting expedition
Shikast	Defeat

Shishmuhull	*Sheesh Mahal;* palace of glass or mirrors
Shroff	*Saraf*; Money changer; banker
Shunkerpore	Shankarpur (town)
Sicca	*Sikka;* coin
Silsila	Link, chain (as in events- not physical chain)
Silsila-e-khair	Social obligation
Silsila-i-Nizamia	Curriculum of Islamic studies of *Firangi Mahal*, Lucknow
Simlah	Simla; Shimla (town)
Sirdar	*Sardar*; Chief; Head - commonly wearing a turban
Sola Topi	A light weight sun hat made from the pith from the *Sola* plant (*Aeschynomene aspera*), formerly worn by the British in India.
Soleyman	Suleiman; name / title
Sonnud; sunnad	*Sanad*; deed, particularly for land holding
Sooltan	*Sultan; medieval (Muslim) ruler*
Soorky	*Surkhi*; pounded brick powder used as mortar
Soubador	*Subedar*; native army rank equivalent to Warrant Officer in colonial army
Soubah; Soobah	*Suba*; *Subah* - Province of the Mughal empire
Sowar	*Sawar*; horseman
Soz; Soz-khwani	Dirge; recitation of dirges (related to Muharram)
Srinugger	Srinagar (city)
Sudder; Sudder Bazar	*Sadar*; *Sadar Bazar*. Military cantonment; market attached to cantonment
Suer; Soour	Pig; hog
Sultan	Sovereign
Sultan- é-Álam	King of the World (honorific title)
Sultanat-é-Mazia	The past kingdom
Sultanpoor	Sultanpur (town)
Sunderbund	*Sundarban;* delta and mangrove forests of Hooghly river in Bengal
Suraiee	*Surahi*; earthen pitcher for storing water
Surajah Dowla	Siraj-ud-Daula, Nawab of Bengal
Surkunda	*Sarkanda*; reed grass
Sutte	*Sati;* custom of widow burning
Sutuun	Pillar; prop
Syce; Sais	One who grooms horses in a stable
Ta'alluqa; Ta'aluqdar; Talookdar	Connection; land or property over which any kind of right or claim existed; person holding such right
Ta'azim, Takriim	Honour, respect
Tabahi	Destruction

Tabarruk	Blessing; Food which is sent to fellow Muslims after a religious ceremony or occasion
Tabasheer	*Tabashir;* medicinal substance from bamboo plant
Tabbaáii	Wisdom; talent
Tabqa	Class, group
Tafrih	Pleasure; entertainment
Tahniyat	Good wishes; to congratulate
Tahzeeb	Culture
Tajurba; Tajurbekar	Experience; Experienced
Takhallus	Pen name; pseudonym
Tal Kathura	Talkatora (area)
Talooka	*Ta'aluka, ta'aluqa*, *taluka*; administrative division of a district; roughly corresponding to the modern day *tehsil.*
Tamanna	Desire
Tamir karna	To build
Tanga; Tonga	Horse drawn carriage for two or more riders
Taqriiz	Favourable criticism or review
Taqvaa	Fear of God; piety; sanctimonious
Tashtari	Plate; salver
Tatviil	Unnecessary long account, prolonged
Tawaif; tavaaif	Prostitute; dancing girl
Ta'zīya; Tazia	Replica of the tomb of Hussain, martyred grandson of Mohammad, carried in processions during Muharram
Tea Cozy / Cosy	Cloth cover for teapot
Teapoy	A small three-legged (tripod) table
Tehalka; Tahalka	Panic; commotion
Tehsil; Tuhseel;Tehsildar; Tahsildar	An administrative sub-division in a district; officer or revenue collector in charge of the *Tehsil.*
Tel-a-Ram	Dilaram Kothi in Lucknow
Thakur	Land owner-cum-local chieftain; ironically may also denote lower caste barbers
Thana; Thannah; Thanedar	Police station; police officer
Thermantidote	Mechanical contraption which blew a current of air inside colonial homes
Thug; Thuggee	Highway robber who also choked / garrotted his victim to death
Thunder Box	Portable, box-like lavatory seat, manually cleaned by scavengers in colonial India
Til-a-ram	Dilaram Kothi in Lucknow (no longer extant)
Tola	Traditional residential area in Lucknow
Tom-Tom	*Tamtam*; native drum

Toofaun	*Toofan;* Storm; hurricane
Toolseepore	Tulsipur (town)
Tope	Cannon
Topkhana	Artillery
Tughra	Calligraphic monogram / seal affixed on official documents like *sanads*, *firmans* etc
Tuhseel	Tehsil
Tulwar	*Talwar*; sword; sabre
Tumasha	*Tamasha;* ostentatious display (often with negative connotations)
Tyear	*Tayyar*; ready
Tykhana; Taikhana	*Tehkhana*; basement
Tyrpowliya	Tripolia, a building or gateway with three entrances
Ugaldān	Spittoon
Ulajhna	To get entangled
Umballah; Umballa	Ambala
Urs	Death anniversary of a *Sufi* saint
Usuf	*Yusuf;* Joseph
Vaasta	Connection; also middleman
Vaasta dena	Come in contact; to be concerned; invoking help or mercy
Vaqat; vakat	*Waqt*; time period
Vasiiqa	Affidavit; deed, legal document
Vizir; Vizier; Vizar; Virzeer	*Vazir*; *Wazir;* Prime Minister
Wafat	Death
Wajib	Reasonable
Wali Ahad; Mirza Wali Ahad Bahadur	Crown Prince; Successor designate; heir to the throne
Waqai Navi; Waqai Nigar; *Sawanih Nigar*	Writer or surveyor providing confidential reports to the ruler
Warq	Foil of silver or gold for edible purposes
Wasifa; Wasiqa	Pension
Waziri	Thoroughbred horse (from Afghanistan)
Wazu; Wazoo	*Wudhu*; cleaning oneself before prayers; ablution
Whitey-brown	See “Anglo-Indian” above
Wizarat	Prime Ministership
Writer	Clerk
Yaad taza karna	Recall; refresh memory
Yeotmal	Yawatmal (town)
Yeshu	Jesus Christ
Zakaat	Alms, charity

Zeminder; Zumeendar; Zmeendaar	*Zamindar*; a landowner, who leases his land to tenant farmers. May not actually own the land, but has tenancy rights, which lapse after his death
Zenana	Seraglio; part of house for the seclusion of women folk
Zihaanat	Intelligence; sagacity
Zillah	*Zila*; district
Zimma; Zimmedari	Responsibility; obligation
Ziyarat; Ziyarat karna	Pilgrimage; to proceed on a pilgrimage
Zumeendaree	*Zamindari* (see above)

Select Bibliography

Ajmad, ML, Kumar, P and Sharukh, M., "Analysing the Re-vitalisation of Hazratganj", *International J. Sc. & Eng.* Research Vol. 10 (3) (2019) pp. 2088 - 2093.

Ali, Darogha Haji Abbas, *An Illustrated Historical Album of The Rajas and Taaluqdars of Oudh* (1880), North Western Provinces and Oude Government Press, Allahabad.

Anderson, G and Subedar, M, *The Last Days of The Company: A Source Book of Indian History, 1818 – 1858* (1918), AH Wheeler, Bombay.

Nevill, HR (*ed.*), *District Gazetteer of the United Provinces of Agra and Oudh*, Vol. XXXVII (1904), Superintendent, Government Press, Allahabad.

Anon (*ed.*), *Imperial Gazetteer of India, Provincial Series: United Provinces of Agra and Oudh*, Vol. II (1908), Superintendent of Government Printing, Calcutta.

Anon (*ed.*), *District Gazetteer of the United Provinces of Agra and Oudh*, Vol. XXXVII (1916), Superintendent, Government Press, Allahabad.

Anon. (*ed.*), *Minutes of The Management Committee from August 1883 to 31st March 1888, The North-Western Provinces and Oudh Provincial Museum, Lucknow* (1888), North-Western Provinces and Oudh Government Press, Allahabad.

Anon. (*ed.), Report of the United Provinces Jails Reform Committee* (1938) Allahabad.

Anon. (*ed.*), *Gazetteer of The Province of Oudh – 3 Vols* (1877), Low Price Publications, Delhi.

Anon. (*ed.*), *Gazetteer of The Province of Oudh – Vol. III – N to Z* (1878), North-Western Provinces and Oudh Government Press, Allahabad.

Anon. (*ed.*), *Hazratganj – A Journey Through The Times* (2011), Bennett & Coleman, Lucknow.

Anon. (*ed.*), *Report on Meteorology, Museum and Horticultural Gardens in the Province of Oudh for 1870 -71* (1871), Oudh Government Press, Allahabad.

Anon. (*ed.*), *Report on Meteorology, Museum and Horticultural Gardens in the Province of Oudh for 1871 -72* (1872), Oudh Government Press, Allahabad.

Anon. (*ed.*), *Report on Meteorology, Museum and Horticultural Gardens in the Province of Oudh for 1872 -73* (1873), Oudh Government Press, Allahabad.

Anon. (*ed.*), *Report on Meteorology, Museum and Horticultural Gardens in the Province of Oudh for 1873 -74* (1874), Oudh Government Press, Allahabad.

Anon. (*ed.*), *Report on Meteorology, Museum and Horticultural Gardens in the Province of Oudh for 1874 -75* (1875), Oudh Government Press, Allahabad.

Anon. (*ed.*), *Report on Meteorology, Museum and Horticultural Gardens in the Province of Oudh for 1875 -75* (1876), Oudh Government Press, Allahabad.

Anon. (*ed.*), *Report on Meteorology, Museum and Horticultural Gardens in the Province of Oudh for 1876 -77* (1877), Oudh Government Press, Allahabad.

Anon. (*ed.*), *Report on The Urban Land Price Scenario – Lucknow* (2005), Industrial and Economic Planning Division, Ministry of Urban Development, Govt. of India, New Delhi.

Anon., *Copy of The Memorandum and Rules and Regulations of the Association of the Prince of Wales Zoological Garden* (1926), Lucknow.

Anon., "A Home away from Home", *An Aesthete's Lament* (2011), at: http://aestheteslament.blogspot.com/2011_09_04_archive.html

Anon., "Canning College", *The Builder*, Vol. 41 (1881) pp. 756 - 766.

Anon., "Hosseinabad Clock Tower", *The Builder*, Vol. 49 (1885) pp. 169 - 170.

Anon., "New Cathedral at Lucknow", *The Builder*, Vol. 65 (1893) pp. 282.

Anon., "Our Goodly Heritage", *The Lal Bagh Jubilee Book* (1870 - 1920), Lucknow.

Anon., "Preservation of Monuments: Monuments of National Importance, *Indian Archaeology 2008 – 09: A Review*", Archaeological Survey of India, New Delhi.

Anon., *A Glimpse of The Monumental Heritage of Lucknow* (2009), Archaeological Survey of India, Lucknow Circle, Aliganj, Lucknow.

Anon., *First Master Plan (2009 – 2018/9), Lucknow Zoological Gardens* (2009), Lucknow.

Anon., *Lucknow: The Garden of India* (1928), GW Lawrie, Lucknow.

Anon., *Memorandum on the Military Works that have been executed at Lucknow in pursuance of Brigadier General Napier's Scheme for the Occupation and Defence of the City* (1859), Military Department, QMG Branch, Calcutta, pp. 1 - 18.

Anon., *Vision for Lucknow (2017) Region, Clean, Green and Prosperous Lucknow* (2017), Lucknow Development Authority, Lucknow.

Asher, Catherine, *Lucknow's Architectural Heritage* (2010), University of Minnesota, digital version at: http://history.ncsu.edu/projects/visualCulture/readings/Asher.pdf

Azmi, AA, *The Annexation of Awadh and its Consequences* (1973), Thesis for Ph.D, Aligarh Muslim University, Aligarh.

Bano, Fozia, "Technical Education in Lucknow - 154 - 1947", *International J. Res. Social Sciences,* Vol. 9 (3) (2019) pp. 2088 - 2093.

Bayly, CA, *Rulers, Townsmen and Bazaars* (1998), Oxford University Press, New Delhi.

Beg, MA, *The Guide to Lucknow* (1911), Asian Educational Services, New Delhi.

Beg, Rubina (*ed.*), *Uttar Pradesh Ki Sanrachna - Abhilekho Ke Sandharbh Se* (2018), UP State Archives, Lucknow.

Beveridge, H and Prashad, B, *A Translation of The Maathir-Ul-Umara - Being Biographies of the Muhammadan and Hindu Officers of The Timurid Sovereigns of India From 1500 to about 1780 AD by Nawwab Samsamuddaula Shah Nawaz Khan and his son, Abdul Hayy, Vol. II* (1941), The Asiatic Society, Calcutta.

Brandreth, AM (*ed.*), "Canning College", *Indian Engineering,* Vol. VIII (1879), Roorkee.

Butler, Harcourt, *India Insistent* (1931) William Heinemann, London, UK.

Butts, HH, *Report of the Land Revenue Settlement of the Lucknow District* (1873), Oudh Government Press, Lucknow.

Carnegy, P, *Historical Sketch of Tahsil Fyzabad, Zillah Fyzabad Including Parganas Haveli-Oudh and Pachhimrath With The Old Capitals Ajudhia and Fyzabad* (1870), Oudh Government Press, Lucknow.

Casci, Simonetta, Casolari, Marzia and Vittorini, Simona, *Cultural and Political Identities in India* (2002), Casa, Milan, Italy.

Chand, TP, *The Administration of Avadh [1858 - 1877]* (1971), Vishwavidyalaya Prakashan, Varanasi.

Chatterjee, Nandlal, *Glories of Uttar Pradesh* (1957), Publications Bureau, Information Department, UP, Lucknow.

Clarke, GR, *The Post Office of India and Its Story* (1920), Mayflower Press, Plymouth, UK.

Croker, BM, *To Let* (1906), JB Lippincott Co., Philadelphia, USA.

Crooke, William, *Ethnographical Handbook for the NW Provinces and Oudh* (1890), NW Provinces and Oudh Government Press, Allahabad.

Crumb, James, *The Highland Brigade: Its Battles and Heroes* (1886), Simpkin, Marshall & Co, London.

Cupples, G, *Memoir of Mrs Valentine, Jeypore. With a Sketch of her Father, Judge Fraser of Lucknow* (1923), James Nisbet, London.

Cuthell, Edith, *My Garden in the City of Gardens: A Memory With Illustrations* (1905), John Lane, London, UK.

Dalrymple, William, *White Mughals: Love and Betrayal in Eighteenth-Century India* (2004), Penguin, New Delhi.

Davies, Philip, *British Architecture in India 1660 – 1947: Splendours of The Raj* (1987), Penguin, Middlesex, UK.

De Silva, Prasannajit, *Colonial Self-Fashioning in British India: Visualising Identity and Difference*, c. 1785 - 1845 (2018), Cambridge Scholars Publishing, Newcastle upon Tyne, UK.

Dronah, *Unesco Creative Cities Network: Inclusion of Lucknow - Interim Report* (2019), Deptt. of Culture, Govt. of Uttar Pradesh, Lucknow.

Eaton, Natasha, "Between Mimesis and Alterity: Art, Gift and Diplomacy in Colonial India, 1770 – 1800", *Comparative Studies in Society and History*, Vol. 46(4) (2004) pp. 816-844.

Eden, Emily, *Up The Country* (1867), Richard Bentley, London, UK.

Fergusson, James, *History of Indian and Eastern Architecture*, Vol. 3 (1876), John Murray, London, UK.

Fisher, Michael H, *A Clash of Cultures: Awadh, the British, and the Mughals* (1987), Manohar Publishers & Distributors, New Delhi; *Idem.*, *The Dynastic History of Lucknow*, http://www.academia.edu/4139086/The_Dynastic_History_of_Lucknow.

Franklin, Michael J, *Romantic Representations of British India* (2006), Routledge, Oxford, UK.

Freitag, Sandra, "A Visual History of Three Lucknows", *J. South Asian Studies*, Vol. 37 (2014) pp. 431 – 453.

Freitag, Sandra, "Postscript. Interdisciplinary Dialogue and Lucknow's Cultural System", *S. Asia Multidisciplinary Academic Journal*, Vol. 11 (2015) pp. 1 - 16.

Gill, RS, Indigenous Spectres, *Subversive Lilas: Encounters Between Nawabi Authority, Colonialism and Popular Ritual in Lucknow* (2003), Thesis for MA, University of British Columbia, Vancouver, Canada.

Gomez, Fernando T, *Cities of Dreams: Examining the Ideology of Colonial Architecture in India* (2009), Thesis for Ph.D, St. Lawrence University, New York, USA.

Gordon, Sophie, *Monumental Visions: Architectural Photography in India, 1840-1901* (2010), Thesis for Ph.D, School of Oriental and African Studies, University of London, London, UK.

Forbes-Mitchell, William, *Reminiscences of the Great Mutiny 1857 – 59* (1910), DK Publishers Distributors, New Delhi.

Gubbins, Martin R, *An Account of the Mutinies in Oudh and the Siege of the Lucknow Residency* (1858), Richard Bentley, London, UK.

Harris, Georgina Maria, *A Lady's Diary of the Siege of Lucknow* (1858), Rupa Publications, New Delhi.

Hasan, Mushirul, *From Pluralism to Separatism: Qasbas in Colonial Awadh* (2012), Oxford University Press, New Delhi.

Hay, Sidney, *Historic Lucknow* (1939), Asian Educational Services, New Delhi.

Herbert, Eugenia W, *Flora's Empire: British Gardens in India* (2011), Penguin, New Delhi.

Hilton, Edward H, *The Tourists Guide to Lucknow* (1894), Murray & Co. and Peake, Allen & Co., Lucknow.

Hollister, JN, *The Centenary of The Methodist Church in Southern Asia* (1956), Lucknow Publishing House, Lucknow.

Hollister, JN, *The Lucknow Publishing House: 1861 - 1961. A Brief History* (1861), The Lucknow Publishing House, Lucknow.

Hoyland, JS and Banerjee, SN, *The Empire of The Great Mogol - A Translation of De Laet's Description of India and Fragment of Indian History* (1928), DB Taraporevala & Co., Bombay.

Irwin, HC, *The Garden of India: Chapters on Oudh History and Affairs* (1880), WH Allen, London.

Jafri, SZH, *Studies in the Anatomy of a Transformation: Awadh from Mughal to Colonial Rule* (1998), Gyan Publishing House, New Delhi.

Jones, Justin, "Urban Mythologies and Urbane Islam: Refining the Past and Present in Colonial-Era Lucknow", *S. Asia Multidisciplinary Academic Journal*, Vol. 11 (2015) pp. 1 – 20.

Joshi, Sanjay, "*Empowerment and identity: The middle class and Hindu communalism in colonial Lucknow, 1880 - 1930* (1995), Thesis for Ph.D, University of Pennsylvania, Philadelphia, USA.

Kabir, N, Naz, N and Qayyum, A, "The Contribution of British Engineer Architect Colonel Samuel Swinton Jacob (1867 – 1902): Proponent of European Indo-Islamic Architecture in Colonial India", *Pakistan J. Science*, Vol. 66 (3) (2014), pp. 282 - 290.

Kataria, I, *Railway Heritage: Indian Railways* (2019), INTACH, New Delhi.

Kaye, JW, *Lives of Indian Officers* Vol. I & II (1867), Strahan & Co, London.

Keene, HG, A Handbook for Visitors to Lucknow: with Preliminary Notes on Allahabad and Cawnpore (1875), Asian Educational Services, New Delhi.

Krishna, Ashima, *The Urban Heritage Management Paradigm: Challenges from Lucknow, An Emerging Indian City* (2014), Thesis for Ph.D, Cornell University, New York, USA.

Laws, RA, *Lucknow: Society and Politics* (1979), Thesis for Ph.D, University of New South Wales, Sydney, Australia.

Llewellyn-Jones, Rosie, *A Fatal Friendship: The Nawabs, the British, and the City of Lucknow* (1992), Oxford University Press, New Delhi.

Llewellyn-Jones, Rosie, *The Last King in India: Wajid Ali Shah* (2014), Random House India, Gurgaon.

Lucknow Appointments, File 805, Manual on Indian Etiquette (1910), UP State Archives, Lucknow.

Lucknow Commissioner Records, File 16, Tablet at Moti Mahal (1891), UP State Archives, Lucknow.

Lucknow Commissioner Records, File 23, Establishment of Art School (1892), UP State Archives, Lucknow.

Lucknow Commissioner Records, File 3, Oudh & Rohilkhand Railways (1891), UP State Archives, Lucknow.

Lucknow Commissioner Records, File 427, Strangers' Home (1895), UP State Archives, Lucknow.

Lucknow Commissioner Records, File 61, Lucknow Water Works (1892), UP State Archives, Lucknow.

Lucknow Commissioner Records, File 789, Strangers' Home (1896), UP State Archives, Lucknow.

Lucknow Commissioner Records, File 941, *Nazul* Buildings (1888), UP State Archives, Lucknow.

Lucknow General Administration Block, File 502 (58), Claim for Restoration of Awadh (1947), UP State Archives, Lucknow.

Lucknow General Administration, File 126, Lawrence Terrace (1910/1912), UP State Archives, Lucknow.

Lucknow General Administration, File 135, Bronze Statue at Gol Darwaza (1892), UP State Archives, Lucknow.

Lucknow General Administration, File 199, Statue of King George V (1936), UP State Archives, Lucknow.

Lucknow General Administration, File 205, Nur Baksh Kothi (1904), UP State Archives, Lucknow.

Lucknow General Administration, File 208, Offices in Lucknow Buildings (1909), UP State Archives, Lucknow.

Lucknow General Administration, File 234, Inauguration of Legislative Council of North-Western Provinces and Oudh (1932), UP State Archives, Lucknow.

Lucknow General Administration, File 279, Plan of Judicial Commissioner's Court, Lucknow (1902), UP State Archives, Lucknow.

Lucknow General Administration, File 27A, Nishatganj Bridge (1900), UP State Archives, Lucknow.

Lucknow General Administration, File 3, Opening Ceremony of Council House, Lucknow (1927), UP State Archives, Lucknow.

Lucknow General Administration, File 35, Lawrence Terrace (1938), UP State Archives, Lucknow.

Lucknow General Administration, File 401, Offices in Lucknow Buildings (1908), UP State Archives, Lucknow.

Lucknow General Administration, File 405, New Council Chamber at Lucknow (1921), UP State Archives, Lucknow.

Lucknow General Administration, File 443, Lawrence Terrace (1915), UP State Archives, Lucknow.

Lucknow General Administration, File 517, China Bazar Gate (1910), UP State Archives, Lucknow.

Lucknow General Administration Proceedings, January to June (1922), UP State Archives, Lucknow.

Lucknow Municipal Block, Files 533/342, 343, 344, Lucknow Improvement Trust, UP State Archives, Lucknow.

Lucknow Municipal Block, Files 500E/32, 34, 35, 36, 40, 44, 46, 47, 48, Lucknow Improvement Trust, UP State Archives, Lucknow.

Lucknow PWD, File 1CB, Maintenance of Memorial of King George V (1940), UP State Archives, Lucknow.

Lucknow PWD, File 307R, Electric Tramway and Lighting in Lucknow (1924), UP State Archives, Lucknow.

Lucknow PWD, File 43CB, Chota Chattar Manzil (1935), UP State Archives, Lucknow.

Lucknow PWD, File 91CB, Marris College (1938), UP State Archives, Lucknow.

Lucknow PWD, File 94CB, Council Chamber Building - Proposed Extension (1935), UP State Archives, Lucknow.

Manisha, "Canning College Educating The Taluqdars?", *Proc. Indian History Congress*, Vol. 70 (2009 - 10) pp. 530 - 536.

Metcalf, Thomas R, *An Imperial Vision: Indian Architecture and Britain's Raj* (2002), Oxford University Press, New Delhi.

Metcalf, Thomas R, *Forging The Raj: Essays on British India in the Heydey of Empire* (2005), Oxford University Press, New Delhi.

Mount, Ferdinand, *The Tears of The Rajas: Mutiny, Money and Marriage in India 1805 – 1905* (2015), Simon & Schuster, London.

Mundy, Capt, *Pen and Pencil Sketches from the Journal of a Tour of India*, Vol. 1 (1833), John Murray, London, UK.

Nagpal, S and Sinha, A, The Gomti Riverfront in Lucknow, India: Revitalisation of a Cultural Heritage Landscape, *J. Urban Design*, Vol. 14 (4) (2009), pp. 489 - 506.

Neville, HR (*ed.*), *District Gazetteers of The United Provinces of Agra and Oudh*, Vol. XXXVII (1904), Govt. Press, Allahabad.

Neville, HR (*ed.*), *District Gazetteers of The United Provinces of Agra and Oudh,* Vol. 4 (1922), Govt. Press, Lucknow.

Newell, HA, *Lucknow -The Capital of Oudh* (1934), HA Newell, Bombay.

Oldenburg, Veena Talwar, *The Making of Colonial Lucknow, 1856 - 1877* (1984), Princeton University Press, New Jersey, USA.

Orlich, LP, *Travels in India including Sinde and the Punjab,* Vol. II (1845), Longman, London, UK.

Oudh General Records No. 1 (1860 - 1890), UP State Archives, Lucknow.

Oudh General Records No. 2 (1859 - 1885), UP State Archives, Lucknow.

Oudh General Records No. 3 (1859 - 1876), UP State Archives, Lucknow.

Oudh General Records No. 4 (1858 - 1890), UP State Archives, Lucknow.

Oudh Records, Lucknow District (1861 - 1879), UP State Archives, Lucknow.

Parkes, F, *Wanderings of A Pilgrim in Search of the Picturesque* (1850), Pelham Richardson, London, UK.

Pender, SR, *The 1857 Indian Uprising and the Politics of Commemoration* (2022), Cambridge University Press, Cambridge, UK.

Qaisar, Ahsan Jan, Verma, Som Prakash and Habib, Mohd. (*eds*.), *Art and Culture: Endeavors in Interpretation*, Vol. 2 (1996), Abhinav, New Delhi.

Qureshi, HA, *The Mughals, The English & The Rulers of Awadh from 1722 AD to 1856 AD. A Kaleidoscopic Study* (2003), New Royal Book Company, Lucknow.

Raj, Jagdish, *The Mutiny and The British Land Policy in North India* (1965), Asia Publishing House, London, UK.

Reddy, AB, Ravindra, C and Maitra, S, *Cantonments: A Transition from Heritage to Modernity* (2017), Directorate General Defence Estates, New Delhi.

Rizvi, SAA and Bhargava, ML (*eds*.), *Freedom Struggle in Uttar Pradesh,* Vol. II*: Awadh 1857 – 59* (1958), Publications Bureau, Information Department, Uttar Pradesh.

Russel, WH, “Life in Lucknow”, *The Times* January 30, (1859), London.

Russel, WH, *My Diary in India In The Year 1858 - 9,* Vol. 2 (1860), Routledge, London.

Sanders, G, *List of Muhammadan and Hindu Monuments,* Vol. 1*: Shahjahanabad* (1916), Govt of India Press, Calcutta; *ibid, idem (1915)*, Illustrations.

Sarkar, PC, “Green Technologies in Nawabi and Colonial Architecture”, *Tree Take*, September (2016), pp. 16 - 18.

Sarkar, PC, *Abode of Fairies - Lucknow's Parikhana* (2022), Kalpaz, New Delhi.

Sarkar, PC, *Lucknow: Buildings, Begums and The British* (2015), Kalpaz, New Delhi.

Sarkar, PC, *Lucknow Chronicles - Memories, Musings, Myths* (2023), Kalpaz, New Delhi.

Sarkar, PC, *Lucknow: Ode To A City* (2021), Kalpaz, New Delhi.

Sarvadhikari, Rajkumar, *The Taluqdari Settlement in Oudh* (1882), Thacker, Spink & Co, Calcutta.

Scriver, P and Prakash, V, *Colonial Modernities: Building, Dwelling and Architecture in British India and Ceylon* (2007), Routledge, London, UK.

Sharma, PM, "Lucknow: A Walk through History", *J. Tourism: A Contemporary Perspective*, Vol. 1(1) (2014) pp. 7 - 12.

Sharma, VC (*ed.*), *Uttar Pradesh District Gazetteers*, Vol. XXXVII (1959), Revenue Department, Government of Uttar Pradesh, Lucknow.

Sheeba, J and Dhas, JTM, "A Study on Indo-Saracenic Architectural Heritage", *Int. J. Pure and Applied Mathematics*, Vol. 118 (22) (2018) pp. 1737 - 1742.

Shorto, S, "Hybrid Accommodations: David Ochterlony, the First Residency and the Mubarak Bagh" in *British Houses in Late Mughal India* (2018), Boydell & Brewer, Rochester, USA, pp. 25-54.

Singh, AA, *Role of Awadh Taluqdars* (2020), New Royal Book Co, Lucknow.

Singh, KA and Bakshi, Pawan, *Ta'alluqdars of Oudh* (2013), Bloomsbury, New Delhi.

Singh, Naresh, *Lucknow Ke Girjaghar* (2010), Hindi Vangmay Nidhi, Lucknow.

Singh, P and Ahmad, LA, "Adaptive Reuse – A Case of Lal Baradari, Lucknow", *Int. Res. J. Engg. Technol.*, Vol. 6 (2019) pp. 7097 - 7105.

Singh, Shalini, *Cultural Tourism In The Awadh Region with Special Reference to Lucknow* (1992), Thesis for Ph.D, University of North Bengal, Darjeeling.

Sinha, Amita, "Bungalows of Lucknow Cantonment, India", *Open House International*, Vol. 24(2) (1999) pp. 56-63.

Sinha, Amita, "Colonial and post-colonial memorial parks in Lucknow, India: shifting ideologies and changing aesthetics", *J. Landscape Architecture*, September (2010) pp. 61-70.

Sinha, Amita, "Greener Pastures", *Indian Architect & Builder*, (2009) pp. 65 - 67.

Soltykoff, Le Prince Alexis, *Voyages L'Inde* (1851), Garnier Freres, Paris.

Speirs, Malcolm, *Lucknow: Families of The Raj* (2013), Amazon, USA.

Srivastava, Manish, *Architecture and Development as Instruments for Political Control and Marginalisation in Lucknow, India* (1997), Thesis for MS, Massachusetts Institute of Technology, Cambridge, USA.

Stark, Ulrike, "Associational culture and civic engagement in colonial Lucknow-The *Jalsah-e Tahzib*", *The Indian Economic & Social History Review*, Vol. 48(1) (2011) pp. 1-33.

Sumama, *Revitalization of Qaiserbagh Heritage Complex, Kaiserbagh, Lucknow* (2019), Thesis for M. Ekistics, Jamia Millia Islamia, New Delhi.

Tandan, Banmali, *The Architecture of Lucknow and its Dependencies, 1722 – 1856. A Descriptive Inventory and Analysis of Nawabi Types* (2001), Vikas, New Delhi.

Tandan, Banmali, *The Architecture of Lucknow and Oudh 1722 - 1856: Its Evolution in an Aesthetic and Social Context* (2008), Zophorus, London.

Tennant, William, *Indian Recreations, Consisting Chiefly of Strictures on the Domestic and Rural Economy of the Mahommedans & Hindoos,* Vol. II (1803), C. Stewart, Edinburgh.

Tieffenthaler, J, Description *historique et géographique del'Inde,* Vol. I (1786–89), CS. Spener, Berlin, pp. 256–57.

Thorn, Adam, *The Upper Ten Thousand: A Biographical Handbook of All the Titled* (1875), George Routledge, London, UK.

Thornton, Edward, *History of The British Empire in India,* Vol. III (1842), WH Allen, London, UK.

Trivedi, DB, *Law and Order in Upper India. A Story of Oudh: 1856 - 1877* (1990), Northern Book Center, New Delhi.

Welch, A, Segger, M and DeCaro, N, "Building for the Raj: Richard Roskell Bayne", *Revue d'art Canadienne / Canadian Art Review*, Vol. 34(2) (2009), pp. 74 - 86.

Welter, Volker M, "Arcades for Lucknow: Patrick Geddes, Charles Rennie Mackintosh and the Reconstruction of the City", *Architectural History,* Vol. 42 (1999) pp. 316-332.

Wyman, FF, *From Calcutta To The Snowy Range* (1866), Tinsley Brothers, London.

Yadav, S, *Lucknow's Tourism in Transition: A Stakeholder's Perspective* (2013), Thesis for Ph.D, Lucknow University, Lucknow.

Yeoward, G, *An Episode of the Rebellion and Mutiny of 1857 and 1858* (1876), American Methodist Mission Press, Lucknow.

Zastoupil, Lynn, *John Stuart Mill and India* (1994), Stanford University Press, Palo Alto, California, USA.

Index

C

D

E

F

G

H

I

J

K

L

M

N

O

P

Q

R

S

T

U

V

W